Readings for Strategies and Tactics of Behavioral Research

Second Edition

Readings for Strategies and Tactics of Behavioral Research

Second Edition

J. M. Johnston
Auburn University

H. S. Pennypacker
University of Florida

LEA LAWRENCE ERLBAUM ASSOCIATES, PUBLISHERS
1993   Hillsdale, New Jersey   Hove and London

Lawrence Erlbaum Associates, Inc., Publishers
365 Broadway
Hillsdale, New Jersey 07642

Library of Congress Cataloging-in-Publication Data

Johnston, James M.
    Readings for Strategies and tactics of behavioral research /
J. M. Johnston, H. S. Pennypacker. — 2nd ed.
        p.   cm.
    Includes bibliographical references and index.
    ISBN 0-8058-0906-6
    1. Psychology—Research—Methodology.   I. Pennypacker, H. S.
(Henry S.)   II. Johnston, James M.   Strategies and tactics of
behavioral research.   III. Title.
    BF76.5.J63   1993
    150′.72—dc20
                                            92-11740
                                            CIP

Books published by Lawrence Erlbaum Associates are printed on acid-free paper, and their bindings are chosen for strength and durability.

Printed in the United States of America
10 9 8 7 6 5 4 3 2 1

to the memory of B. F. Skinner

Contents

Preface

The Preface of *Strategies and Tactics of Behavioral Research* explains our approach to this revision. *Strategies and Tactics* provides a basic treatment of the topic suitable for a wide range of students. In order to do this, certain specialized and advanced material covered in the original work had to be set aside. Points that could be satisfactorily treated in a few paragraphs were moved to supplementary boxes. In other cases, however, the material at issue was chapter length but warranted continued availability. Three such chapters are included in *Readings for Strategies and Tactics of Behavioral Research*.

Since writing the first edition, we have also published a number of papers and chapters concerning behavioral research methods. Although these publications are otherwise available, bringing them together in a single volume allows them to augment students' mastery of *Strategies and Tactics*. Furthermore, we had accumulated a number of methodological papers that had not yet been published (or, in some cases, finished), and these are included to broaden the coverage of this volume.

The 13 readings are primarily intended to serve a supplementary function for readers of *Strategies and Tactics*. Although they are organized under the *Strategies and Tactics* part headings, they cannot by themselves present a coherent picture of behavioral research methods. Furthermore, although each reading is related to some chapters in the first volume more directly than to others (e.g., the discussion of probability in Reading 5 clearly follows chapter 5 on dimensional quantities and units), each chapter does not have an associated reading, and some readings are directly related to multiple chapters.

Those readings that have already been published have been revised in minor ways. Some changes were literary in nature, mostly breaking up long paragraphs and editing awkward phraseology. Occasionally, a phrase was rewritten to make a point more or less conservatively than in the original, although we avoided the tempting opportunity to revise arguments. Other changes were made merely to facilitate their service as supplementary readings. Thus, citations of the original volume have been replaced with references to the appropriate chapters of *Strategies and Tactics*. However, we did not refer to chapters in the first volume at every opportunity, under the assumption that readers would already be familiar with them and because such citations would have been excessive.

Although we intend these readings to serve instructional functions, we have not treated them in entirely the same way as *Strategies and Tactics'* chapters. For instance, we have not provided a detailed outline at the beginning, partly because each reading's headings were often not constructed for textbook purposes. Neither did we write a study guide for each reading. *Readings* is more likely to be assigned in graduate courses, which may make such study aids less necessary or likely to be used. Finally, we did not compose a *Readings* glossary because it would be almost entirely redundant with the one in *Strategies and Tactics*.

These readings were mostly written over a period of more than ten years as journal articles and chapters for edited books. Collectively, they therefore lack the consistency of style, purpose, and integration of *Strategies and Tactics* chapters. Nevertheless, they are especially valuable supplements to *Strategies and Tactics* because they are thematically consistent with the material covered. Some provide important background for *Strategies and Tactics'* chapters (e.g., Readings 1, 2, 3, and 7), and others show how the framework explained in the first volume can be extended to diverse methodological issues (Readings 4, 5, 6, 10, 11, and 12). Still others abandon *Strategies and Tactics'* generally positive tone and openly challenge certain traditional practices or conceptualizations (e.g., Readings 8, 9, and 13). Together, these two volumes provide a coherent and thorough explication of research methods for investigating behavior.

—*J. M. Johnston*
—*H. S. Pennypacker*

Acknowledgments

Some of the readings in this volume have been published previously and we gratefully acknowledge permissions to reprint them. Furthermore, the readings involve varying authorship, including additional authors, and we wish to acknowledge these contributions as well.

Johnston, J. M. Why behavior analysis is a natural science (this volume).

Johnston, J. M. The development of behavioral research methods: Contributions of B. F. Skinner (this volume).

Johnston, J. M., & Pennypacker, H. S. (1980). Traditions of behavioral measurement. In Johnston, J. M., & Pennypacker, H. S., *Strategies and Tactics of Human Behavioral Research* (pp. 55–78). Hillsdale, NJ: Lawrence Erlbaum Associates. (rev. ed.).

Johnston, J. M., & Hodge, C. (1989). Describing behavior with ratios of count and time. *The Behavior Analyst, 12*(2), 177–185. (rev. ed.). Reprinted by permission of the Society for the Advancement of Behavior Analysis.

Johnston, J. M. Probability as a scientific concept (this volume).

Johnston, J. M., & Pennypacker, H. S. (1980). The problem of limited accessibility. In J. M. Johnston & H. S. Pennypacker, *Strategies and Tactics of Human Behavioral Research* (pp. 171–197). Hillsdale, NJ: Lawrence Erlbaum Associates. (rev. ed.).

Johnston, J. M., & Pennypacker, H. S. (1980). Traditions of experimental design. In J. M. Johnston & H. S. Pennypacker, *Strategies and Tactics of Human Behavioral Research* (pp. 79–92). Hillsdale, NJ: Lawrence Erlbaum Associates. (rev. ed.).

Johnston, J. M., & Pennypacker, H. S. (1986). Pure versus quasi-behavioral research. In A. Poling & W. Fuqua (Eds.), *Research methods in applied behavior analysis* (pp. 29–54). New York: Plenum Publishing Co. (rev. ed.). Reprinted by permission of the Plenum Publishing Co.

Johnston, J. M. (1988). Strategic and tactical limits of comparison studies. *The Behavior Analyst, 11*(1), 1–9. (rev. ed.). Reprinted by permission of the Society for the Advancement of Behavior Analysis.

Hodge, C., & Johnston, J. M. Measurement scales and the description of behavioral variability (this volume).

Terrell, D. J., & Johnston, J. M. (1989). Logic, reasoning, and verbal behavior. *The Behavior Analyst, 12*(1), 35–44. (rev. ed.). Reprinted by permission of the Society for the Advancement of Behavior Analysis.

Johnston, J. M. (1979). On the relation between generality and generalization. *The Behavior Analyst, 2*(2), 1–6. (rev. ed.). Reprinted by permission of the Society for the Advancement of Behavior Analysis.

Johnston, J. M. (in press). Within subject versus between groups designs: Comparing experimental outcomes. In D. B. Gray & T. Thompson (Eds.), *Destructive Behavior: Epidemiology, Measurement, & Information Management*. Newbury Park, CA: Sage Publications.

PART ONE

THE NATURAL SCIENCE
OF BEHAVIOR

Why Behavior Analysis is a Natural Science

DISTINCTIONS BETWEEN NATURAL AND SOCIAL SCIENCE

B. F. Skinner viewed the study of behavior as a part of biology (Skinner, 1978, chapter 6) and, as such, a natural science. Behavior analysts have always seemed fond of this categorization because it helps differentiate their field from the social sciences—an association they sometimes find embarrassing. More politely, this distinction is generally important to behavior analysts because the social sciences embody certain conceptual and methodological practices that are antithetical to those of behavior analysis.

A distinction between the natural and social sciences is not easily made, however, at least not to everyone's satisfaction. There is a sizeable literature concerning the nature of science that ranges from philosophical to sociological (e.g., Carnap, 1966; Kuhn, 1970; Nagel, 1961; Popper, 1959), but it is impossible to find a consensus on this point. One distinction that is almost colloquial is that the social sciences study human affairs (allowing an exception for the study of animal behavior in experimental psychology) at the level of the intact organism, and the natural sciences study everything else. This bifurcation is so superficial and arbitrary as to be useless, however; it is especially unsatisfying to behavior analysts because it leaves them squarely within the social sciences.

More thoughtful examinations of this issue consider formal philosophical/ methodological criteria. The nature of scientific theories, falsifiability of constructs, and countless other such concerns offer potentially worthy standards, but there are at least two difficulties in reaching a clear categorical decision. First, scientists simply do not work the way that philosophers and sociologists say they work. They do not consider philosophical niceties when they theorize and reason, for example (see Reading 11). In fact, they just behave as everyone else does. Although their formal training as researchers has undeniable propaedeutic value, it does not change the fundamental orderliness of their behavior as human beings. Second, the variety of methodological practices across all areas of scientific study are enormous, and finding enough consistent differences to usefully distinguish between the natural and social sciences may be impossible. Almost any practice more or less characteristic of the social sciences can probably be found in use somewhere in the natural sciences.

Another approach to the problem admits that the variety of methodological practices across all sciences makes a consistent distinction between natural and social categories unfeasible. Instead, it may be useful to consider more basic or general features of each putative category that might contribute to what could be called a scientific "style." Such generalities suffer the usual risks, of course, but the arguments may be more useful.

For example, at the heart of any science is the way in which its practitioners define its subject matter. Natural scientists are consistent in attending only to physical phenomena—events that are known or at least strongly suspected to exist. Furthermore, they attempt to explain physical phenomena only in terms of other physical phenomena. Although philosophers of science write complicated tomes about such matters, this generality is not difficult to comprehend, especially by contrast to the social sciences.

Social scientists study behavior, which is certainly a physical phenomenon. Indeed, it may be argued that this is all that is available for study, given that the other biological features of organisms are already "taken" by specialties that are generally viewed as natural sciences (biochemistry, physiology, biomechanics, neuroscience, etc.). Their approach to behavior as a subject matter requires a more thorough examination, however.

Social scientists often study behavior only as a means to a very different end. Behavior is likely to be viewed as an epiphenomenon caused by mental events, which are often the real subject matter of interest. Measures of behavior are assumed to represent these mental activities, which apparently cannot be directly measured. In recent years, the same mental activities have also been indirectly approached through measures of biochemical and neurological events. It takes only passing familiarity with psychological or other social scientific literatures, however, to appreciate that the theoretical underpinning of most social science research depends upon a universe of mental phenomena whose invention is clearly cultural (Skinner, 1971, 1978, chapter 8).

EFFECTS OF A NONPHYSICAL SUBJECT MATTER

Does this justify a categorical distinction between natural and social sciences? Are the effects of this difference so important as to require a formal bifurcation of scientific activities? After all, natural scientists routinely theorize about and study phenomena that cannot be directly measured, sometimes without any certainty that they actually exist. Furthermore, natural scientists view their own scientific behavior no less mentalistically than their social science colleagues. The crux of the matter is not about the use of theoretical constructs or indirect measurement, however, or even the researcher's ability to avoid mentalism in how they conceptualize their own behavior. It is about the side effects of pursuing a nonphysical subject matter.

Remember that both the subject matters of the natural science and their explanations remain within the physical realm, however novel or uncertain they may sometimes seem. Proposing an extraphysical universe as a source of both primary subject matter and explanation for physical events is unique to the social sciences. Because this mental universe is not bound by any physical laws, it is especially troublesome. It provides an endless source of theories about and explanations for behavior that cannot ultimately be falsified.

The consequences of a mental subject matter in the social sciences are pervasive and serious. In an effort to build a natural science of behavior that avoided this scourge, Skinner wrote extensively about the effects of mentalism in the study of behavior (e.g., 1953, 1974), and others have extended his arguments (e.g., Moore, 1981). It is these consequences that collectively contribute to a style of social scientific inquiry that may lie at the root of the informal but persistent distinction from the natural sciences that is so widely assumed.

For instance, although both natural and social sciences rely on theory to summarize and guide research, there is a perceptible difference in the foundation upon which theories are constructed. In the natural sciences, theory is generally built upon and therefore constrained by pertinent laws, facts, and empirical generalizations. Because the natural sciences have amassed a vast body of evidence about the way the world works, these constraints are considerable. With a dominant interest in a mental universe, theory in the social sciences is more likely to ignore established evidence in favor of the predilections of the theorist. If there is contradictory evidence, it is easy to change the theory to avoid the problem. Natural science theories also change to accommodate new experimental evidence, but in the social sciences, a style of theorizing seems to have evolved in which theories are also free to ignore facts that are inconvenient. It is almost as if the theories are more important than the facts.

Another consequence of a primary interest in a mental subject matter concerns the fact that social scientists frequently measure behavior in ways that violate some of its fundamental qualities. It is not that the particular measurement techniques are necessarily improper or unique to the social sciences, but that they are unsuitable for the task at hand. As a result, the data may not represent all or even any of the fundamental qualities of behavior, with the resulting cost to the accuracy and generality of the findings. This *faux pas* may be more understandable, though no less costly, if one remembers that the real interest lies in mental "phenomena."

The impact of a nonphysical subject matter on research methods and experimental style accumulates quickly. Lacking the availability of falsifiability as a touchstone, the social sciences have developed a style of experimental design that is notable more for its formality than its functionality. This approach is remarkably dependent on inferential statistical design models, in spite of increasing evidence that they are often inadequate if not counterproductive.

The fact that experimental findings are often unsuccessful in describing orderly relations among behavioral phenomena in turn enhances dependence on theory.

There is no better evidence in support of these criticisms than the technological track record of each scientific approach. The natural sciences have spawned technologies that have dramatically transformed the human culture, and the pace of technological development only seems to increase. The social sciences have yet to offer a single well-developed technology that has had a broad impact on daily life. The best that might be proposed is a fledgling behavioral technology that is actually based on the natural science of behavior analysis (Estes, 1979).

Over time, the accumulation of these and other effects of mentalism in the social sciences has created a scientific mileau that is represented by a set of overarching attitudes about scientific endeavors that stand in stark contrast to those of natural scientists. For example, natural scientists seem to take the enterprise quite seriously in the sense that experiments are genuine efforts to discover new things about nature. Lacking a comparable history of success, social scientists may be no less serious but often seem to approach research more as a means to a theoretical or extraexperimental end than as the primary mechanism of discovery. In the natural sciences, researchers are always seeking improved experimental methods, and experimental control is the holy grail of this search. In the social sciences, methodological issues are more likely to be approached by following tradition, and statistical "control" over the data is substituted for control over independent and extraneous variables. In the natural sciences, theories are killed on the experimental battlefield, but in the social sciences, they die of experimental neglect and old age.

THE AFFILIATION OF BEHAVIOR ANALYSIS

Is the field of behavior analysis a natural science? Yes, in that it scrupulously avoids the insidious temptations of mentalism in the definition and explanation of its subject matter. More generally, it also seems to function more like a natural than a social science. Experimentation tends to dominate theorizing; measurement usually respects the characteristics of behavior as a subject matter; experimental methods enhance opportunities for improved control; and experimental design is approached functionally with a primary interest in discovery of natural relations. Behavior analysis has suffered from growing up in a social science neighborhood (psychology), however. Its applied "wing," for example, has made less progress than it might have because it has been driven more by the contingencies of the marketplace than by the needs of a science-based technology (Johnston, 1991, in press).

What is the point of making this categorical distinction between the social and natural sciences? An "us against them" attitude is unlikely to be productive but it is important for behavior analysts to appreciate the place of their discipline among the other sciences. Psychology is in the midst of fundamental disciplinary changes and behavior analysts need to have a sound sense of the nature of their science and its role in Science. Behavior analysis has always seemed like an orphan or a changeling, being raised by in a home where it did not belong. It has worried about its proper place among the other sciences (e.g., Barry, 1986; Epstein, 1984; Fraley & Vargas, 1986; Leighland, 1985; Malagodi & Branch, 1985), and the arguments presented here, however informal and undocumented, may help.

The Development of Behavioral Research Methods: Contributions of B. F. Skinner

INTRODUCTION

The experimental methods of behavior analysis are one of the hallmarks of this field. The ways that behavior analysts ask experimental questions, measure behavior, create experimental comparisons, analyze data, and draw conclusions are often strikingly different from those exemplified in most psychological research, although they share many features with methods used in the natural sciences. In fact, these differences underlie, not only the development of behavior analytic journals (Dews, 1987; Herrnstein, 1987; Skinner, 1959), but the resulting citation patterns (Krantz, 1971).

The origins and rationale of this approach may be unfamiliar to those who are not trained in this field. These methods emerged from natural science traditions that predated Skinner's contributions (for example, see Bernard, 1865/1957). However, his creative laboratory research transformed unclear and uncoordinated methodological practices into a coherent set of strategies and tactics for studying behavior. These were eventually elaborated by Sidman's volume, *Tactics of Scientific Research* (1960).

The rationale for these experimental methods stems from two converging influences on Skinner's work. First, he viewed the study of behavior as a natural science and he adopted a set of scientific values that had long been productive in the natural sciences. Second, Skinner approached his research in the context of a set of facts, empirical generalizations, and assumptions about the nature and workings of behavior. These influences are detailed in a later section but it should be noted that the defense of the resulting research practices is more empirical than rational. The use of these practices by Skinner and his students has evolved and persisted because these methods are effective at describing the relations between environmental variables and behavior. This paper focuses on (a) how these methods developed in the work of Skinner and his colleagues, (b) how they are related to our understanding of behavior, and (c) how they collectively constitute a set of attitudes about the scientific study of behavior.

ORIGINS

Many of the investigations of behavioral phenomena in the late 19th century might be called preexperimental. Even as behavioral research became more formal and systematic during the early 20th century, however, there was no distinctive approach to measuring behavior, arranging comparisons between control and experimental conditions, and drawing conclusions that dominated experimentation. Researchers usually followed the lead of predecessors in their specialty, incorporating variations of their own as necessary. Although the influence of inferential statistics was growing rapidly, Fisher had not yet published his seminal work, *The Design of Experiments* (1935).

This was the situation when Skinner arrived at Harvard for graduate study in the fall of 1928. As chronicled in the second volume of his autobiography (Skinner, 1979), his exposure to the psychological traditions of the day was thorough. Nevertheless, he grew increasingly interested in studying the behavior of the intact organism for its own sake, instead of for what it might reveal about hypothetical inner processes.

Skinner described his earliest experimental activities and their impact on him in a paper he wrote for a meeting of the Eastern Psychological Association in 1955, which was published in the *American Psychologist* in 1956. It was eventually reprinted in *Psychology: A Study of a Science, Vol. II*, edited by Sigmund Koch, and then again in Skinner's *Cumulative Record* (1959). "A Case History of Experimental Method" provides a strikingly informal (the figures and diagrams are hand drawn) and revealing picture of Skinner's thinking as he moved from one curiosity and handmade apparatus to another. The paper is personal and almost casually iconoclastic, while showing the first experimental steps of one of psychology's most influential scientists and scholars.

In the paper, he outlined and exemplified a number of "principles" he discovered that are not formally recognized by scientific methodologists:

1. "When you run onto something interesting, drop everything else and study it" (p. 81).
2. "Some ways of doing research are easier than others" (p. 82).
3. "Some people are lucky" (p. 85).
4. "Apparatuses sometimes break down" (p. 86).
5. "Serendipity—the art of finding one thing while looking for something else" (1959, p. 88).

His examples of these principles in his research describe his invention, discovery, development, or emphasis of free operant procedures, the operant chamber, the cumulative recorder, experimental control, schedules of reinforcement, steady state responding, and within subject comparisons.

UNDERLYING CONVICTIONS

Skinner's ground-breaking, early research was summarized in *The Behavior of Organisms* (1938). As his career as a researcher and teacher flourished, the experimental style so charmingly described in "A Case History" became the *modus operandi* for an entire field. Sidman's influential book (1960) facilitated this development by helping to insure that the next generation of behavioral researchers would understand what had become some of the defining features of behavior analysis.

The natural scientific values that Skinner learned from his study of biology in particular that are evident in his research may be summarized as follows:

1. Experimental questions should ask about the subject matter and the variables that influence it (rather than about theory).
2. Variability in the data is a measure of the degree of experimental control achieved.
3. The value of the data is directly related to the degree of experimental control achieved.
4. Generality emerges from understanding controlling variables.
5. Experimental methods must be adapted to the characteristics of the subject matter.

Whether based on established facts, empirical generalizations, or assumptions, the convictions about behavior that guided Skinner's experimental tactics include the following:

1. Behavior is an important subject matter in its own right.
2. Behavior is a phenomenon that results from interactions between individual organisms and their environments.
3. Behavior–environment interactions occur through time.
4. The natural unit of behavior analysis is the response class.
5. The model that best describes behavior is the three-term contingency.
6. Behavior is orderly when controlling variables are properly managed.
7. The experimenter's behavior must be viewed and managed in the same way as the subject's behavior.

One principle pervaded Skinner's experimental efforts more thoroughly than any others. He was unfailing in his respect for and relentless in Skinner's pursuit of orderly data. This is especially clear in "A Case History," where he reports how his decisions to invent or modify a piece of apparatus, control a variable, create a certain procedure, or analyze data were guided by evidence of, or at least the possibility of, more orderly data. He was even clear in his credit: "I had the clue from Pavlov: control your conditions and you will see order" (Skinner, 1959, p. 80). When this invaluable methodological touchstone is combined with a clear sense of the methodological needs of the subject matter, it will eventually lead an investigator to discover effective experimental methods, which is exactly what Skinner did.

FOUNDATION FOR BEHAVIOR ANALYTIC METHODS

Experimental Questions

These underlying convictions of Skinner and his intellectual progeny collectively provide a foundation for the defining features of behavior analytic research methods. (Description of a coherent and convincing rationale for these tactics is well beyond the scope of this paper, however.) For example, the most consistent feature of behavior analytic experimental questions is, not surprisingly, that their primary interest is in behavior for its own sake. They also tend to focus on a particular response class (or classes) and the environmental variables that might influence it. Typical phraseology takes the form, "What are the relations between Response Class X and Variable Y?" or "What are the effects of Variable Y on Response Class X?" This phraseology signals that their interest in the relations between particular pieces of behavior and environment is usually fairly open-ended. Instead of presupposing what will be found by stating formal hypotheses, they remain open to whatever might be revealed by the data. This experimental approach is far from purely inductive, however, and behavioral researchers usually have reasoned guesses about what might happen and why. However, its emphasis is more on asking questions about behavior than making theory driven predictions.

This approach to asking experimental questions is based on the conviction that behavior is an appropriate subject matter for investigation, not as an epiphenomenon, but in its own right. The focus on particular response classes comes from understanding that this is the natural unit of analysis for the study of behavior. The interest in learning about how certain environmental variables may influence the response class lies in the belief that behavior is largely the result of environmental variables. The construction of questions that ask about behavior without formally forecasting possible or preferred results is based on the realization that the question is part of the set of contingencies that control the experimenter's behavior. Questions that ask more about nature rather than theory encourage the investigator to design and conduct a study that is not biased toward a certain outcome but open to whatever can be discovered about behavior.

Behavioral Measurement

There are a number of characteristics of behavioral measurement that have come to distinguish this methodological approach. As suggested by the focus of experimental questions, what is measured are response classes defined in functional terms, rather than broad categories of possibly different behaviors based on colloquial labels. In laboratory research, response classes are likely to be created by contingencies designed to assure that exactly the same behavior is measured for each subject. In applied research in which there may be no choice about the target behavior, the researcher at least attempts to define the response class functionally, rather than topographically, to assure consistency in controlling variables across subjects.

In addition to accommodating the literature describing the way behavior seems to be organized, these definitional practices attempt to assure that variability in the data does not reflect the effects of experimental variables on a mixture of different response classes, which may have differing sources of control. Measurement of distinct response classes also encourages the investigator to be cautious about extending interpretations to response classes that were not studied.

Following the natural science practice of dimensional measurement, it is not the response class that is actually measured but certain dimensional quantities of it, which are quantified in terms of standard and absolute units of measurement with as much precision as possible. By helping to obtain accurate measures of responding, this tactic decreases the likelihood of variability resulting from imprecise measurement.

Whether detection and recording of the occurrence of the defined response classes is accomplished by equipment or human observers, measurement most often involves counting or timing individual responses. Because the resulting data represent the events of inferential interest, the question of the data's validity is avoided, leaving only accuracy to be assessed. This kind of observational approach minimizes variability contributed by the observational process.

One of the most notable features of the approach to behavioral measurement that Skinner developed concerns the practice of measuring the targeted response class repeatedly under each experimental condition. This usually involves both sampling behavior for extended periods on each occasion, as well as repeating such sessions many times in succession for each condition. This practice accommodates the observed fact that the effects of environmental variables on behavior occur over time. Obtaining a clear picture of behavior change therefore requires sampling thoroughly over time. Furthermore, this tactic is a prerequisite to achieving a high degree of experimental control.

Finally, all of these measurement practices are implemented individually for each subject in a study. This means that at least some decisions may be made separately for each subject, such as the details of response class definition or the timing of observation periods. However, the most revered tactic is separately observing and recording each subject's behavior. In fact, the data are usually retained in individual form throughout at least the initial, if not all stages of analysis.

Skinner was quite clear about the importance of collecting and maintaining individual data, which, even in the early 1930s, contrasted with prevailing traditions. The biological fact that behavior is an intraorganism phenomenon requires this approach, and Skinner found it revealing in his earliest experimental efforts. The goal of orderly data that guided his research tactics was clearly served by this practice and generations of behavior analysts have discovered that this result encourages attending to extraneous influences and identifying reliable and general experimental effects.

Experimental "Design"

For Skinner, experimentation was an evolving process of exploration: "... science does not progress by carefully designed steps called 'experiments' each of which has a well-defined beginning and end. Science is a continuous and often a disorderly and accidental process" (1959, p. 98). His research exemplified this opinion, and he observed, "If I engaged in Experimental Design at all, it was simply to complete or extend some evidence of order already observed" (1959, p. 89). He was primarily concerned with discovering how environmental variables influenced the behavior of individual organisms, noting, "So far as I can see, I began simply by looking for lawful process in the behavior of the intact organism" (1959, p. 80).

His methods yielded orderly behavioral data that were usually unmistakably clear in their message without mathematical processing required by elaborate interpretive rules. When data were too variable or changes too subtle for unambiguous analysis, his solution was to continue searching for ways to improve control over independent or extraneous variables rather than to force a conclusion that he saw as premature. The static conception of experimental design that was becoming popular seemed to him to interfere with what was a dynamic process that, when properly done, needed little or no statistical assistance.

This approach to experimental design begins with the collection of repeated measures of each subject's performance under each condition. This facilitates a concentrated effort to establish a high degree of experimental control. The orderliness of the data under each supposedly constant condition is a metric of the experimenter's control over relevant variables, and this is therefore an occasion for taking whatever steps are necessary to augment such control. Skinner simply said, "I never faced a Problem which was more than the eternal problem of finding order" (1959, p. 88).

Determining how many observations are needed under each condition is an instance of the steady state strategy. Each subject is exposed to a condition until stable data can be produced, which usually requires different numbers of sessions for each subject. Stability is defined, both by general standards, as well as by criteria that are specific to the experiment and the individual subject. The goal is to generate, not just orderly data, but data that represent the full effects of each condition on the behavior of each subject.

Skinner mentioned that he learned about steady states from physical chemistry (1959, p. 87), and he saw them as fundamental to the study of behavior. They provide the investigator with an unhurried opportunity to obtain a satisfactory level of variability, which often requires an active effort to improve experimental control rather than merely waiting until stability emerges. In the process, the data create an evolving and eventually complete picture of the effects of a condition, usually giving the investigator a choice of effects to consider. Although attaining stable responding can take some time to accomplish, there is no better way to gather orderly data that represent the effects of each condition on the behavior of individual subjects.

For Skinner, the essence of design—the comparison of control and experimental conditions—had to be conducted separately for each subject. Not only did his conception of behavior as a subject matter require this approach, his early experiences described in "A Case History" showed him that this tactic provided a clearer picture of the effects of experimental variables than could be obtained by collating data across individuals in some manner. He emphasized this point repeatedly in "A Case History," as well as in other observations on research method.

Not only does this alternative avoid mixing variability resulting from the treatment with intersubject variability, it again encourages the investigator to focus on variable data and address its causes. Excessive variability in individual data serves as a prompt for locating and controlling its sources, instead of for grouping data across individuals and resorting to statistical procedures that use variability as a metric of the size of the difference between conditions. Skinner (1959) made this priority clear in the following example:

> Suppose that measurements have been made on two groups of subjects differing in some detail of experimental treatment. Means and standard deviations for the two groups are determined, and any difference due to the treatment is evaluated. If the difference is in the expected direction but is not statistically significant, the almost universal recommendation would be to study larger groups. But our experience with practical control suggests that we may reduce the troublesome variability by changing the conditions of the experiment. By discovering, elaborating, and fully exploiting every relevant variable, we may eliminate *in advance of measurement* the individual differences which obscure the difference under analysis. This will achieve the same result as increasing the size of groups, and it will almost certainly yield a bonus in the discovery of new variables which would not have been identified in the statistical treatment. (p. 91)

His reference to "practical control" concerns his observation that in applied situations we have little choice but to identify and control the factors that will produce the desired behavior change in a particular individual. He observed:

> When you have the responsibility of making absolutely sure that a given organism will engage in a given sort of behavior at a given time, you quickly grow

impatient with theories of learning. Principles, hypotheses, theorems, satisfactory proof at the .05 level of significance that behavior at a choice point shows the effect of secondary reinforcement—nothing could be more irrelevant. No one goes to the circus to see the average dog jump through a hoop significantly oftener than untrained dogs raised under the same circumstances or to see an elephant demonstrate a principle of behavior. (1959, p. 90)

He proposed that researchers take the same approach in controlling the behavior of their subjects in order to see the effects of experimental variables.

Data Analysis and Interpretation

Skinner (1959) found the increasingly popular statistical conception of data analysis both unnecessary and harmful. He wrote:

> . . . it is a mistake to identify scientific practice with the formalized constructions of statistics and scientific method. These disciplines have their place, but it does not coincide with the place of scientific research. They offer *a* method of science but not, as is so often implied, *the* method. As formal disciplines they arose very late in the history of science, and most of the facts of science have been discovered without their aid. It takes a great deal of skill to fit Faraday with his wires and magnets into the picture which statistics gives us of scientific thinking. And most current scientific practice would be equally refractory, especially in the important initial stages. It is no wonder that the laboratory scientist is puzzled and often dismayed when he discovers how his behavior has been reconstructed in the formal analyses of scientific method. He is likely to protest that this is not at all a fair representation of what he does. (p. 78)

Instead, Skinner simply examined the data from control and experimental conditions individually for each subject, and his persistent pursuit of experimental control meant that these data were sufficiently orderly to facilitate meaningful interpretation.

If Skinner had a "method" of data analysis, it could be called graphical. The data he analyzed were usually displayed in the form of cumulative records. Even in the computer age, the standard cumulative recorders are still a common adjunct to data handling software and graphics packages, although their role is often limited to monitoring session activity. Whether in laboratory or applied research, however, the overwhelmingly dominant approach to data handling remains graphical, as it is in many other natural sciences (see Iverson, 1988 for discussion of the growing appreciation of this approach). Descriptive statistics are often useful supplementary aids, but graphic displays of individual data in the temporal sequence of their occurrence are the first analytical priority. This should not suggest, however, that quantitative analytical procedures, including inferential statistics, do not have a well-earned place among a behavioral researcher's tools.

To those primarily accustomed to inferential statistical procedures, graphical analysis of data may seem unacceptably flexible or even casual; to those trained in these methods, however, it encourages attention to the relations of interest while providing demanding limits on interpretation. More to the point, graphic analysis of individual subject data helps to bring the investigator's behavior under control of the subject matter in ways that lead to accurate and general inferences.

Skinner was struck by how clearly relationships could be seen in graphed, individual data, which was exactly what he wanted to see. He noted, "The organism whose behavior is most extensively modified and most completely controlled in research of the sort I have described is the experimenter himself" (1959, p. 98). He was concerned that the outcome of inferential statistical techniques created a picture of the data that was unlikely to control the investigator's reactions in the same way as graphs of individual subject data (also see Michael, 1974).

Finally, Skinner's approach to generality is implicit in his focus on the individual: "We are within reach of a science of the individual. This will be achieved . . . through an increasing grasp of relevant conditions to produce order in the individual case" (1959, p. 95). He understood that generality did not come from increasing the size of experimental and control groups, but from identifying and understanding the role of variables that influenced the relations in question for each subject. His methodological practices were therefore shaped by successive approximations to order at this level of description and analysis.

Attitudes of Scientific Discovery

These various strategies, tactics, and their rationales may also be collectively described as a set of attitudes about the scientific study of behavior. These attitudes were evident in Skinner's research and writing, as they are today in the work of many behavioral researchers. For instance, one such attitude is the optimistic conviction that behavior can be studied with appropriate experimental methods as successfully as can other natural phenomena. This attitude holds that this subject matter and its influences are no more complex or resistent to analysis and understanding than other natural phenomena.

Another scientific attitude is that control is everything. Whatever the methods required by a behavior in an experiment, it is difficult to give too much attention to controlling variables (whether extraneous or independent) that have or might have some influence on the dependent variable. Control provides clarity, and a corollary view is that nothing can substitute for achieving high levels of experimental control. More importantly, control implies an understanding of the variables that "cause" the behavior.

With this approach to control, a related attitude is that variability is a window through which we can see how behavior works. Variability in behavior either shows us what we need to control (extraneous variables) or the fruits of successful control (independent variables). We want to do everything we can to see behavioral variability more clearly. When we are successful, the only variability we see is that which we have induced by manipulating independent variables, and this helps answer the experimental question.

Perhaps the most overarching attitude is that our scientific methods must always respect and accommodate the subject matter. To be effective, our behavior as scientists must come largely under control of our subject matter, which is one of Skinner's most important scientific achievements. This is why he ended *A Case History* by saying:

> We have no more reason to say that all psychologists should behave as I have behaved than that they should all behave like R. A. Fisher. The scientist, like any organism, is the product of a unique history. The practices which he finds most appropriate will depend in part upon this history. . . . When we have at last an adequate empirical account of the behavior of Man Thinking, we shall understand all this. Until then, it may be best not to try to fit all scientists into any single mold. (1959, pp. 99–100)

PART TWO

MEASUREMENT

Traditions of Behavioral Measurement

INTRODUCTION

Measurement is the cornerstone of all scientific activity. The history of science is coextensive with the history of measurement of natural phenomena because without measurement, science is indistinguishable from naturalistic philosophy. To the extent that natural phenomena yield to measurement, they are removed from the domain of philosophical discourse and emerge as the subject matter of scientific inquiry.

Scientific measurement of natural phenomena involves quantification of observations with respect to a reference scale defined by units that are both absolute and standard. The absolute and standard character of measurement units is important in assessing contemporary research strategies.

One can readily trace the history of science in terms of the history of the invention and application of units of measurement. The history of mathematics is closely related to this history, which may be viewed as a system of rules for combining and manipulating the results of quantified observations. Science and mathematics have therefore developed in a more or less symbiotic fashion.

This reading begins by tracing the development of measurement in science to the end of the 19th century. Our purpose is to convey the richness and continuity of the measurement tradition that has since been adapted to the needs of a natural science of behavior. This preparation also enables us to contrast these traditions with measurement traditions common in the social sciences. The result will be a clear picture of two fundamentally different approaches to the problem of behavioral measurement and their distinct and pervasive implications for other methodological practices.

EARLY HISTORY OF SCIENTIFIC MEASUREMENT

Measurement Prior to the 17th Century

The earliest records of scientific measurement date from around 3000 B.C. and are found in the remains of the Sumerian civilization of the Tigres-Euphrates Valley (Mason, 1953). This culture left cuneiform records indicating the development of a number system and a modest algebra, which permitted them to perform the physical calculations necessary for surveying and building. The Sumerians had apparently both developed the concept of number and applied it to the dimensional quantification of length.

From the Egyptian and Babylonian civilizations, we observe the beginnings of the measurement of time, which is coincidental to the origins of the science of astronomy. The Egyptians, for example, developed the calendar and decimal number system, and around 2000 B.C., the Babylonians developed the 7-day week, as well as our present system of days, hours, and seconds as units of time.

Refinements in measuring space and time were the principal contributions to measurement made by the ancient Greeks. Their major scientific contribution appears to have been in the collateral areas of astronomy and geometry. Hipparchus (ca. 130 B.C.) combined Babylonian observation procedures with Greek geometry to produce the basic system of astronomy, which, as later codified by Ptolemy, survived until the 16th century. Hipparchus also invented the practice of representing points on the earth's surface by geometric coordinates, the foundation of Descartes' analytic geometry. Both Archimedes and Euclid are known to have used the degree as the unit for measuring angles, and Euclid's geometry remains as an elegant example of a formal mathematical system that is valid both logically and empirically.

Historians do not regard the Middle Ages as a period of great advancement in either science or mathematics. Nevertheless, further refinement of the techniques of measuring physical distance facilitated major advances in the technology of navigation, which spawned the Age of Exploration. The essential phenomena of magnetism had been discovered by the 13th century, so that voyagers such as Columbus and Magellan were able to navigate with the aid of a magnetic compass.

The Medieval period is best remembered for the contributions of a handful of natural philosophers, notably Roger Bacon, Robert Grosseteste, and Nicolaus Copernicus. The questioning of certain fundamental assumptions by Copernicus concerning the arrangement of the heavens paved the way for the explosion of scientific inquiry that began in the late 16th and early 17th centuries with Galileo. It is important to note that Bacon and Grosseteste began inquiry into the nature of light and, in the process, pioneered the earliest technology of optics (Crombie, 1961). Bacon, moreover, was among the first to speak of ''laws of nature'' and to suggest the possibility of describing such laws mathematically. It had previously been customary, in the wake of Aristotelian philosophy, to regard both the physical world and mathematical systems as logical ideals to be contemplated. Roger Bacon's work in optics in the 13th century was probably the first instance of an effort to employ mathematics to elucidate principles of nature induced from observation.

Measurement in the 17th Century

Advances in scientific measurement in the 17th century are clearly too numerous to catalog here, and we shall mention only a few of the major developments that bear directly on the emergence of an overall strategy of scientific measurement. In addition to the contributions of Galileo and Descartes, the 17th century witnessed the beginnings of the science of chemistry with the work of Boyle (1627–1691) and Cook (1635–1703). In 1628, William Harvey revealed his discovery of the circulation of the blood with what remains one of the classic demonstration experiments in the history of experimental biology, building on the earlier work of Hippocrates and Galen and the careful anatomical studies of Leonardo da Vinci.

Early in the 17th century, Napier (1550–1617) introduced the idea of continuous measurement of proportion and, in doing so, invented the logarithm. A number of people then developed logarithmic tables, which greatly reduce the computational labor involved in physics and astronomy. The slide rule was developed in 1622 and still consists of two logarithmic scales sliding over one another. Pascal and Leibnitz later developed the first calculating machines, which were essentially mechanical abacuses.

The 17th century also witnessed the development of instrumentation, both as an extension of the senses and as an aid to measurement. Of course, Galileo's perfection of the telescope was the critical event in the development of astronomy, and this technology for manufacturing lenses immediately spawned the microscope, which was probably invented in Holland. In any case, it was the Dutch scientist Leeuwenhoek (1632–1723) who first observed bacteria and spermatozoa with the aid of magnifying lenses.

Other basic instruments were developed or improved during this period, notably the barometer and thermometer. It was with such instruments that new types of measurement units (e.g., the Fahrenheit degree) were defined in terms of the calibrated operation of standardized instruments. In other words, the 17th century marked the beginning of scientific measurement of phenomena that cannot be detected without the aid of instruments and whose units are, therefore, at least partly defined by known properties of the instrument. It should be clear that the existence of such phenomena was not a consequence of the invention of the instruments, only that the units in terms of which they were measured sometimes reflected characteristics of the instrument. By the 18th century, such measurement became commonplace, especially as experimentation with electricity began. Such units as the ohm, watt, volt, and ampere carry the names of the men who invented the devices with which to measure those phenomena that could be detected only by application of such instruments.

Another major occurrence of the 17th century was the development of non-finite mathematics, notably the calculus, invented independently by Newton in England (1666) and Leibnitz in Germany (1675). This development, when coupled with Descartes' earlier refinement of Hipparchus' invention of physical coordinates into analytical algebraic geometry, provided the language for theoretical description and measurement of continuous phenomena such as motion, acceleration, and various limiting processes. With this tool, Newton was able to synthesize the known facts of physics and astronomy into a theory of mechanics that survived intact until the early 20th century. Moreover, the calculus provided a mathematical system in which formal deductions could be restated in the form of scientific predictions to be verified by measurement.

An important by-product of the invention of the calculus was not realized until the 18th century, although the problems were well formulated by 17th-century mathematicians such as DeMoivre, Fermat, and Pascal. The impetus provided by economists, administrators, and gamblers concerned with such uncertain matters as annuities, insurance, and the outcomes of games of chance led to the development of the calculus of probabilities and, eventually, to modern inferential statistics. We see later that this development constitutes the origin of social science measurement, which blended the calculus of probabilities with the social philosophy prevalent in the 18th and 19th centuries.

SUMMARY AND IMPLICATIONS

Let us summarize and elaborate on the implications of early scientific measurement that emerged between the time of the early Egyptians and the later 17th century. Three more or less distinct stages are discernible in the history of scientific measurement. The most primitive stage involved the development of number systems, conventions for enumeration (counting), and standard units of the physical dimensions of time and space. These developments were necessary as science moved from the act of mere classification of sense data to the level of quantitative description implied by measurement. In other words, precise measurement systems permitted objective classification of shared perceptions and provided the basis for meaningful discourse concerning those perceptions.

The second major feature of this history is the parallel development of mathematical systems and models. Throughout the development of the natural sciences, applying the tools of mathematics was usually preceded by accumulating extraordinary amounts of factual data. The nonfinite calculus developed by Newton and Leibnitz was not developed in the abstract. Rather, the calculus and Newton's consequent Laws of Motion may be regarded as the final chapter in the story of direct physical measurement, which took over 5000 years to unfold.

There has been an unsettling tendency in the 20th century to ignore this fact. Formal mathematics has now developed into a separate discipline and is no longer exclusively the consequence of a need to organize vast accumulations of scientific data. As a result, it has become fashionable to attempt to reverse the traditional process by first borrowing or creating a mathematical system and then initiating a search for data that it will organize. Although it is true that Newton's calculus permitted systematic formal deductions that could be translated into scientific predictions, it is not true that every mathematical system necessarily displays this degree of correspondence to the workings of the universe.

The mathematical model building enterprises of today often lack the extensive naturalistic data base that gave Newton's calculus its enormous descriptive and predictive power. For example, predicting the exact time and location of a comet's appearance is not a triumph of the calculus alone, but requires a vast body of data describing the relative positions of the numerous entities in our galaxy. Unfortunately, elaborating the mathematical model will not compensate for the absence of an objective, independently verifiable data base. The discipline of macroeconomics enjoys access to the most sophisticated mathematical models in history, yet remains unable to forecast precisely significant oscillations in the major elements of our national economy.

The third significant facet of the history of scientific measurement is the emergence of measurement through instrumentation. Although the development of instrument technology was well under way by the end of the 17th century, it fairly exploded in the late 18th and 19th centuries during the Industrial Revolution. The development of scientific instrumentation, particularly in the life sciences, has made a valuable set of measuring devices available to the behavioral scientist.

The urge to refine measurement devices remains properly vigorous. An important cautionary note must be sounded, however. The development of measuring instruments almost always followed the isolation and identification of the phenomenon that the instruments were designed to measure. Although new phenomena have been discovered with instruments designed for another purpose, this remains the exception rather than the rule.

Nevertheless, fascination with instrumentation has sometimes led scientists to define phenomena *solely* on the basis of the behavior of instruments. This extreme form of operationalism[1] is typified by the practice of attempting to study human cognition by computer simulation. Programming a computer to "solve problems" in ways that seem to mimic human efforts inextricably involves the computer circuitry in both the model and the process. Such metaphors of computer technology as input, output, storage, coding, retrieval, and so on, appear to have acquired the status of biological reality and have become the subject matter of a highly specialized "science." Actually, these terms have no necessary biological referents, and the "behavior" of a computer resembles that of a human in only a limited sense. Originally, it was hoped that such activity would have heuristic value in guiding research into nervous system functioning, but the supremacy of fascination with the computer, as evidenced by the distinctive emerging language, has rendered this ideal all but unattainable.

---

[1]Briefly, *operationalism* is the doctrine that scientific constructs are defined by the operations through which they are measured.

It may be argued that a similar fascination with biomedical instrumentation has occasionally misdirected the efforts of many interested in studying behavior. Again, naive operationalism gives rise to a synthetic reification of ancient constructs that Descartes discarded in the Middle Ages for their lack of explanatory utility. For example, modern electronic technology has given us the capability of monitoring with astonishing precision the minute electrical phenomena that are attendant to all living tissue. Investigators therefore confidently attach electrodes to various surfaces of the human body and observe the correlation between potential or resistance changes and various events in the surrounding environment. In attempting to explain those correlations, however, some researchers invent names for the systematic and orderly fluctuations in the data, then ascribe process or explanatory status to their inventions.

As an illustration, a drop in skin resistance coupled with accelerations in cardiac and respiratory activity defines arousal, which is also used to explain the drop in skin resistance, and so on. Unfortunately, fluctuations of a solid state polygraph bestow upon the concept of arousal no greater scientific utility for the explanation of behavior than Hippocrates' concept of humors contributed to the science of physiology.

It is important to understand the implications of these historical points for the development of a natural science of behavior. The evolution of the natural sciences of matter was largely coextensive with the development of instrumentation and language systems for measuring and describing their independently defined subject matter. The development of instrumentation within each discipline is still dictated primarily by the nature of the phenomena studied by that discipline, and the science of behavior must follow the same strategy.

As we see later in this reading, the tradition established by the measurement strategies of early natural science continues uninterrupted to the present day in the natural science of behavior. During the late 18th and early 19th centuries, however, a number of intellectual developments coalesced to prompt a major departure from the tradition of natural scientific measurement. This deviation has its origins in a problematic philosophical conception of the nature and the causes of variability, and it has evolved into a set of measurement strategies that constitute the animus of the modern social sciences.

THE ORIGINS OF VAGANOTIC STRATEGIES

Preliminary Developments

We noted earlier that late in the 17th century mathematicians began using the principles of Newton's calculus to formulate the theory of probability. Support for this work came in part from the wealthy patrons of the mathematician–scientists of the time. These benefactors often sought a return on their academic investment in the form of increased revenue at the gambling tables.

During the same period, concern with the reliability of measurement began to emerge. The study of error appears to have its origins in 1806 in the work of Legendre, who, along with Euler and Gauss, developed the least squares method for extracting the best measure of a physical event from a set of measures that displays variability. In 1778, Laplace produced the continuous equation of the law of error, and the connection with the calculus was made. The mathematics of probability had become as formally rigorous as the mathematics of motion.

The importance of Laplace's provision of a nonfinite calculus of probability can hardly be overemphasized in considering the subsequent application of this mathematical system. Nonfinite mathematics embodied the notion of limits, from which it is but a short step to the notion of approximation of an ideal. Thus, the mathematics of probability provides a way of estimating a "true" value from quantitative assessment of the dispersion among empirically measured estimates of that value. An elementary theorem in probability theory holds that as the sample size upon which such estimates are based becomes larger, the error of estimate of the true moment of the distribution becomes smaller. The consequences of this theorem for measurement practices was profound. The possibility of discovering and even defining true values out of apparently uncontrollable variation rendered quantifiable a vast range of phenomena that had previously been discussed only in qualitative or metaphorical terms.

Descriptive Use of the Normal Law of Error

The use of the mathematics of probability to estimate true values fascinated the Belgian statistician Adolphe Quetelet (1796–1874), who is regarded by many as the founder of the social sciences.[2] While still in his 20s, Quetelet discovered the earlier efforts of Laplace and Fourier to apply statistical techniques to the description of census data. Although trained as an astronomer, Quetelet had a profound interest in human affairs and quickly grasped the possibility of using the calculus of probability to estimate the ideals of measurable human characteristics, much as calculus provided defined quantitative descriptions of the motions of the planets.

It was Quetelet's notion that every individual represented an attempt by nature to achieve perfection but that, like a person shooting at a target, nature's aim was never exact. For example, by collecting a large number of measures of people's heights and observing that the distribution closely resembled the curve of the Normal Law of Error, Quetelet could easily calculate the "ideal" height. He went on to suggest (quoted by Lazarfeld, 1961) the use of this technique to "measure the qualities of people which can only be assessed by their effect" (p. 170). Quetelet suggested, for instance, that we might measure the attribute of drunkenness by observing the frequency with which a given

---

[2]The contributions of Quetelet are beautifully summarized by Paul Lazarfeld (1961).

individual gets drunk. Again, large numbers of such observations would yield a distribution from which it would be possible to estimate the natural idea or at least provide a stable description of the prevalence of the tendency in the society.

It is important to note the teleological assumptions underlying Quetelet's work. The existence of natural norms or ideals was assumed, not demonstrated, and the results of the statistical manipulations upon the variability of direct observation only served to affirm the consequent. In doing so, Quetelet was merely reflecting the philosophical temper of his day. His first major work, *Sur l'homme et le developement de ses facultés*, was published in 1835—nearly 25 years before the appearance of *The Origin of Species*. No sacred oxen were gored by Quetelet's assumption of natural ideals being imperfectly achieved in the individual case. To the contrary, the existence of error in the moral sense justified the religious and social authority of the day. No doubt great comfort was drawn from the use of error of a different sort to describe social phenomena.

Of more concern to us is Quetelet's willingness to use variability as the basis for defining latent entities or characteristics. Although Quetelet was apparently careful to avoid attaching causal significance to such characteristics, his successors have not been so cautious. It is easy to see how Quetelet's work gives the prestige of quantification to such supposed determinants of human behavior as traits, personality attributes, and so on, which were already prominent in the language of the culture. Quetelet thus accidentally arranged the conditions for reintroducing into science, albeit by different names, a whole class of explanatory variables whose origins are philosophical or religious rather than empirical.

Psychophysics

Quetelet's use of observed variability was primarily for the purpose of estimating ideals or norms as well as propensities and dispositions. It was Gustav Fechner (1801–1887) who, working in an entirely different tradition, developed the idea of combining observed variability with the mathematics of probability to create units and scales of measurement. Fechner was interested in establishing a correspondence between changes in the physical energy directed at a human observer and the private experience of that observer. Ernst Weber had earlier shown that the ability of the observer to detect a change in physical stimulation was a constant function of the proportion by which the stimulating energy was increased or decreased. Thus, the amount by which one light must vary in intensity in comparison to a reference light before a subject will report seeing two lights of differing intensities depends on the intensity of the reference light. In making such determinations, the intensity of the comparison light is adjusted until the subject reports a difference.

Fechner proceeded to make a large number of such adjustments until he found a difference value for which the subject reported noticing a difference on 50% of the occasions the stimulus was presented. The corresponding physical difference between the two lights then defined one sensory scale unit or JND (Just Noticeable Difference). Stevens (1957) referred to this procedure as "measurement by confusion," because variability in the subject's behavior is clearly the substrate from which the measurement units are defined.

Let us underscore the importance of this development. The contributions of Quetelet and Fechner constitute the basic point of departure for entirely new definitional measurement strategies in science. Observed variability in measured natural phenomena is described with the aid of the calculus of probability and, from these descriptions, not only are new phenomena defined, but units for scaling them are created. Two separate procedures (that do not necessarily occur together) are involved here, and both may be described as *vaganotic*.[3] Vaganotic definition denotes the practice of defining phenomena into existence on the basis of variation in a set of underlying observations. Similarly, vaganotic measurement refers to the creation of scales and units of measurement on the basis of variation in a set of underlying observations.

We can find no precedent in the natural sciences for this method of defining phenomena and their units of measurement.[4] The use of procedures wherein the phenomena being measured or the units of measurement are defined in terms of variability characterizing a set of otherwise direct observations seems peculiar to the social sciences. This is one of the most fundamental differences between the natural and social sciences. Not only does this difference dictate a vastly different approach to defining and quantifying subject matter, this difference has profound implications for the tactics of experimental design, control, and interpretation.

---

[3]Vaganotic is derived from the Latin *vagare* (to wander) compounded with the Latin *notare* (to designate with a brand of mark) and hence conveys the characteristic of instability in the meaning of the entity thus described. Although we generally eschew the practice of introducing new terms into the scientific vernacular, precision and economy of exposition, together with the overriding importance of differentiating among scientific measurement strategies, justifies it in this case. Furthermore, the distinction we draw has been anticipated by other writers, notably Boring (1920), but has not previously been reduced to categorical description. Such dimensions as ideographic-nomothetic and ipsitive-normative have been offered to furnish a basis for discussing the general issue of individual versus group sources of data, but do not embrace the underlying question of units of measurement.

[4]However, we can invent one to highlight the absurdity of such a practice were this to be applied in the natural sciences. Let us imagine a scientist who needs to determine the length of a certain object. No scale unit such as the centimeter exists, and, thus, there is no calibrated ruler with which to perform the measurement task. The resourceful scientist has a large ball of string, however, and proceeds to cut lengths of string that match all of the objects in the laboratory and surrounding buildings, thus ensuring a large representative sample of string bits. The scientist collects the string segments and presents all possible pairs of them to a panel of trained judges with the instruction, "Tell me which one is longer." Using the method of paired comparison analysis, the scientist can extract from these judgments a scale of subjectively judged lengths and can then assign to the object the scale value obtained for the matching piece of string. If the scientist wished, he or she could even assign a unit name to the string length that matches the object and proceed to measure other objects in terms of this unit. No problem exists until another scientist in another laboratory wishes to investigate the same phenomena and faces the task of measuring the lengths of other examples of the same kind of object. The same process used to arrive at scale values and a unit in the second case will obviously yield different values and a different unit, with fatal effects on the discovery of facts about the class of objects under study.

Fechner's work launched the discipline of psychophysics, the history of which has been well documented by Boring (1942, 1950, 1961). Boring (1961) points out that Fechner's dubious assumption that the JND provided a unit of subjective magnitude impeded progress in psychophysics until the development of direct scaling methods by Stevens in the 1950s.

Mental Measurement

An even greater impact of Fechner's thought on the contemporary scene may be traced through the work of Francis Galton. Galton (1822–1911), a cousin of Charles Darwin, synthesized the ideas of Quetelet with those of Fechner and launched the mental measurement movement. Galton was evidently impressed by Quetelet's vast accumulation of instances in which the Normal Law of Error also described the distribution of various characteristics in the human population. He assumed, as Quetelet probably had, that mental ability was similarly distributed. Following Fechner's innovation, Galton mapped the theoretical normal distribution onto a 14-step, equal-interval scale and in one grand gesture invented, not only the concept of intelligence, but a means of measuring it as well.

This idea was put to immediate practical use by Binet (1857–1911) in France and Cattell (1860–1944) in the United States. These men created tests composed of items selected for their ability to prompt performances that would display variability across a number of individuals. Because this variability was distributed in accordance with the Normal Law of Error and because Galton has defined mental ability in those terms, it was natural to assert that these were tests of mental ability. The sustained impact of this activity on American psychology is due in no small measure to the entrepreneurial abilities of Cattell, who founded or edited a number of prestigious journals in addition to forming the Psychological Corporation for manufacturing and selling mental tests. Mention of Cattell's early leadership in the American Psychological Association completes our account of the forces that forged virtually unified adoption of the strategies of vaganotic definition and measurement early in the history of psychology.

Statistical Scaling

The story of the Normal Law of Error as a basis for description has one final catholicizing installment—the use of the techniques of statistical inference for purposes of scaling. In 1889, Galton published *Natural Inheritance*, in which he observed the existence of what he called "co-relation" between certain variables measured in the population (e.g., the heights of fathers and sons). He also noticed the phenomenon of regression toward the mean, and according to Boring (1961), gave the problem to F. Y. Edgeworth for mathematical solution. Edgeworth developed the index of a correlation, from which Karl Person worked out the product moment method of linear correlation in 1896.

In hindsight, it is clear that Pearson's development of the mathematics of correlation was a crucial step in the history of vaganotic practices. Correlational procedures enable the investigator to separate variability that is shared from that which is unique among variables. From the implicit assumption that variability may be used to define and measure phenomena, the investigator is then encouraged to invent names for these components of variability, investigate their relation with other similarly defined entities, and so on, *ad infinitum*. Current practices in factor analysis and multidimensional scaling illustrate this strategy. Not surprisingly, a proliferation of jargon results from the problem of finding names for all the little particles of variability created by these methods.

Vaganotic measurement of differences, which has become the standard device for evaluating experimental effects in American psychology and education, emerged from the work of Ronald Fisher and his student, W. S. Gosset. Gosset elegantly demonstrated in 1908 that the error in using a sample mean as an estimate of a population mean could be inferred probabilistically from the variability of the sample observations. This made possible the actuarial assessment of differences among sample means, again with reference to the Normal Law of Error.

The logical rationale underlying this practice derives from the device of proof by contradiction. It is assumed that the variability observed in a set of experimental observations is not due to the operation on a specified experimental treatment. One then calculates the probability of obtaining the observed differences among means under these conditions. If that probability is sufficiently small, one concludes that the observed differences are the result of something other than natural variability, thus contradicting the original assumption. The experimental treatment is then selected as the most likely explanation.

The fact that this procedure constitutes vaganotic measurement in exactly the same sense as does Galton's 14-point scale of mental ability may not be immediately obvious. To understand why this practice, usually referred to as *hypothesis testing*, extends the measurement practices of Galton, one need only carefully examine the conventional use of formulae for calculating the *t*-ratio.[5] The standard formula for calculating *t* is given by:

$$t = \frac{(\bar{x}_1 - \bar{x}_2) - (\mu_1 - \mu_2)}{S_{\bar{x}_1 - \bar{x}_2}}$$

where $\bar{x}_1$ is the mean of the first sample, $\bar{x}_2$ is the mean of the other sample, $(\mu_1 - \mu_2)$ is the hypothesized difference in population means (usually 0), and $S_{\bar{x}_1 - \bar{x}_2}$ is the standard error of the difference in means.

Critical to our discussion is the quantity $S_{\bar{x}_1 - \bar{x}_2}$. Known as the estimated *standard error of the difference*, it is calculated as follows:

$$S_{\bar{x}_1 - \bar{x}_2} = \frac{S_1^2}{n_1 - 1} + \frac{S_2^2}{n_2 - 1}$$

---

[5]An identical argument can be made in the case of the *F*-ratio as used in the analysis of variance.

where S_1^2 is the sample variance of the first sample, S_2^2 is the sample variance of the other sample, and n_1 and n_2 are the respective sample sizes.

The quantities S_1^2 and S_2^2 are measures of the variability observed in the two samples and are completely determined by the measures that comprise the samples. Calling the quantity $S_{\bar{x}_1 - \bar{x}_2}$ a standard error does not make it standard in any but the most local and temporary sense. It is "standard" only with respect to the samples of observations obtained and thus owes its fleeting existence entirely to whatever variability characterizes the samples. As a reference value against which the magnitude of the numerator is compared, this "standard error" is determined by the same set of measurements that define the quantitative differences it is proposed to assess.

The actual assessment process is removed one step from computation of t. The decision whether the obtained difference in means is large enough to warrant rejection of the null hypothesis is made by consulting a table of probabilities associated with various values of t under conditions where the true difference is 0. The tabled values relate variation in t to probability values in a perfectly legitimate mathematical manner. However, the use of these values tends to be binary and categorical; a result is significant if the associated value does not exceed a certain amount, usually .05.

In summary, obtained variability is again used to devise a scale whose units are mappings of discrete densities under the curve describing the Normal Law of Error, exactly after the fashion of Galton and Fechner. The resulting scale is composed of only two categories—significant and nonsignificant—and assignment to one or the other bears no fixed relation to the absolute size of the difference under examination.

Fisher, Gosset, and their numerous followers in the discipline of mathematical statistics should not be held responsible for the fact that their mathematically valid procedure for assessing deviations of a random variable have been subverted for use as measuring devices in the social sciences. Fisher could hardly have anticipated that, in his discussion of fiducial limits, his arbitrary example of .05 would become the index point of a rigid binary scale for measuring the quality of scientific research. This unfortunate degradation has nevertheless become the ultimate consequence of the 19th-century insight that variability could be used not only to define otherwise nonextensive phenomena, but simultaneously to create units and scales for their measurement.

THE ORIGINS OF IDEMNOTIC STRATEGIES

The tradition of scientific measurement that insists on enumeration in terms of exact, standard, and absolute quantities or units was by no means stifled by the activities of Quetelet, Fechner, and Galton in the 19th century. As a matter of fact, with the exception of the undue attention paid their work by philosophers of science in the early 20th century, we may conclude that the vaganotic tradition inspired by these men has been largely ignored in natural scientific circles.

It would be beyond both the scope and purpose of this reading to attempt to summarize the vast array of developments that occurred in scientific measurement during the 19th and early 20th centuries. Instead, we pick up the thread of innovation that begins with Legendre's attempt to smooth measurement error as it winds its way through the scientific and technological revolution of the 19th century, eventually presenting us with the rudiments of a technology for direct measurement of behavior.

As an astronomer, Legendre was concerned with the fact that simultaneous observations by different observers displayed variability. As we have seen, he approached the problem by using the calculus of probability to compute a value about which the variation was minimized. Although probably improving the accuracy of estimated measurement, this solution did nothing to control or eliminate the variability among observers. Of course, at no time did Legendre rely on observer variability to define the subject matter of his inquiry. His legitimate use of descriptive statistics to quantify measurement error should not be misconstrued as an early precursor of vaganotic definition, because the phenomena to be studied existed prior to any measurement.

A subsequent 19th-century astronomer, F. W. Bessel, noticed that different observers reacted with different latencies to the appearance of a star in their telescopic field of view. By carefully equating the aiming point of each observer's telescope, Bessel found that part of the variability in the observer's latencies was constant for each individual. The notion of reaction time thus came into being and with it, the impetus for technical refinement of timing devices capable of measuring very short intervals. Better experimental estimates of personal reaction times were made by having people observe a swinging pendulum, an innovation also attributed to Bessel. Bessel may have been among the first to measure directly a universal dimension of behavior, its latency.

Measurement of reaction time also played a critical role in the experimental psychology of Wilhelm Wundt (1832–1920). Wundt trained in medicine and physiology, and his pioneering work in perception clearly extended these disciplines. As a disciple of Helmholtz, Wundt knew the value of proper experimental control, and there is reason to doubt that he was overwhelmed by Fechner's indirect psychophysical scaling techniques (although he did use Fechner's methods in his studies of perception). From our point of view, Wundt's principal contribution lies in his attempt to develop a "mental chronometry." He evolved an elaborate scheme for timing (and, presumably, measuring) what he thought to be conscious processes. He gradually complicated the stimulus array and response requirements for a particular subject and reasoned that, by subtracting the successively longer reaction times, he could get a measure of the time required for such processes as apperception. Regardless of what Wundt thought he was measuring with these methods, his units of measurement remained standard and absolute. He was unquestionably measuring a characteristic of overt human behavior that changed in orderly ways as a result of controlled changes in the environment. In addition, further advances in the instrumentation for behavioral timing came from Wundt's laboratory.

The use of simple counting to measure behavior, an idea also suggested by Quetelet, developed further in the late 19th century. Both Galton and Binet were prodigious counters and were obliged to count the occurrences of certain behaviors in order to obtain a measure of test behavior in response to test items, although the variability obtained in their data was not subject to further experimental analysis. Perhaps the first investigator to experimentally isolate the sources of variability in counts of behavior was Hermann Ebbinghaus (1850–1901). In 1885, Ebbinghaus began using numerical frequency of verbal recall as a measure of strength of association or memory. He was influenced by Fechner to the extent that Fechner suggested the possibility of measuring psychological events, but he did not incorporate Fechner's notion of scaling. Instead, he invented a novel experimental independent variable, the nonsense syllable and defined and investigated the phenomena of learning and memory in terms of simple, direct counting procedures (number of trials to completely learn a list, number of items recalled as a function of the passage of time, etc.).

The extension of the natural science approach to measurement to animal behavior has its origins in the work of E. L. Thorndike (1898) who, in pursuing an understanding of animal intelligence, arranged puzzles for animals to solve and recorded both the time for solution and the number and nature of unsuccessful attempts. Although the object of Thorndike's inquiry was not directly accessible to measurement, it is important to note his reliance on environmental control and his use of absolute units to describe behavior.

Probably the earliest and still among the most elegant uses of instrumentation in the measurement of animal behavior is in the work of Pavlov. In describing his measurement procedures, Pavlov (1927) wrote:

> The secretory reflex presents many important advantages for our purposes. It allows an extremely accurate measurement of the intensity of reflex activity, since here the number of drops in a given time may be counted or else the saliva may be used to displace a colored fluid in a horizontally placed graduated glass tube. (p. 17)

One of the first reports of automatic behavioral recording may also be found in Pavlov's (1927) writings:

> As the saliva flows into the hemispherical bulb the colored fluid is displaced along the graduated tube where the amount of secretion can be read off accurately. Further it is not difficult to fix up an automatic electrical recording device which will split up the displaced fluid into drops of exactly equal volume and reduce any lag in the movement of the fluid to a minimum. (pp. 18–19)

Three important features characterize the work of Wundt, Thorndike, Ebbinghaus, and Pavlov and place it squarely in the natural scientific tradition. First, their units of measurement were standard and absolute. None went the route of Fechner and Galton and developed vaganotic scale of measurement. Second, all apparently viewed variability as the scientific window through which to observe the workings of basic controlling relationships. All four of these investigators were admittedly concerned with phenomena other than behavior, but none succumbed to the temptation to mix behavioral variability with the theory of probability and produce a substance from which to fashion tools of measurement.

The third feature that characterizes the work of these four investigators is their shared tactic of collecting a large number of observations from each of a relatively small number of subjects. Ebbinghaus is known to have used only one subject, himself. Surprising as it may seem to some readers, the quality of their science did not suffer as a result of such small sample sizes. These investigators were concerned with establishing the relations between controlled aspects of the experimental environment and the behavior of their subjects, not with describing the variability of static characteristics in a population.

From the standpoint of the development of a science of behavior, the work of Wundt, Ebbinghaus, Thorndike, and Pavlov established the feasibility of applying traditional scientific measurement strategies to behavioral phenomena. Inasmuch as the measurement practices differ so dramatically from the vaganotic strategies common in the social sciences, it is important to have a single descriptor for the type of measurement we are now considering. We have chosen the term *idemnotic*[6] to denote the type of measurement that incorporates absolute and standard units whose existence is established independently of variability in the phenomena being measured. The implications of this measurement strategy for the scientific study of behavior are pervasive. We argue that the measurement strategy adopted influences the resulting tactics of subject matter definition, experimental design, reduction and analysis of data, and interpretation.

As in the case of vaganotic practices, the term idemnotic could be used to refer to the manner in which phenomena are defined, as well as to the nature of measurement units. Thus, an idemnotic definition would be made without reference to variability in a set of observations made along some underlying dimension. This usage would certainly not be inappropriate in that attention would be called to the separate functions in scientific analysis of named properties of events and their variability. Except for the historical digression occasioned by the emergence of the vaganotic tradition, however, this clarification seems largely unnecessary. The fact that virtually all natural scientific definitions are idemnotic has implications for other methodological issues that are of at least equal importance to the consequences of idemnotic measurement.

SIGNIFICANCE OF MEASUREMENT STRATEGY

Further Idemnotic Characteristics

We shall now consider a few of the more general consequences of adoption of a vaganotic as opposed to an idemnotic strategy for the enterprise of knowledge production. Although these comments are particularly relevant to

---

[6]Idemnotic is derived from the Latin *idem* (the same) compounded with the Latin *notare* (to designate with brand of mark) and thus communicates the stability of meaning of a unit of measurement that is standard and absolute.

generating scientific knowledge about behavior, we believe their applicability extends to all domains of natural phenomena.

The idemnotic–vaganotic distinction is a simple bifurcation of a highly complex historical dimension. We can better appreciate the significance of the schism if we briefly explore two additional facets of the idemnotic strategy—standardization and anchoring to arbitrary constants. The earliest forms of idemnotic measurement involved inventing standard units for the description of the three physical parameters—distance, mass, and time. Very shortly thereafter, new phenomena were described and investigated in terms of compound units resulting from algebraic combinations of the basic three. For example, the Greeks worked with velocity (distance/time) and density (mass/distance).

Beginning in the 16th century, new units of measurement, often associated with special instruments, were described. An attempt was made to standardize such units by defining them with respect to common elements. For example, we define the Newton (N) as the force required to give a mass of 1 kg an acceleration of 1 m/sec^2. Pressure units are force units divided by area units, for example, N/m^2. A convenient reference is the force of atmosphere pressing on the earth. Thus, a unit called the atmosphere (atm) is advanced, its value being 10.3×10^5 N/m^2. Measurement of atmospheric pressure is often in terms of millimeters of mercury (mm *Hg*), one of which is the pressure exerted by a column of mercury 1 mm high. It is also equivalent to 1/760 atm and came into being through the invention of the mercury barometer in 1643 by Torricelli. Clearly, this unit can be reduced to a combination of the three basic dimensions—distance, mass, and time.

During the Age of Reason, the French attempted to anchor all physical measurement in natural phenomena, thinking that by doing so they would achieve an invariance dictated by the constants of nature. For example, in adopting the metric system in 1791, they defined the meter as the distance from the equator to either pole $\times 10^{-6}$. Nowadays, length and time can be anchored to atomic phenomena by reference to certain wavelengths of light and atomic vibrational phenomena, but no such natural standard exists for measuring mass. This poses no problem, however, because standards for the meter, kilogram, and second exist independently of natural referents.

The desire to anchor units of measurement in natural phenomena may have been partly responsible for Quetelet's efforts to divine the existence of social phenomena out of observed variation. Had it been possible to establish the existence of such phenomena independently of behavioral variability, a constant value could have been selected as an anchor for an idemnotic scale. This was not the case, of course. The existence of sensation was established by observing behavioral variability (from which Fechner defined the JND), but the existence of the atmosphere was not similarly established by observing pressure variations. Because the atmosphere was defined and known to exist prior to measurement of pressure variations, an arbitrary but absolute value of pressure could be selected as a reference value for a standard scale. Fortunately, behavior, like the atmosphere, is an objective phenomenon whose existence does not depend on inference from a more basic substrate.

Contemporary Behavioral Usage

This idemnotic measurement tradition finds full expression in the contemporary natural science of behavior. Behavior possesses many of the characteristics of matter in motion, and the same principles of measurement are applicable. Units have been developed for describing frequency and acceleration, as well as the dimensional quantities of speed and latency. Unfortunately, a large segment of the scientific community that considers behavior its subject matter has its origins in the vaganotic tradition of the social sciences and has been unable to reap the benefits of measurement based on standard and absolute units.

Contemporary vaganotic measurement practices may be distinguished by the presence or absence of a formal, labeled unit and the extent to which variation is either implicit or explicit in the construction of the scale. For example, the Thurstone Case V method of paired comparisons for scaling preference makes explicit use of the variability in the preferences of observers making pairwise comparisons among a set of objects but does not attach an independent unit label to the numerical outcome. Perhaps a more widely known illustration is found in such aptitude tests as the Graduate Record Examinations, the Scholastic Aptitude Test, and so forth. On the other hand, statistically averaged performance on achievement tests is used to define performance expectation for various grade levels and these quantities are invested with a time label—for example, 5.2 years.

Determination of mental age norms for certain intelligence tests follows the same practice. The underlying variability is often only assumed and does not enter into the calculation of scale values. Technically, such measurement is not even vaganotic as we have defined it, although most of the criticisms obviously apply. "On a scale from 1 to 5, how do you like this dessert?" typifies this practice. There is no answer to the question, "One to 5 what?," so it is obvious that no unit label is imparted to such numbers. Variability is nonetheless assumed and enters the measurement process when the allowable range is decided. For example, "3" on a scale from 1 to 10 presumably means something different from "3" on a scale of 1 to 5. In order to evaluate the response, "3," it is necessary to know the limits of possible variation.

It is difficult to find cases in which the underlying variability is only assumed, but a formal unit label is nevertheless present. Informally, "points" on various scales serve the linguistic function of a unit and this practice is widespread. Classroom achievement tests, developmental rating scales ("Score *1* if the student does it, *0* if the student does not"), and many trait inventories are but a few examples of measuring devices that are not derived from explicit variability but nevertheless yield results that connote a unitary dimension.

Variability

The fundamental task of all science is to account for variability within and among natural phenomena. A necessary first step in the accounting process has always been quantifying observations to obtain an accurate description of

the variation that occurs. Unfortunately, using variability as the sole determinant of scales of measurement almost forces, for the sake of consistency,
the assumption that such variability is both inherent and invariant in the
phenomenon under consideration.

Either of these assumptions is practically fatal to the development of an exact science, although, in combination, they are comforting to the proponents
of the view that an exact science of behavior is an a priori impossibility. The
assumption that variability is inherent, as Sidman (1960) capably pointed out,
discourages the search for its causes. The strategic essence of the experimental method in science involves treating variability as the subject matter to be
understood and explained. But understanding and explaining must be preceded by measurement, and this measurement must be in terms of units that are
not defined by the same variability as the phenomenon they are designed to
quantify.

The widespread use of vaganotic measurement procedures in the social
sciences has lent tacit support to the implicit contention that human behavior
is inherently variable and thus qualitatively different from other natural
phenomena. We must recognize that as a consequence of vaganotic measurement, this assertion has come to be accepted by definition rather than by
demonstration. The assumption of inherent variability has become tantamount
to proclaiming a scientific sanctuary for the philosophical doctrine of indeter-
minism, a critical proposition of the body of invented knowledge from which
many prevailing conceptions of the causes of human behavior are drawn.

The alleged uniqueness of human behavior among natural phenomena has
long been proffered as justifying the development of methods of investigation
different from those of the natural sciences. The results of applying these
methods further encourages the assertion of inherent variability because they
are inevitably characterized by the presence of unexplained residual variance
that is often measurement induced. Because the phenomena under study are
constantly changing, vaganotically obtained units of measurement are changing as well, and the discovery and communication of lawful relations becomes
virtually impossible.

For example, vaganotic definition and measurement of intelligence ensures
that whatever is represented by any proposed unit (such as an IQ point) varies
with each restandardization of the test. As a result, such questions as the role
of genetics in the determination of intelligence will never be answered at the
population level because as the independent variable (genetic composition)
changes, so do measures of the dependent variable. In addition, any discourse
concerning vaganotically defined phenomena is confusing at best. At its worst,
it is meaningless, an assessment of such terminology being rendered with increasing frequency by the lay and professional public. Many people who have
become accustomed to measuring their own weight in pounds and their con-
sumption of electricity in kilowatt hours have difficulty comprehending a measure of their child's academic achievement given in terms of other children's
academic achievement expressed as a unit of time.

Perhaps the best illustration of the strategic differences stemming from vaganotic versus idemnotic measurement is in the resulting methods of handling the variability among individual characteristics within a population, which so fascinated Quetelet and Galton. As we have seen, both Quetelet and Galton took this variability as given. The former measured and described it; the latter used it as a means of scaling the entity to which he attributed its existence.

In contrast, Gregor Mendel (1822–1884) viewed the obvious morphological variability among members of a species as something to be explained and, along with Galton, suspected that heredity might be partly responsible. In his classic experiments with garden peas, Mendel showed that by controlling the principal factor responsible for heredity, one could produce populations of garden peas whose mathematical distributions of characteristics were not only predictable but changeable at will. As a result, research in the physiology and chemistry of reproduction was greatly stimulated, and we now have a rather exact science of genetics. It is doubtful that the subsequent benefits to humanity would have resulted had Mendel been disposed to regard the variability in color and conformity of garden peas as the basis for the creation of a scale for measuring "peaness."

Other Methodological Decisions

Another issue concerns the extent to which acceptance of vaganotic or idemnotic measurement strategies influences other basic methodological decisions. This influence is pervasive, usually unrecognized, and often quite powerful in its ultimate effects on the characteristics of the data that are generated and on our interpretations of their meaning. It should be clear that the general measurement strategy is seminal for other decisions by limiting, permitting, encouraging, and sometimes requiring the selection of various tactics.

For example, a vaganotic approach encourages measuring the behavior of a relatively large number of subjects, which in turn necessitates defining responses that can be observed in a manner compatible with large groups. These tactics come close to requiring group comparison experimental designs, which usually force the use of inferential statistics to assess variability and determine interpretative conclusions.

By comparison, idemnotic measurement is somewhat less forceful in its influence, not so much encouraging or requiring subsequent decisions as permitting the possibility of measurement, design, and interpretative tactics that can lead to markedly superior data characteristics. The use of standard and absolute units allows the definition of response in a form that facilitates direct and continuous observation of a small number of subjects individually, thus permitting the use of more powerful experimental designs that approach variability in a vastly different and more productive manner. These tactics lead to data that actually constitute a different subject matter with characteristics allowing a strikingly dissimilar interpretative process.

Subject Matter

One impact of measurement strategies merits special attention. A subtle but significant reciprocity distinguishes the relation between the conception of the subject matter under investigation and the measurement strategy chosen to approach the investigation. Answering the "chicken or the egg" question raised by the relations between subject matter definition and measurement strategy is less important than understanding the relations and their implications. Whichever comes first or exerts more control, it is clear that the conception of the nature of the subject matter to be investigated is a major consideration in selecting a measurement strategy. Defining behavioral events that are hypothetical, inferred, or otherwise beyond direct observation encourages the choice of indirect measurement practices that are usually vaganotic in style. Interest in overt behavioral events prompts describing them with standard and absolute units of measurement. Furthermore, establishing criteria for observational and measurement reliability becomes far less difficult when the units of measurement are stable.

The correlation between subject matter definition and measurement strategy is less than perfect, and conflicting examples are not difficult to find. However, the assumptions with which we approach a subject matter are potent sources of control over many experimental decisions, the first and most important of which is selecting a guiding measurement strategy.

On the other hand, the impact on subject matter of the measurement strategy to which a research program is committed is probably less obvious and well understood. The vaganotic strategy guarantees that the data upon which interpretations are based will be minimally composed of both the variability that is imposed by the treatment and the variability that results from the repeated measures required to define the scale and units. Such data actually constitute a *qualitatively* different subject matter from those generated by idemnotic measurement, which, under ideal application, exhibit only treatment-imposed variability.

This discussion of the "pure" case does not acknowledge the influences on the data of other methodological practices encouraged by these two strategies. For example, vaganotic measurement usually predisposes the researcher toward using a relatively large number of subjects across whom the repeated measures are made. The resulting data are then collapsed statistically so that an estimate of the treatment effect is furnished by a group or cell mean. Of course, an extraneous source of variability—that attributable to differences between subjects—has been allowed to enter into determining the treatment effect, even if only as an error term against which to scale differences.

The necessity of evaluating mean differences against an error term also highlights the major weakness of vaganotic measurement—no absolute unit exists in terms of which to describe any difference that exists. The use of a small number of subjects, each serving as its own control, not only avoids these problems, but encourages attempts to describe, identify, and control extraneous sources of variability so as to clarify the environment–behavior relation as it applies to a single individual.

Finally, differences in the process of interpretation highlight the differences in what have become two fundamentally different subject matters. In both cases, conclusions are drawn about the effects of manipulated variables that are intended to apply to the individual case. However, only with the tactics encouraged by idemnotic strategies has the subject matter been preserved in an undiluted form that facilitates interpretations legitimately generalizable to the individual. The practices often associated with vaganotic measurement require that interpretations be controlled by the end result of a statistical digestive process that completes the transformation of what were once individual data into a homogenized subject matter no longer entirely a natural phenomenon. Many writers (e.g., Krantz, 1972) have lamented the apparent chauvinism and lack of integration of the disparate literatures that have arisen to accommodate these two distinct subject matters. The underlying differences, however, are largely irreconcilable because the differences in the basic strategies of measurement are unresolvable.

Technology

The hope for an effective technology of behavior is predicated on developing an exact science of behavior. Such a technology must have the same applicability to the individual case as does its parent science. It is only by discovering and describing in general form the behavioral relations governing the interaction between single organisms and the environment that specific technological applications of these relations can be created.

It is plausible to assert that the abundance of technology emanated from the natural sciences is partly the result of the reliance of these sciences on idemnotic measurement. The availability of standard, absolute units has facilitated accumulating and refining knowledge in a fashion that is simply foreclosed by reliance on varying measurement scales. Only when relations have been demonstrated to be stable and general can they be extended and relied upon for technological innovation. We argue that such demonstration is virtually impossible in the absence of stable measurement, and therein lies a partial explanation of the failure of any vaganotically based approach to the study of behavior to bestow upon the culture any but the coarsest of screening and labeling technologies.

We contend that there are no justifications for measurement *strategies* being different in any setting or for any behavioral question. Furthermore, this argument can be extended beyond technological development to technological application, in which the only questions raised are those involving maintenance. A common measurement strategy that is as applicable to the single instance as to the general case is a prerequisite for an effective technology at both levels.

Once the tactics of idemnotic measurement become commonplace in the realm of technological development and application, a mutually productive interplay with the parent science will be enhanced. Discoveries and innovations applicable to the single case may be described in a manner conducive to analysis and eventual generalization, the province of the basic scientist. As such generalizations are firmly established, we can anticipate a profound revolution in our understanding and management of behavioral phenomena.

Describing Behavior With Ratios of Count and Time

DIMENSIONAL MEASUREMENT

Describing behavior with ratios of count and time has long been an extremely popular practice among behavior analysts. Popular traditions and unexamined practices warrant careful consideration of how such ratios are constructed and used, however. It may be that some of these practices actually lead us to miss features of our data that might be important. The ubiquity of count and time ratios has also led to some confusions about how we use certain terms. These problems may constrain our ability to interpret data as thoroughly as might be possible.

Constructing ratios involving count and time is a component of dimensional measurement, which is the way that all natural sciences observe and record phenomena. This feature of scientific method requires specifying the facets of a physical event or variable that are the focus of interest and how these features will be quantified. Properties, dimensional quantities, and units of measurement constitute the foundation for dimensional measurement. Properties are fundamental qualities of objects or events that can be represented in distinct dimensions, whereas dimensional quantities, also referred to simply as dimensions or quantities, are quantifiable aspects of properties (see chapter 5 in Volume I). The distinction between properties and dimensional quantities is often not clearly drawn in practice, however, and experimental interests are usually expressed in terms of quantities (see Ellis, 1966, chapter 2, for a discussion of this issue; as well as McDowell, 1988). Units of measurement are determinate amounts of dimensional quantities, usually defined as a fixed and standard amount of each. When scientists attach a number to a unit so as to describe the amount of a quantity that is present, the result is called a measure of that event.

For example, an object may have the property of physical extent, which

43

in turn can be described by quantities such as length and weight. These quantities are measured in terms of basic units such as meters and grams. The list of such quantities and units routinely used in science and technology is extensive (e.g., see Chertov, 1964; Cook & Rabinowicz, 1963; Zebrowski, 1979), and there is a sizeable literature concerning this critical aspect of measurement (e.g., Ellis, 1966; Ford & Cullmann, 1959; lpsen, 1960). This literature addresses the origin and definition of quantities and units, as well as the tactics guiding their use.

As a physical event, behavior can be described in dimensional terms. Although there are a great many established quantities that may be used to describe different dimensions of behavior, attention has traditionally focused on a relatively short list of possibilities. These include countability, latency, and duration (all of which characterize the single response, as well as rate and interresponse time (which apply only to multiple instances of behavior, such as a response class. Of these, rate is one of the most popular quantities used in the analysis of behavior.

RATIOS OF COUNT AND TIME

Interest in Count and Time

One of the reasons for the popularity of rate in the analysis of behavior is probably Skinner's seminal use of it as a measure of response strength (Skinner, 1938). In contrast to traditional preparations of the era, Skinner measured behavior under conditions in which the organism was "free" to respond at almost any time. Rate of responding captured the dynamic character of behavior better than the latency or duration measures usually associated with discrete-trials procedures (Skinner, 1966). The extensive reliance on rate and its usefulness throughout the field's more than 50 years of experimental literature assures this measure a continued primacy among dimensional quantities.

Rate may have been found useful because it conveniently integrates two different quantities of interest in the form of a ratio that provides more information than either quantity considered separately. If a sample of responding is described by either the number of responses emitted or the total duration, but not both, in each case we are likely to find ourselves wanting the other quantity in order to make more sense of the one we have. For instance, knowing that a student correctly completed five math problems is of little value unless we know how long it took to do so. Similarly, knowing that a client tantrumed for 45 minutes during the day would be interpreted differently if this aggregate duration had resulted from one tantrum versus nine.

A preference for both count and time information may also reflect our appreciation that how often behavior occurs is one of the most general and useful features to know about it (but cf. Nevin, 1974, 1979, for example, regarding resistance to change). An integration of the quantities of count and time is implicit in the connotation of "oftenness." However, depending on what temporal features are described and how the ratios are constructed, these two quantities allow a variety of possible ratios, each of which describes a somewhat different aspect of behavior.

This reading examines some derived quantities of count and time, some of which are quite common in the behavioral literature and others of which are still relatively untried. It focuses on what each ratio tells us, why we may wish to use one instead of another, and what terminological issues these quantities raise. In addition, the reading briefly considers related issues such as derived quantities, dimensional analysis, advantages and disadvantages of ratios, and how to select useful quantities for measurement. Throughout, count and time ratios are considered in the context of the goal of describing behavior, rather than variability in behavior. The use of ratios for describing variability in sets of observations raises other issues that will not be treated here.

Count and Total Time

Count Over Total Time. Certainly the most common ratio of count and time is obtained by dividing the total number of occurrences of the target behavior by the total time that observation occurred. This quotient is called either *frequency* or *rate*, each of which has a long history of varying scientific and colloquial usages. Before Skinner emphasized rate (which he sometimes termed frequency), the use of the terms rate and frequency had already become thoroughly confused.

The *Oxford English Dictionary* acknowledges that the two words have generally been used interchangeably in scientific contexts. Although references to frequency as a ratio of the number of times an event occurs in relation to time (e.g., cycles per second in measuring the frequency of a tone) can be found more than a century ago, statistical references to frequency as the number of times an event occurs in a given sample were also used (Boole, 1854). The extensive use of statistics in psychology and the social sciences may make frequency more familiar as countability than this usage is in the natural sciences. On the other hand, in scientific contexts, rate more consistently refers to some measure of count over time, although rate probably has more varied colloquial usages than frequency.

Given that behavior analysis has its origin in psychology and yet looks to the natural sciences as its model, it is understandable that behavior analysts may often be confused about the meaning of frequency. As suggested in Box 5.2 in *Strategies and Tactics*, either term is acceptable as a reference to this ratio, but it is important to be clear which definition is being used in each case.

Terminology aside, there is a more important problem with this type of count/time ratio. Using the total time of observation as the time measure inextricably mixes two behaviorally distinct "kinds" of time. The total time during a period of observation is fully composed of the duration of each response, as well as the interresponse time (a type of latency) between the end of each response and the beginning of the next.[1] These two temporal quantities have very different behavioral implications. Duration is time during which the response class is occurring. Assuming that only one response in the class can occur at a time, no other instance is possible when one response is already occurring. In contrast, interresponse time is time during which responding can presumably occur, given other prerequisites for responding.

Because duration and interresponse time represent importantly different aspects of behavior, combining them in a total time measure can only risk obscuring relations of possible interest when rate is calculated by dividing count by total session time. If a series of rate measures decreases across sessions, for instance, it will probably be important to know if the reduction occurred because the duration of responses increased or the interresponse times increased. In other words, if the rate of an employee's performance on a task decreases, it would probably be important for someone interested in understanding this decrease to know whether it results from an increase in the duration of work responses or an increase in the time between responses (during which incompatible and inappropriate behavior may occur).

When either or both quantities are free to vary and such variations might be interesting, using this ratio may obscure relevant information. Much human behavior seems to vary significantly in duration and interresponse time, and such variations may be independent.[2] When data describing rate of responding have been calculated using total session time, it is impossible to know to what extent variations in rate measures are due to variation in duration, interresponse time, or both.

Although mixing duration and interresponse time has this inherent disadvantage, it is not always serious. For instance, whenever one of the temporal quantities is known to be relatively constant or extremely brief, this commingling may be unimportant. This might be true if durations or interresponse times were knowingly constrained by some aspect of the situation. This may be the case when the nature of the response class assures that the quantity is relatively trivial (i.e., as with the duration of a pigeon's key peck), or when some aspect of the environment produces either consistent or trivially brief values (e.g., very brief presses on a word processor keyboard aided by both

---

[1]Technically, the session is started during the interresponse time between the first response and the last one that occurred before timing began. Similarly, the session is ended during the interresponse time between the last response and the one that follows after the session. These "pseudolatencies" contribute a small degree of distortion into rate measures, although the errors tend to cancel each other (see *Strategies and Tactics,* chapter 5, for further discussion of this point).

[2]It might appear that these quantities are necessarily dependent within a session because total duration plus total interresponse time equals total session time. This is true for any one session length, however, only if total duration and interresponse time are being considered. If individual durations and interresponse times are of interest, these values can vary between sessions of the same length. Furthermore, if session lengths vary, even total duration and interresponse time can vary independently. Finally, these relations are true by definition when the behavior can only occur during sessions. However, when the behavior can also occur independently of experimental sessions, which are then an arbitrary imposition of measurement, these quantities may vary independently.

the return spring under each key and the aversive effects of holding a key down).

Having examined some interpretive consequences of mixing duration and interresponse time in total session time calculations of rate measures, we now revisit the original terminological problem from a slightly different perspective. Although it may be argued that our label for a quantity is less important than clearly understanding what it does and does not tell us, calling the ratio of count over total session time *rate* seems to involve some inconsistency between colloquial connotations and technical language. If rate is generally intended to refer to "oftenness," then using this label for a quantity that incorporates duration is misleading. Oftenness implies a quantity of "being able to occur" or "oftenness given possible occurrence." Our ability to detect this aspect of behaving is limited by the extent of the total duration of a sample of responding, and the ratio of count over total time can be misleading. Practically speaking, however, rate (or frequency) seems unalterably attached to the count/total time ratio. However, *total rate* or *overall rate* will distinguish this construction from other forms of rate.

Total Time Over Count. If total count over total session time expresses the number of responses emitted per unit of session time, the inverse ratio describes the average amount of session time per individual response. As with its sibling ratio, this quantity is potentially useful within the limits just described. However, we may be unaccustomed to looking at count and time information in this form, so such measures may seem confusing or, at best, only vaguely interesting. Perhaps the popularity of count over total time has discouraged examining the utility of total time over count, or perhaps we are simply more interested in count than time.

Another possibility is that this ratio makes the confusion caused by mixing duration and interresponse time too obvious to accept. With this ratio, a description of "seven minutes per response" plainly raises the question of "seven minutes of what?" (i.e., duration or interresponse time). The answer must confront the awkward duration–interresponse time dilemma. The analogous description of "seven responses per minute" associated with count over total time does not seem to offer a comparable problem, though, only because we customarily omit reference to the proper unit of measurement for countability—the cycle. The technically proper expression is, "seven cycles per minute," and then asking for the referent of cycles may be answered by identifying the response class.

Whatever the reason for the apparent lack of interest, this ratio would seem to have descriptive potent equal to that of the count/total ratio. There is no general reason why countability should be more important than temporal quantities, although it may be a challenge to identify situations in which mixing duration and interresponse time is important or even desirable. If this is the case, one of the "cleaner" ratios discussed will always be preferable.

Finally, the ratio of total time over count has no accepted name in psychology. "Average session time per response" is as close as we tend to come, and this is more description than label. In the natural sciences, it is referred to as *period* (as in "the period swing of a pendulum") and this may be an appropriate label.

Ratios of Count and Duration

Count Over Duration. This ratio describes the average number of responses per unit of total duration. Although it may seem similar to the traditional concept of rate (count over time), it is fundamentally different. Whereas rate connotes the average number of times that a response occurs per measurement interval during which responding is possible, count over duration describes average count during periods when responding is already occurring. Although such a ratio may well describe features of responding that are useful in some experiments, it seems to make less behavioral sense than count over interresponse time.

Many investigators are not accustomed to this quantity, and most probably find it difficult to conceptualize. This may be because of the previously cited fact that an operant generally cannot occur when it is already occurring. It seems meaningful to look at total count averaged over the time available for it to occur (i.e., rate), but averaging count over time when responding cannot occur is difficult to interpret. For instance, if we divide the total number of math problems correctly answered by their total duration, the same measure that seems clear in the case of rate (i.e., responses per minute) is now confusing.

However, when the contingencies for initiating a response are different from those for ending a response, this ratio may be more clearly interpretable. (The variables controlling initiation of watching a television that is already on might be auditory, whereas the variables controlling cessation of watching a television might be visual. Such a ratio may represent response initiations or terminations per unit of duration, which might provide useful information under some conditions. Nevertheless, the ratio of count over duration has no established name. Perhaps *response continuity* is closest to what this ratio describes.

Duration Over Count. The inverse of total count over total duration, on the other hand, expresses the familiar and usually more behaviorally meaningful quantity of average duration per response, which is usually called *average duration*. Examples are common in the behavioral literature (e.g., average time spent playing, studying, etc.).

Ratios of Count and Interresponse Time

Count Over Interresponse Time. This ratio might be said to be the quantity that we ought to call rate. It avoids the difficulty described in interpreting a quantity that places count over duration plus interresponse time. Total count over total interresponse time simply describes the average number of responses that occur during periods when responding is possible. For example, a ratio of the number of inhalations of cigarette smoke over the total number of minutes not actually inhaling is a form of rate corrected for periods during which responding cannot occur (i.e., duration). Because the term rate is often assigned to the ratio involving total session time, this quantity has no unique identifier. If count divided by total session time is qualified as *total* or *overall rate*, it would permit count over interresponse time to be called, simply, rate, although some distinctive modifier may be necessary.

Interresponse Time Over Count.   Because this quantity uses a measure of the time during which responding can occur, it makes more behavioral sense than duration over count. Total interresponse time over total count describes the average time between responses and is appropriately labeled *average interresponse time.*

Other Count and Latency Ratios.   Of course, interresponse time is only one type of latency. The time between a stimulus event and a subsequent response is another quantity that may be informative with some experimental preparations (e.g., the time between an alarm going off and a corrective action being taken). Accordingly, the two quantities placing count and this type of latency in ratios may sometimes describe useful aspects of responding.

USING COUNT AND TIME RATIOS

Other Ratios Involving Count and Time

The quantities of duration and latency are in the category of quantities that are called *substantial variables* (Ipsen, 1960) or *fundamental variables* (Chertov, 1964; Ellis, 1966; Ford & Cullmann, 1959) because they may be measured directly and their units have been defined independently in terms of some artificial standard. (The nature of the quantity of countability does not require an independently defined unit because it merely requires enumeration of instances, although it is still usually considered a fundamental quantity.) The count and time ratios discussed above are termed *simple natural variables* (Ipsen, 1960) or *derived quantities* (Chertov, 1964; Ellis, 1966) because they are derived from fundamental quantities on the basis of physical relationships.

Any of these ratios can themselves participate in other ratios as either numerator or denominator. The familiar quantity of acceleration is a good example of this practice. It may be defined as a ratio of rate (count over time) over time, or count divided by time squared. In the case of behavior, acceleration and deceleration (increasingly referred to in behavior analysis as *celeration*, as proposed by Pennypacker, Koenig, & Lindsley, 1972) described the change in the rate of responding over time. Many ratios of count and time are possible, but there is no a priori guarantee that any particular ratio will be meaningful in the study of behavior.

One method of obtaining clues about meaningful functional relations is through dimensional analysis (Bridgeman, 1922; Barenblatt, 1987). The process of creating derived quantities will result in some that lack units of measurement and are thus called *dimensionless* variables, quantities, or numbers (e.g., the Mach number, which is the ratio of the speed of an object to the speed of sound in the medium through which it travels). *Dimensional analysis* is a technique for deriving dimensionless numbers that may lead to promising or interesting experimental findings through the delineation of all viable functional relations. For example, dimensional analysis can show that the period swing of a pendulum is independent of its mass and depends on length, acceleration, and swing amplitude (Ellis, 1966; Ford & Cullmann, 1959). Thus, dimensional analysis may be used to aid the search for physical relationships.

Dimensional analysis cannot preempt empirical analysis, however, because empirical evidence is always required to confirm any supposed functional relation. For example, it is conceivable that the period swing of a pendulum may depend on mass or length in a way different from that specified by the dimensional formula. That is, the relationship suggested by dimensional analysis may not exist under all conditions (such as varying atmospheric conditions), or it may be modified by a dimensionless constant. Furthermore, meaningful functional relations may be implied through the use of dimensional analysis, but its use will not lead to the discovery of "basic" laws such as gravity. Fundamental physical relations are not always derivable from other relations, and they are often not unitless (Ellis, 1966). Therefore, dimensional analysis may be used to propose experimental directions that must be tested empirically or as a check on the meaningfulness of calculations.

The field of behavior analysis has not often attempted dimensional analysis (cf. Nevin, Mandell, & Atak, 1983). Such analyses would involve examining various combinations of fundamental quantities in an attempt to learn something new about particular facet of behavior. The quantities that were suggested by the literature as relevant would be combined in different ways and candidate dimensionless numbers obtained. Each would then be applied to the analysis of actual data in a search for orderly relations. However, order per se may not always be meaningful (i.e., useful). The features of behavior described by a dimensionless quantity must also be shown by experimental research to be important to our understanding of behavior.

Disadvantages of Ratios

When two or more fundamental quantities are combined in a ratio, the viewer's behavior can no longer be controlled by the original quantities (unless, of course, those quantities are retained separately in some form). Although this may well be an intentional and valuable analytical tactic, it nonetheless involves a "loss of information" that can hinder effective interpretation. For instance, when the total number of self-injurious responses per observation period is divided by the total interresponse time to provide an experiment's sole data, viewers cannot know either total count or total interresponse time.

Whether this omission is important will depend on the particulars of each such case, but the risk certainly exists that the use of these fundamental quantities only in the form of such a ratio will limit interpretation.

A related limitation of ratios is that the viewer has no information about how each of the underlying quantities contributes to changes in the ratio. The point is illustrated by Fig. 4.1, which displays a series of session values representing two different quantities (Q1 and Q2, bottom) and the quotients resulting from dividing one quantity by the other (Q1/Q2, top). It is easily seen that a description of the sequential change in Q1/Q2 would improperly represent change in either of the quantities that were combined to form the ratio.

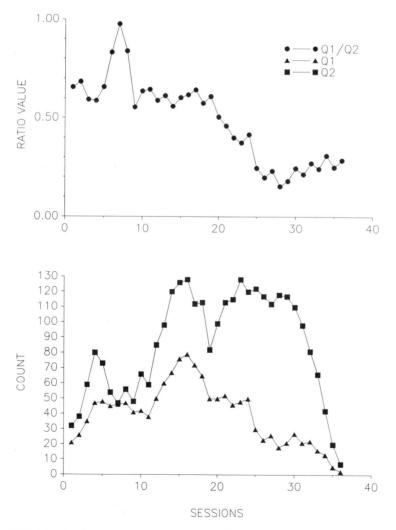

FIG. 4.1. Session values representing two different quantities (*Q*1 and *Q*2, bottom) and the quotients resulting from dividing one quantity by the other (*Q*1/*Q*2, top).

For example, most would describe the data points in the top panel approximately between sessions 10 and 20 as relatively stable. However, this stability is produced by sharply increasing and decreasing transitory sessions in $Q1$ and $Q2$, with $Q2$ having much higher values. This limitation (which applies to a all ratios) can be serious, and should at least be acknowledged in interpretations. When describing ratio data, the customary phrase, "Responding showed such and such a pattern . . ." should always be qualified by reference to only the particular derived quantity under analysis (i.e., *Rate* of responding showed . . .). Of course, either of the contributing quantities can be independently analyzed, thereby avoiding this problem.[3]

Selecting Useful Ratios

Which ratios involving count and time will be important in the analysis of behavior? In spite of the popularity of rate (as traditionally calculated), there can be no general answer to the question. The quantity that reveals variability that helps to answer the experimental question may not even involve count or time (e.g., force). Although it may be possible to exclude certain quantities before the fact (as when some aspect of procedure makes the variability in a certain quantity meaningless or trivial), it is more difficult to be sure which will show variability that turns out to be important.

The conservative solution to this problem is to measure all of the reasonably relevant fundamental quantities so that all candidates and their possible ratios will be available for analysis. This is not as challenging an option as it might seem. If observation can detect the beginning and end of individual responses and therefore create a record of the number of responses and all of the resulting intervals (i.e., durations and interresponse times), all quantities based on count and time will be available. If it is not possible to identify individual response cycles (e.g., if it is only possible to know when the behavior is occurring, as with the behavior of watching TV), only duration can be measured.

Having all quantities based on count and time at one's analytical disposal is encouraging, but it does not mean that any possible ratio that shows systematic variability within or across phases is automatically behaviorally meaningful. As discussed, some ratios may be uninterpretable for the study of behavior and others may be inappropriate or trivial in the case at hand. If any set of data describing fundamental count and time quantities is subjected to sufficient examination, it is likely to exhibit some kind of order. However, the meaningfulness of the resulting derived quantity must be convincingly shown and the generality of the relations must then be experimentally established.

In summary, ratios of count and time can bring the viewer's interpretations

---

[3]The points in this section fully apply to ratios in which numerator and denominator represent like quantities (e.g., percentages).

under control of aspects of responding that might not otherwise be evident. However, casual selection or automatic construction of such ratios can lead to interpretative limitations and errors. Cautious use, guided by the focus of the experimental question and possibly supplemented with other displays of the same raw data, may augment our analytical skills.

Probability as a
Scientific Concept

USE IN BEHAVIOR ANALYSIS

The Definitional Problem

It has been said that Bertrand Russell once told a class, "Probability is the most important concept in modern science, especially as nobody has the slightest notion what it means" (cited in Bell, 1945, p. 587).[1] Although one might quibble about Russell's priorities, there is no evidence that his assessment of this definitional state of affairs is dated. Certainly it is still the case in the field of behavior analysis that the concept of probability has multiple and conflicting meanings of uncertain utility. For example, a recent survey of the editorial staff of the *Journal of the Experimental Analysis of Behavior*, the *Journal of Applied Behavior Analysis*, *The Behavior Analyst*, and *Behaviorism* conducted by Johnson and Morris (1987) allowed respondents four broad categories of meanings. As if these were not enough, 23% even checked a fifth category (*other*) and 40% checked two or more categories.

The problems that issue from such variety are the same as would follow from any technical scientific terms that share the curse of definitional ambiguity. In contrast with the language of the culture, the language of science is at least intended to be especially precise and spare; scientific definitions of technical terms are formal, complete, and narrow. When this is not the case, confusion and misunderstanding occur, which in turn lead in one way or another to inaccurate inferences and wasted scientific resources. Although it might be argued that probability is either more or less than a technical term, in fact it is often used in a manner similar to technical terms called dimensional quanti-

---

[1]This quote was taken from Johnson and Morris (1987).

ties (frequency, duration, latency, etc.). Whatever its formal or informal meanings, it is difficult to argue that precision of reference is unimportant.

B. F. Skinner

The term probability in behavior analysis was clearly assigned its major role by B. F. Skinner. In his early work, he discussed operant behavior in terms of its "strength," which he related to frequency: ". . . appeal must be made to frequency of occurrence in order to establish the notion of strength. The strength of an operant is proportional to its frequency of occurrence . . ." (1938, p. 21).

In a paper delivered in 1949, Skinner seemed to have relegated "strength" to a more minor role, and "probability" had begun to replace it in importance. For example, in "Are theories of learning necessary?" he wrote: "If we are to predict behavior (and possibly to control it), we must deal with *probability of response*. . . . Rate of responding is not a 'measure' of probability, but it is the only appropriate datum in a formulation in these terms" (1959, p. 46).

A few years later, Skinner's references to probability seemed to grow more frequent. Some illumination of his thinking is also revealed by two quotes from *Science and Human Behavior*:

> Suppose now we bring someone into a room and place a glass of water before him. Will he drink? There appear to be only two possibilities: either he will drink or he will not. But we may speak of the chances that he will drink, and this notion is the probability that he will drink. This may range from virtual certainty that drinking will occur, to virtual certainty that it will not. The very considerable problem of how to measure such a probability will be discussed later. For the moment, we are interested in how the probability may be increased or decreased. (1953, p. 32)

> To get at the core of Thorndike's Law of Effect, we need to clarify the notion of "probability of response." This is an extremely important concept; unfortunately, it is also a difficult one. In discussing human behavior, we often refer to "tendencies" or "predispositions" to behave in particular ways. Almost every theory of behavior uses some such term as "excitatory potential," "habit strength," or "determining tendency." But how do we observe a tendency? And how can we measure one?
>
> If a given sample of behavior existed in only two states, in one of which it always occurred and in the other never, we should be almost helpless in following a program of functional analysis. An all-or-none subject matter lends itself only to primitive forms of description. It is a great advantage to suppose instead that the *probability* that a response will occur ranges continuously between these all-or-none extremes. We can then deal with variables which, unlike the eliciting stimulus, do not "cause a given bit of behavior to occur" but simply make the occurrence more probable. We may then proceed to deal, for example, with the combined effect of more than one such variable. (1953, p. 62)

In a lecture given in 1955, Skinner suggested problems, however: "Probability of responding is a difficult datum. We may avoid controversial issues by turning at once to a practical measure, the *frequency* with which a response is emitted" (1959, p. 102). In *Schedules of Reinforcement*, he and Ferster continued this convenient substitution: "Our basic datum is the rate at which a response is emitted by a freely moving organism. . . . Such a datum is closely associated with the notion of probability of action. Among the independent variables which modify this rate or probability are some which are not primarily at issue in a study of intermittent reinforcement" (1957a, pp. 7–8).

In his book, *Verbal Behavior* (1957b), Skinner made only two references to probability:

> Some parts of a verbal repertoire are more likely to occur than others. This likelihood is an extremely important, though difficult, conception. Our basic datum is not the occurrence of a given response as such, but the probability that it will occur at a given time. Every verbal operant may be conceived of as having under specified circumstances an assignable probability of emission—conveniently called its "strength." We base the notion of strength upon several kinds of evidence. (p. 22)

> Although the English language contains many expressions which suggest that the concept of probability of response is a familiar and useful one, certain problems remain to be solved in using it in the analysis of behavior. Under laboratory conditions probability of response is easily studied in an individual organism as frequency of responding. Under these conditions simple changes in frequency can be shown to be precise functions of specific variables, and such studies supply some of the most reliable facts about behavior now available. But we need to move on from the study of frequencies to a consideration of the probability of a single event. The problem is by no means peculiar to the field of behavior. It is a basic one wherever the data of a science are probabilistic, and this means the physical sciences in general. Although the data upon which both the layman and the scientist base their concepts of probability are in the form of frequencies, both want to talk about the probability of a *single forthcoming event*. In later chapters of this book we shall want to consider the way in which several variables, combining at a given time, contribute strength to a given response. In doing so we may appear to be going well beyond a frequency interpretation of probability, yet our evidence for the contribution of each variable is based upon observations of frequencies alone. (p. 28)

All of the aforementioned quotes were from no more than passing references to the issues surrounding probability. More recently, Skinner discussed response probability at somewhat greater length in *Contingencies of Reinforcement* (1969):

> We are not so much concerned with the topography of a response as with the probability that it will be emitted. Probability is a difficult concept. For many purposes we may be content with rate of responding, but this is awkward when a single instance of behavior is attributed to more than one variable. Similar problems arise, together with many others, when probability is inferred from the occurrence or nonoccurrence of a response in a given "trial." . . . A common practice is to evaluate probability of response in terms of magnitude of an *in-*

dependent variable. A response evoked by a brief stimulus, for example, is felt to be stronger than one which requires a longer exposure. The probability seems to lie on a continuum between the time which guarantees a response and the time at which no appropriate response is ever made. . . . Probability of response is also sometimes inferred from how quickly the response is acquired or brought under stimulus control. If a response of complex topography is acquired only slowly, it is assumed that it began in very low strength. When an organism has been conditioned to respond to a given pattern, the probability that it will respond to a different pattern is sometimes argued from the speed with which it forms a discrimination. If it learns to distinguish patterns quickly, it is assumed that learning to respond to one pattern does not make a response to the other highly probable. Speed of learning is also sometimes used to measure probability attributed to deprivation or aversive stimulation. . . . Speed of forgetting is also, as we have noted, used to infer probability; a response which can be recalled a long time after acquisition is presumed to have been stronger when acquired. (pp. 91–92)

Finally, in an undated entry in his *Notebooks*, Skinner commented in reaction to a review in *Scientific American* that suggests that "there is a tendency to think of a probability as being inherent in the event rather than in something the individual who is trying to predict the event has done":

Is probability "inherent" in anything? The word shows the uneasiness with which probability is discussed. If we assume that a response is strong because upon similar occasions it has been reinforced on a given schedule, then the probability is: a. "inherent in the event" in the sense of due to the scheduled contingencies, b. "something the individual . . . has done" in the sense of the exposure to these contingencies, and c. a matter of "trying to predict the event" in the sense of the strength of the behavior itself (strong if the event is "confidently predicted") or in the sense of formulating the contingencies in a rule for future action. The statement that "probabilities we assign . . . become reflections of our preferences" means that the probabilities *are* the preferences. (1980, pp. 331–332)

The view of probability that emerges from these references leaves much to be desired. For Skinner, probability seemed to be more or less interchangeable with strength, although neither was clearly defined. However, probability was not seen as synonymous with rate or frequency. In fact, rate or frequency was not even seen as a measure of probability, although he wrote of some unspecified association that this dimensional quantity has with probability. Probability was apparently to be simply inferred from the status of the independent variable or from measures of responding.

Given these uncertainties, the basis for the importance of the concept of probability to Skinner is not entirely clear. Although he referred to the difficulties of describing the all-or-none aspect of single instances of behavior and offered probability as a continuous alternative, it is not evident how this solves the referential problem. His concern for dealing with the single operant response alerted him to the fact that the existing scientific verbal practice involving probability as a dispositional quantifier was appropriate to his own purposes. In almost all cases, his earlier term, response strength, could simply be replaced by response probability without changing any of the implications. The definition of probability was problematic for Skinner, but no more so than for physicists. Furthermore, probability seemed much less susceptible to interpretation as an internal entity or intervening variable.

A Survey of Contemporary Opinions

The term probability is ubiquitous in all areas of the contemporary literature of behavior analysis. The recent survey of the editorial staff of four major journals in the field already mentioned (Johnson & Morris, 1987) certifies the extant definitional problems. When respondents were asked to indicate agreement with one or more of four general meanings that were listed, 54% checked *relative frequency of response*, 41% checked *a number obtained from observed data to predict future behavior*, 25% chose *strength of response*, and another 25% selected *a degree of belief or opinion regarding the occurrence of a response*.

In addition, 23% either checked an *other* category or qualified the previous categories. Johnson and Morris described these additional responses as falling into three subcategories. The first subcategory included "restatements in terms of likelihood, chance, tendency, belief, and response potential, with emphasis on the conditions, contexts, and circumstances controlling the occurrence of a response" (1987, pp. 9–10). A second subcategory expressed response probability as "a ratio of target responses relative to opportunities to respond . . . [which] should then be used to aid in the prediction of future behavior, based on degree of situational similarity" (p. 10). A third grouping of reactions suggested that "it would be more effective to note the conditions under which the verbal response 'response probability' occurs, rather than attempt to specify any particular definition" (p. 10). In addition, remember that 40% of the 92 respondents checked two or more categories.

The second question of the survey asked if probability was a useful concept and why. Although 71% said that it was useful in behavior analysis, 16% said that it was not and 13% indicated that it could be useful if properly defined but was not useful because it was "conceptually confusing" and "inexact." It is striking that more than a quarter of this respected sample of the field's leaders felt that such a widely used term was not useful. Furthermore, the reasons reported by Johnson and Morris that were offered by some of the respondents for their answers to these two questions indicated a broad and conflicting variety of opinions on this definitional issue.

DEFINITIONAL POSSIBILITIES

Dimensional Quantity

In the science of behavior, probability most often refers to some aspect of a response class, therefore, it is natural to consider whether it can be classed as a dimensional quantity. A *dimensional quantity* is a quantifiable aspect of a property of a natural phenomenon and should not be confused with a unit of measurement, which specifies a fixed and standard magnitude or amount of a quantity (see chapter 5 in *Strategies and Tactics*).

Can probability qualify for membership? What are the requirements for a dimensional quantity? There would seem to be two requirements for any candidate: (a) its relation to one or more fundamental properties of the phenomenon must be clearly traceable, and (b) it must be quantifiable in terms of a fixed and standard unit of measurement. Perhaps it should be added that any candidate should not be redundant with a quantity already well established.

What, then, is the property (or properties) of behavior that probability quantifies? In order to examine this question, we must turn away from quantitative definitions to the colloquial connotations of the term. Probability generally refers to uncertainty surrounding the occurrence of an instance of a response class. Of course, the occurrence of a single response depends on the status at any moment of all of the variables that influence it. Thus, probability would seem to refer more to a coalition of controlling variables than to behavior directly. Uncertainty just does not seem to be a legitimate, fundamental property of behavior upon which probability can define its status as a quantity, however. Some reassurance about this conclusion comes from the other natural sciences, which have not found the need for a property of uncertainty. Other possible properties that probability alone could be said to quantify are simply not evident, suggesting that by this criterion probability is not a quantity.

Remember, however, that a quantity can reference multiple properties, as does frequency or rate, which is related to both temporal locus and repeatability. On the chance that probability could qualify in this manner, let us consider the second (and third) requirement(s) for a dimensional quantity. What would be the fixed and standard unit of measurement that would specify the amount of probability present in any instance and that is not already used to measure any other dimensional quantity? The most common answer (according to the Johnson & Morris 1987 survey) is *relative frequency of a response*. However, there are two problems with this candidate.

First, this expression raises long-standing confusions about the term *frequency*. Following colloquial connotations, the term in the natural sciences most often refers to a quantity describing the occurrence of an event in relation to time, as is suggested by its unit of measurement, cycles per unit time. Thus, the term *relative frequency* might seem to refer to a ratio of two frequencies. However, the term is also sometimes used to refer to number or count, especially in the fields of philosophy, mathematics, and statistics. It is this usage that tends to appear in discussions of probability. The customary referent of the term relative frequency, then, is a ratio of two counts, which might be more clearly described as *relative count*.

This awkwardness aside, there is second complication that is not so easily remedied. According to basic mathematics, when two measures sharing the same unit of measurement are expressed as a ratio and divided, the units cancel and the quotient is a unitless number. At this point, all reference to the original dimension is lost, which creates a number of potential interpretative complications when attempting to describe behavior. So, whether probability is defined in terms of rates (frequencies) or counts, the result is a *dimensionless* quantity. Although dimensionless quantities have their place in science, reference to fundamental properties is not one of them.

There is still another possibility. Probability could be defined as a dimensional quantity referencing two or more established properties of behavior and measured in terms of a ratio of two unlike units of measurement, as is rate, interresponse time, and quarter-life, among others. The term probability could be attached to a ratio that is presently unnamed or in a shuffle of redefinitions of existing quantities.

For example, as Reading 4 points out, there are three obvious ratios in which some measure of countability serves as the numerator and some measure of time serves as the denominator: (a) the ratio of countability to interresponse time, (b) the ratio of countability to duration, and (c) the ratio of countability to total session time (interresponse time and duration added together). The third ratio is how response rate is often calculated in practice, presumably because it does not require timing the onset and offset of each response. If this convention were retained, the other two ratios would be available for naming and empirical evaluation. The ratio of countability to duration might be called something like *response continuity*, and the similar ratio of countability to interresponse time might then be called *response probability*.

This could be defended as an official definition of probability as a dimensional quantity if only because it meets the criteria just listed. However, this ratio is already called rate (or, sometimes, frequency), even though this label insures some confusion with other count/time ratios. Furthermore, the term probability is so ubiquitous and ill-defined, both in science and in the lay culture, that simply redefining it might be doomed to failure. In other words, this ''proper'' usage might be overwhelmed by unofficial connotations, much as has been the case with many technical terms in behavior analysis that also have broad colloquial usage. This is widely agreed to be a serious problem, and it would seem to unwise to ignore it here.

In summary, the term probability could be arbitrarily defined as a dimensional quantity, though not without raising questions and exacerbating present confusions. This may not be the best resolution to the definitional issues surrounding this term, however. A thorough consideration of these issues must probe other directions.

Mathematics and Philosophy

The concept of probability is hardly a conundrum for the field of behavior analysis alone, of course. Philosophers and mathematicians have been arguing among themselves about the meaning of probability since at least the 17th century, and any sort of general agreement still seems centuries away (Durbin, 1968).

For example, Salmon (1966) surveyed five leading interpretations of probability and assessed each according to three criteria of adequacy. The classical or a priori definition originated with Simon Laplace and is one of the oldest and best known; it defines probability as the ratio of favorable to total, equally possible cases and is the basis of theoretical mathematical probability. The subjective interpretation is that probability is simply a measure of a degree of belief. The logical interpretation approaches probability as the degree of confidence that would be rationally justified by the available evidence. The personalistic theory of probability

> allows . . . that the fundamental probabilities are purely subjective degrees of actual belief, but the probability calculus sets forth relations among degrees of belief which must be satisfied if these degrees are to constitute a rational system. Although the fundamental probabilities are subjective, their relation to derived probabilities is objective. (Salmon, 1966, p. 79)

Finally, the frequency or a posteriori interpretation defines probability "in terms of the limit of the relative frequency of the occurrence of an attribute in an infinite sequence of events" (Salmon, 1966, p. 83). This approach thus requires probability to be defined empirically: As a result of an actual series of tests, probability is the ratio of the number of times an event occurs to the number of trials. Not surprisingly (and for reasons that only philosophers and mathematicians could understand and appreciate), Salmon finds all of these interpretations of probability inadequate according to one or another of his criteria.

Philosophical hair-splitting aside, three broad and easily distinguishable traditional definitions of probability are commonly identified: classical (a priori), frequency (a posteriori), and subjective (Durbin, 1968). What implications do they have for use in a natural science of behavior? The classical approach (a ratio of favorable to total, equally possible cases) is easiest to assess. This definition requires assuming that the cases under consideration are equally possible. Although formal evidence could be marshalled in support of such a contention, the evidence is likely to be extremely hard to come by, even for common examples such as tossing coins (see Kolata, 1986). In the case of behavior as a subject matter, there is often good reason based on what is known about behavior in general or about a particular circumstance to avoid the assumption of equal possibility, although the available evidence may fall short of satisfying the requirements of the frequency definition of probability.

For example, most would agree that assuming an individual is equally likely to chose each of the four alternatives of a multiple choice question is quite risky, although there are unlikely to be any data available for a particular individual and a particular question. Therefore, calculating probability in this manner essentially requires ignoring any past or current evidence about actual occurrences of the events of interest. Nevertheless, when data are unavailable, this formulation of probability may offer a better prediction than the subjective approach, although the opposite may be true.

Although the classical definition of probability may have some utility to mathematicians, when there are any data pertinent to calculating the ratio between favorable and total cases, it is tempting to leave the a priori calculation behind in favor of the a posteriori or frequency approach. Although this definition has the advantage of an empirical basis (the ratio of the number of occurrences to the number of trials or opportunities), there are still complications. For instance, although it is easy enough to determine the number of occurrences of a response (presuming a proper definition of the response class and accurate measurement procedures, which should not be very quickly presumed), how does one determine the denominator?

For this value, the frequency definition requires an infinite sequence of events (responses) whose relative frequency is known to approach a limit value. In the case of behavioral probabilities, the questions are: (a) How must this class of events be defined and measured? and (b) How can we determine this value? In the case of a discrete trials procedure, the answers seem obvious—count the total number of trials. However, this tactic assumes that each trial is, in fact, an identical opportunity for a response and that the trials are the only opportunities for that response class. Even more difficult in this regard (and more common) are "free operant" circumstances in which there are no trials or well-defined opportunities that can be unambiguously counted. Worse still, what can be done when the need is to calculate the probability of a single response? Finally, the whole business of estimating the limit of the relative frequency of an infinite sequence solely on the basis of observations of the initial portion of the sequence bothers philosophers more than a little bit (Salmon, 1966). These are not simple issues, although this is apparently the most common definition of probability in behavior analysis (Johnson & Morris, 1987).

At this point, the subjective definition of probability may appear a rather weak alternative for scientific purposes, in spite of the difficulties of the a priori and a posteriori interpretations. It allows no formal calculation on the basis of principle or fact and therefore does not permit technical applications. Nevertheless, even though the subjective definition may never define the vertical axis of a graph, it may well be the most used sense of probability in daily scientific discourse; in fact, this ubiquity should suggest greater importance than its nonquantitative nature implies.

The reason for our comfort with a subjective assessment of probability may lie with its origins in our accumulated experience. Subjective probabilities are as empirically based as are frequency-based probabilities; it is merely the source of control over the two types of assessments that differs. In the case of relative frequency probability, the control is narrowly restricted by the definition of the ratio to our experiences in determining the numerator and denominator. For subjective probability, control is exerted by any or all of our experiences with the response class and circumstances in question as well as our accumulated personal and professional experience with behavior, each in a sense weighted in a nonexistent formula defined by our unique amalgam of experiences.

The lack of a formal method of calculation is both valuable and harmful. It is valuable in that we can take into account any variables that we know are relevant to the assessment and weigh them as experience and present circumstances dictate. It is harmful in that we are likely to be influenced by factors that worsen the accuracy of the prediction, such as our desire for a certain outcome.

These interpretations of the concept of probability are about all the help that can be expected from the disciplines of mathematics and philosophy, although this is admittedly an extremely brief summary of what are very complex positions in a large literature. Of course, neither mathematicians nor philosophers work in the "experimental trenches" every day, so it might be expected that their perspectives about the concept of probability would be somewhat different from those of practicing scientists. What uses of probability are common in the natural and social sciences?

Natural and Social Sciences

Natural Sciences. An examination of a variety of introductory texts in physics, chemistry, and biology shows not even a single definitional mention of probability. The few references to the term make merely passing mention of probability in particular contexts, such as to weather forecasting. Furthermore, books addressing the technical aspects of measurement in the natural sciences also make little mention of probability (e.g., Bridgeman, 1922; Chertov, 1964; Ipsen, 1960). In fact, the only general and substantive discussions of probability in the context of scientific method are in philosophy of science texts, written by philosophers specializing in this area (e.g., Kyburg, 1984).

Research journals "paint" a similar picture. For instance, an informal examination of *Science*, one of the most respected multidisciplinary journals in the world, shows only infrequent references to probability. They encompass all three common interpretations (classical, frequency, and subjective), but most of these few references occur in the context of inferential statistical interpretation of experimental data.

Social Sciences. Although, the term probability appears much more often in the literature of the social sciences, this greater usage is almost entirely due to the pervasive role of inferential statistics in the social sciences. Tests of hypotheses are, in principle, made by selecting a subjective probability for which it will be accepted that the obtained difference between the sample means occurred by chance (actually, that the difference is due to factors other than the experimental treatment). Methodological texts are usually either primers for statistical training (e.g., Neale & Liebert, 1980) or fully developed manuals for teaching the rationale and procedures of inferential statistics (e.g., Kerlinger, 1986). References to probability are therefore common in these research literatures, psychology being a good example as the epitome of a well-developed experimental social science. However, if all of the statistical uses of the term are put aside, there again remain only the same scattered and very infrequent references to probability observed in the natural science literature.

These observations of the paucity of substantive uses of probability in everyday science are revealing. They suggest that the concept of probability may be far less useful and important to the conduct of science than philosophers would have us believe. In particular, the lack of widespread usage of technical applications of the concept (classical or frequency definitions), even in an idiosyncratic manner from one field to another, urges the conclusion that there may be little need to refer to ratios of this sort and that such ratios do not describe relations of great usefulness.

This assessment contrasts dramatically with the role of dimensional quantities in science, especially in the natural sciences. These quantities, also often in the form of ratios, are at the heart of scientific measurement, presumably because they represent aspects of the phenomena under study that are both real and demonstrably useful. Uses of the term probability, on the other hand, only partly refer to the subject matter under study. The frequency definition, for example, has as its numerator a real aspect of the phenomenon (its countability), but the denominator's definition in terms of "opportunities" is actually a reference to an unknown conglomeration of influences that constitute such opportunities. In other words, unlike dimensional quantities, probability does not narrowly refer to real aspects of a phenomenon, and scientists seem to find relatively little practical use for the concept in their routine conduct and interpretation of experiments.

If the concept of probability has limited utility for working scientists for this reason, perhaps it will be fruitful to examine the meaning of the concept in terms of the behavior of scientists rather than the behavior of their subject matter. Indeed, probability is fundamentally a behavioral concept, and any responsibility for its meaning must be borne by the science whose subject matter includes the behavior of scientists.

Verbal Behavior

From the perspective of a science of behavior, probability can be most usefully analyzed as verbal behavior. Certainly, probability does not exist in a physical sense, as does a chair. This does not mean that there is nothing real that is referred to by the term, however. The measure of the countability of a response class that serves as the numerator in the relative frequency definition is real enough as a quantifiable dimension of behavior, although it is more somewhat more difficult to define the real dimension referred to in the denominator by trials or opportunities. Whatever the word may refer to, however, probability is also a verbal response. As such, what are its sources of control?

First, in the cases in which probability has been calculated according to a formal definition, the verbal response is a tact of those calculations (see Skinner, 1957b, chapter 5). However, it seems that the most everyday uses of the term are not this narrow. Colloquially, the response may be a tact of unpredictability or uncertainty, presumably due to lack of strong control by one or more variables. We say that "He will probably get angry" when the variables that will control his getting angry are unknown, either in general or at least for the moment in question. If a particular influence over his getting angry was known to be both sufficient and present, we would drop the "probably" and merely predict that "He will get angry." This usage is modulated by crude efforts at quantification, as in "There is little chance that Mary will arrive on time," "It is quite probable that John will be here tonight," or "It is highly unlikely that Jane will call you." This function of the response probability may be as a descriptive autoclitic of the strength of the speaker's tact, as in "That's probably Bill" or "I'll probably be there."

Michael (1988) suggested that it would be helpful to view probability from a dispositional perspective. For Michael, a dispositional term is a "type of functional relation where the form of a speaker's response is not primarily controlled by an immediately prior stimulus situation, but rather by other verbal and nonverbal stimuli, some possible private" (p. 2). He analyzes Skinner's references to response probability in this context, concluding that, for Skinner, "it became the dispositional concept of choice, functioning as a more precise replacement for operant strength" (p. 16). However, Michael's overriding concern with probability is that the disadvantages associated with its formalistic, philosophical, excess baggage make it less preferable than response strength.

SUMMARY AND RECOMMENDATIONS

What, then, has this review of the scientific uses of the concept of probability shown? It has revealed that there are three, more-or-less official definitions of probability that are recognized by mathematicians, philosophers, and scientists. Two of the three refer to formulae that express a simple ratio. One ratio is based on a count of the possibilities of an event's occurrence in relation to the sum of those possibilities plus a count of nonpossibilities, all made without taking into account any influences that might affect either class of events. This is the classical or a priori definition, and its formal uses are fairly narrowly limited to mathematics and philosophy, presumably because anyone else would prefer biasing the counts with any pertinent evidence. This influence is formalized in the second ratio, in which the numerator and denominator come from counts of actual occurrences of the classes of events under supposedly similar, if not identical, circumstances. This is the relative frequency or a posteriori definition.

Although only this latter usage is commonly referred to as empirical in nature, both are actually empirical to the same degree. In both cases, counts are made of the events and nonevents of interest; they are merely made under different circumstances. Of course, it cannot be known which set of circumstances will provide the best prediction in any particular case because the variables that will determine the actual outcome are unknown either in general or in that instance. This limitation suggests that these interpretations of probability are not really different from the subjective meaning—a degree of belief. Here, there is no pretense of quantification. Under control of a conglomeration of influences stemming from experience, one just attaches an adjective, either qualitative or quantitative, to the term. This definition, too, is thus importantly empirical in nature.

The important observations regarding these traditional definitions of probability is that

1. They are all empirical.
2. Their methods of empiricism do not make one inherently superior to the others in any or all cases.
3. They all attempt to predict events under conditions of some ignorance.
4. This prediction is controlled by an assessment of, not just the events of interest themselves, but the variables that influence them.
5. They do not, therefore, refer solely to quantifiable dimensions of the phenomenon.

This last observation suggests difficulties in any effort to add to these traditional definitions a further definition of probability as a formal quantity. Instead of narrowly referring to real aspects of the phenomenon, the definition actually describes the behavior of the experimenter interpreting the results. Although one could define probability as the ratio of countability to interresponse time, such a definitional direction would seriously conflict with more well-established definitions. Furthermore, it would be difficult to eliminate other existing uses of the term.

The fact that scientists seem to have little practical use for the concept of probability might be predicted on the basis of the aforementioned list of characteristics. Probability is simply a less useful concept in daily scientific practice that the frequency of the term in informal scientific discourse might suggest. It does not clearly and narrowly refer to important features of a natural phenomenon. Instead, it indirectly refers to unknown variables and conditions and thus serves more colloquial than technical functions in the special language of science. From the perspective of Moore (1981), the term may be more under the control of discriminative stimuli and reinforcers in the general cultural (social) environment than under control of discriminative stimuli (operations and contacts with data) and reinforcers (outcomes leading to prediction and control) in the scientific environment.

This analysis leaves us with some rather behavioral observations about probability. An examination of the term's use makes it clear that it is like the term *chance*—a synonym for our ignorance. As a analysis in terms of verbal behavior suggests, it is either a tact or an autoclitic related to uncertainty, and the reasons for such uncertainty lie in a lack of knowledge of variables that would allow certainty. More behaviorally, it seems to refer to a lack of control over our verbal behavior by those variables that actually control the phenomenon. Whatever label serves this function will never qualify as a useful scientific term because its emission as a verbal response cannot be consistently controlled by real features of the phenomenon. As Skinner pointed out, "Scientific verbal behavior is most effective when it is free of multiple sources of strength" (1957b, p. 420).

Therefore, it would seem most helpful for the development of the natural science of behavior for this concept to be avoided as a technical reference. For example, when a ratio of the number of responses to the number of opportunities is described, *proportion* seems a better label than probability. References to probability may best be left to the subjective or colloquial meaning of ''a degree of belief.'' In fact, because this modal use of the term seems culturally controlled, it is unlikely that this use could be changed by fiat anyway. In any case, it is important that the term not masquerade as something more than it is, and it is no more than a reference to the speaker's uncertainty.[2]

---

[2]An excellent discussion of probability by Johnson and Morris (1987) written independently of, but at the same time as, this paper reached a similar cautionary conclusion regarding the term's use by behavior analysts.

The Problem of
Limited Accessibility

A GENERAL STRATEGY

Most often, the portions of behavior and environment of scientific interest are public or accessible by more than one person. However, the experimenter's interest may sometimes lie with investigating functional relations between responses and environmental events, either or both of which are private or accessible by only the subject.[1] These special circumstances present some serious problems for a scientific approach to experimentation built upon control and replication. The caution in this area prevalent among some behavioral scientists today may be a justifiable reaction to the abuses that characterized earlier approaches to the study of private events and that are still widespread in the social sciences.

Historical Perspective

Given its origins in philosophy and its special, inherited concern with the epistemological problem, 19th- and early 20th-century psychology is largely defined by attempts to study private events and various attendant "phenomena"—consciousness, the mind, awareness, and so on. An overview of this mammoth effort (e.g., Boring, 1950) makes clear that historical attention should be focused on two principal aspects: content and method. Furthermore, although little lasting illumination has been cast on the chosen subject matter, certain methodological considerations have substantial bearing on contemporary behavioral approaches to the study of private events.

---

[1]The conceptions in chapter 17 of Skinner (1953) are basic to this reading.

The distinction between method and content is perhaps best typified in the work of E. B. Titchener (1867–1927). According to Boring (1950), Titchener recognized that a particular stimulus would occasion different observational reports depending on the point of view the observer took. If the observer took what might be called the "physical" point of view or set, the stimulus event was described in detached, objective terms. Lacking this set, the observer described the stimulus event in more subjective terms, including reference to feeling quality. Verification of the operation of these different sets was obtained in tests of two-point thresholds, in which a blindfolded observer was asked to report whether one or two needle points were being applied to the skin. At a given physical separation of the two points, the subject responded differently when asked to report what "is" from what "it feels like."

Recognizing this characteristic of human observers, Titchener could train his observers to report only what "is" and thus act as neutral transducers of the sensory consequences of controlled stimulus events. This is similar to the demands imposed on an observer of private stimuli and is exactly the demand placed on any scientific observer of public events, whether they are instrument dials, cells on a slide, or responses.

A second methodological characteristic of certain early, psychological traditions closely resembles the inferential practices of modern physics. Although Wundt's "mental chronometry" mentioned in Reading 3 did not produce data of unimpeachable interpretability, it was, nevertheless, an attempt at descriptive measurement of phenomena whose existence and influence can only be inferred from effects observed under carefully controlled experimental conditions.

Millikan's well-known oil drop experiment furnishes a physical illustration of this tactic (Miller, 1972). The charge of a single electron is measured as a deductive consequence of careful measurement and control of all but one variable, whose effects are then quantified in terms of variation in the known parameters. More simply, electrons themselves are known only by their effects on photographic plates and cloud chambers, not by direct observations; yet the operations by which these researchers detect effects are sufficiently controlled and replicable as to leave little doubt as to the existence and reliability of the underlying phenomena.

Of course, the precision of idemnotic measurement in modern physics is sufficient to make the existence of an event such as an electron a compelling inference for the sake of completeness and parsimony. As indicated in Reading 3, the early attempts at quantitatively demonstrating various mental phenomena did not enjoy the benefits afforded by precise idemnotic measurement, and the scientific status of these "phenomena" remains in dispute.

These two strategies, proper training and instructing of observers and deductive inference from observable functional effects, hold promise as components of a natural scientific strategy for the study of behavioral events whose accessibility may be severely limited. In order to consider properly the role of these components in such a general strategy, we first consider the dimensions of the problem posed by limited accessibility.

Accessibility Continua

In order to discuss the methodological difficulties involved in investigating relations between behavioral and environmental events that are difficult to detect, it is useful to propose a public–private continuum of accessibility for both behavior and the environment. These continua are depicted graphically in Fig. 6.1. In our usage, the concept of *accessibility* is a combination of the likelihood that the event exists at all coupled with the difficulty of observing it, given that it does exist.

Describing behavioral and environmental events in terms of an accessibility continuum underlying the discrete categories of public and private provides a dimension (susceptible to at least ordinal measurement) for analysis of a problem that has often been viewed as largely semantic or philosophical. The terms *public* and *private* refer to adjacent nominal regions of the accessibility dimension, much as the terms *hot* and *cold* describe portions of the dimension of temperature. Even though for any single observer a particular event at any point in time either is or is not detectable, over a number of measurement occasions the accessibility of the event in question may vary for a variety of reasons within or across public or private regions.

One explanation for this variation in accessibility lies in our conditioning history. We may not detect certain events because we have not been conditioned to respond to a particular class of stimuli. A skilled worker such as an inspector in a manufacturing plant has been trained by the employer and conditioned by natural contingencies to detect and respond differentially to stimuli that are indeed public, but that others would not be able to detect in the absence of such a conditioning history.

In another case, a class of events such as the behavior of swallowing may fall in the public region for any observer who is present (movement of Adam's apple invariably accompanies the internal movements that we call swallow-

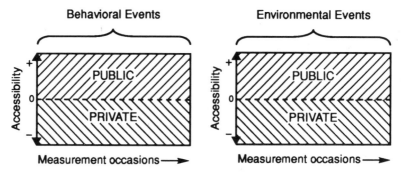

FIG. 6.1.   Schematic representation of accessibility continua for behavioral and environmental events over measurement occasions.

ing). However, it might strain the devotion of the most ardent observer to remain in a position to see every such movement by a subject for extended periods of time. The limitation on accessibility here is clearly only logistical, but it remains a limitation nevertheless.

Finally, Skinner (1953) pointed out the third justification for the schematic representation in Fig. 6.1: "The line between public and private is not fixed. The boundary shifts with every discovery of a technique for making private events public" (p. 282). Advances in scientific measurement technology repeatedly expand the accessibility of the universe of public events by augmenting our sensory capabilities through magnification (in a generic sense) of some aspect of the event. Many behavioral events that occur inside the skin are routinely made public by measurement advances originating in medicine. These advances constitute a rich opportunity for expanding the frontiers of the science of behavior.

It should be clear, then, that the public or private nature of a behavioral or environmental event is not a characteristic of the event itself. Rather, this reference to accessibility is a statement about the likelihood of an observer's behavior of detecting or responding to the event. The fact that an event cannot under some circumstances be detected does not mean that the event is inherently different from events that can usually be detected, nor does it mean that the event has the "property" of being private. The most parsimonious assumption is that the "private" event is in no way different from "public" events and that any supposed difference lies only in the degree to which we have access to it.

The major benefit of this perspective lies in how it guides the investigation of events whose occurrence is difficult or presently impossible to detect. Because the assumption is that such events are not different in their basic nature but merely raise problems of detection, the measurement problems forced by selecting such phenomena for study are not in any way different, regardless of traditional or a priori assumptions about the phenomena or the reasons for their inaccessibility.

Figure 6.1 suggests that the public and private regions of accessibility apply to both behavioral and environmental events. There are therefore four possible circumstances of measurement distinguishable by this analysis, and each requires a somewhat specialized strategy for achieving accurate measurement and functional analysis. Let us examine these strategies individually.

Public Stimuli and Public Responses. When both the subject's movement and the part of the environment to which it is related are observable by the experimenter and others, there are no special difficulties other than the considerations discussed in *Strategies and Tactics*. It is appropriate that public events have been the predominant focus of early behavioral research and fortunate that the demands for technology have been of a similar nature.

Public Stimuli and Private Responses. When the functional relation of interest involves stimuli that are public but responses that are private, scientific investigation might seem impossible. In fact, careful behavioral research ers using nonhuman subjects in controlled laboratory settings routinely draw conclusions about private behavioral events without hesitation. They study visual or auditory behavior of pigeons or rats or monkeys, for example, and accept the data as accurately reflecting private visual or auditory responses in spite of the direct inaccessibility of these events to the experimenter. They do this by teaching the animal to make a particular public response to experimenter controlled presentations of relevant environmental stimuli. Confidence in the accuracy of the public response is gained by the orderliness of correlations between the emission of the public responses under successive manipulations of the environmental stimuli.

For example, a pigeon may be exposed to contingencies in which pecking a key results in the occasional presentation of grain only if the key is green; if the key is red, no grain ever appears no matter how much pecking occurs. Once this pattern is established and the pigeon only pecks when the key is green, we may safely infer that the private response of "seeing green" is occurring. The experimenter may then gradually change the color of the red key (holding other dimensions such as intensity constant) until its wavelength is very close to green and note when the pigeon resumes pecking. In this fashion, the pigeon's ability to differentiate or "see" colors in the spectrum can be assessed. This tactic is now commonplace, and through it we have learned about the sensory capabilities of various species in precise detail (Blough, 1966).

The tactic is used in an identical fashion to measure the same private responses to auditory and visual stimuli in humans of all ages. We teach a public response (such as hand raising or vocalizing) appropriate to the subject and the task and vary different characteristics of the stimuli (intensity of auditory stimuli or size of visual stimuli) in a systematic sequence. We trust the resulting evidence of the unobserved private responses (hearing and seeing) enough to prescribe prosthetic devices (hearing aids and glasses) that could be harmful if improperly fitted.

There is, then, an underlying strategy for investigating behavioral events of limited accessibility that has demonstrated success. First, train or bring under stimulus control a public response appropriate to the subject and task. Then arrange to bring that response under the control of a particular stimulus that it also accessible to both the subject and the experimenter. The demonstration that the resulting public responses are indeed highly correlated with the private responses depends on the orderliness of the resulting data in relation to repeated manipulations of the public stimuli.

Private Stimuli and Public Responses.   The third combination includes responses of interest that are public but stimuli that are inaccessible. As before, this does not present an insoluble problem to the investigator. The well-respected tactic is to take advantage of the relation between the private environmental event and a public one. For example, consider a patient reporting repeated migraine headaches to a physician. The physician is interested in minimal use of pharmacologic agents and must therefore have confidence in the relation between the patient's reports of pain and actual pain. After noting that aspirin and other mild drugs do not change the patient's reports of pain, the physician takes advantage of the well-known effects of morphine by administering a substantial dose under controlled conditions (taking care not to inform the patient of possible effects). If the patient reports the disappearance and return on the pain consistent with the known time course of the drug's analgesic effects, the physician's confidence in the relation between the public response and its prompting private stimulus is increased.

It is important to caution against falling into a trap. Successfully applying this tactic requires a known and demonstrable relation between some public environmental event and its private counterpart (in this case, morphine and its effects on pain). This is not always available, and the researcher must never be in the position of hypothesizing the relation or, worse yet, the private stimulus itself in the absence of any such knowledge.

Private Stimuli and Public Responses.   Finally, we may consider the case in which the investigator is primarily interested in functional relations between responses and stimuli, both of which are observable only by the subject. If this was truly an unalterable situation, it would indeed pose a problem at present not approachable scientifically. The tactic in the two previous cases, in which either environmental or response events were inaccessible, was to make them public by applying measurement technology or by selecting other stimulus or response events whose correlations with the private events are either known or can be clearly demonstrated. Combining those tactics may move doubly inaccessible relations into the scientific arena so they can be subjected to the same quality of analysis as other behavioral phenomena. The following laboratory example provides an especially creative and rigorous attack on the problem of inaccessibility of both stimulus and response events.

In an ingenious and elaborate series of experiments with rhesus monkeys, Adams and his co-workers (Adams, Hall, Rice, Wood, & Willis, 1975) succeeded in reproducing by electrical means the private stimulus correlates of specific public stimulus displays. These investigators developed a complex procedure, of which the following is a simplified variation. Monkeys were initially taught to respond on one of three levers depending on whether one, two, or three dots appeared on a screen. If anything else (or nothing) appeared on the screen, the animal pushed a fourth lever. Appropriate lever responses were reinforced with food. At this stage, the experiment resembles the pigeon experiment already mentioned, in which the private response of seeing is arranged to occasion key-pecking responses.

Adams and his colleagues went further, however. After the monkey was trained to a high criterion of accuracy (always pushing the correct lever corresponding to the number of dots displayed), a blackout condition was arranged and patterns of mild electrical stimulation were applied directly to the animal's visual cortex. Varying the pattern of this stimulation produced lever responses previously correlated with dot displays, supporting the inference that the private event previously produced by dots can be reproduced by cortical stimulation. The availability of the fourth lever allowed the animal to respond when whatever it "sees" was not dots, thus increasing confidence in the existence of the private correlate of public dots.

It should be noted that a two-stage inference is involved here, supported entirely by the amount of control over the animal's lever pressing established in the training phase of the experiment. The first is the inference that the same private response of "seeing dots" is occurring in the blackout condition. The second is the inference that the private event evoked by the electrical stimulation at least closely resembled that which previously occurred when dots were presented before the eyes in normal light. The fact that differential lever responding was observed in the absence of light but only in conjunction with cortical stimulation supports both inferences. The purpose of this research was to develop an electronic prosthesis for the blind. Refinement of the technique may lead to the ability to transform signals generated by a miniature television camera into cortical stimulation that will elicit private visual experiences that are tightly determined by what the camera sees.

The strategy underlying this research is similar to that used to investigate subatomic particles in modern physics. The private events that the monkey sees are not formally assumed to exist beforehand. The existence of the private events is the most parsimonious explanation of certain experimental effects observed under conditions that render any other cause unlikely. In physics, when certain data can be reasonably explained only by positing the presence of an electron of a specific charge, that electron is identified by its effects. Similarly, the private stimulus, two dots, is identified by its effects on the monkey's behavior; it is unlikely that the monkey would, given this experimental history, strike that lever if any other event were the result of the specific cortical stimulation.

If a problem of double inaccessibility remains unapproachable by the tactics described, it may be time to call a temporary halt for purposes of regrouping while gathering reinforcements or planning a flanking movement. Reinforcements in this context might include developing new measurement technology or new tactics for describing correlations with public events. A flanking movement might embody redefining the problem of interest so that the question can be approached in a slightly different manner that will still provide valuable information.

The work of M. K. Goldstein and his associates at the Gainesville, Florida, Veteran's Administration Hospital provides an illustration of such a tactical redirection of efforts. A persistent logistical problem in the delivery of health care services involved attempting to monitor patients in their home and work environments to verify that they are complying with medical instructions ("Get more exercise." "Take one of these three times a day," etc.). This monitoring has traditionally been attempted through haphazard and infrequent contacts with the physician, usually initiated by the patient in response to renewed distress. Alternatively, some psychologists have relied on systematic verbal reports, either by mail-in questionnaires or telephone conversations, both necessitating the researcher to make an ill-founded inference of correspondence between the verbal report and compliance behavior.

By approaching the verbal report itself as the initial phenomena of interest, Goldstein experimentally analyzed its determinants and developed techniques for establishing controlled calibration so that eventually, by exclusion, the only determinant of variability in the verbal report were the actual details of the recent behavioral history (Goldstein, Stein, Smolen, & Perlini, 1976; Stein, Goldstein, & Smolen, 1976). In other words, correspondence between the public verbal report and the less accessible behavioral history was arranged experimentally, rather than assumed or taken for granted.

Whatever alternatives are pursued, behavioral scientists should not be embarrassed at the necessity of a temporary halt in the face of measurement limitations. This decision has a long and respected tradition in the history of science. It is one thing to be on the leading edge of one's science, but it is quite another to be beyond it. It is far preferable to admit the present limits of our knowledge and measurement technology than to ignore such limits and begin abandoning the strategies and tactics that have brought behavioral researchers this far.

Further Strategic Considerations

Although there are some superficial similarities, the general strategy proposed here for investigating phenomena of limited accessibility is very different from that of Wundt, Titchener, and the other early investigators whose legacy remains evident in the contemporary social sciences. The problem of limited accessibility was so fundamental to their interests that 19th-century researchers were easily convinced that an entirely different subject matter had emerged, occasioning abandonment of the established methods of the natural sciences. With hindsight, it is clear that this was an incautious overreaction to a problem of degree, not of kind. The troublesome demands of limited accessibility do not relieve the requirement of firm adherence to all other demands of careful natural scientific investigation. The basic strategy rests firmly on a scientifically sound technology of public measurement and dictates only supplementary cautions, not variations in basic conceptions.

The active investigation of less accessible behavioral phenomena has also properly lagged well behind the study of public behavioral events. This has allowed a considerable body of secure, basic knowledge about behavior to emerge as a foundation for research on less accessible events. The importance of this chronology lies in the accumulated empirical support for the parsimonious scientific assumption that private behavioral events differ from public ones only in their accessibility (Skinner, 1953). This cautious position would have to have been relinquished only with the utmost reluctance, and such a surrender now seems quite unlikely.

It is important to encourage a cautious respect for difficulties inherent in this kind of research. The central complication stems from the difficulties of observing less accessible stimuli or responses. Solving this problem will require a more strenuous effort than the same investigation of more public phenomena.

The general recommendations in this reading must be accompanied by special efforts in response definition, observation, recording, and experimental design.

As a final caveat, investigators should carefully consider whether struggling with the problems of limited accessibility is unavoidably required by the research interest. An honest and searching examination of the research question will often lead to an alternate version that can be answered through experimentation with public phenomena. Meaningful behavioral research is difficult enough without borrowing unnecessary complications.

MEASUREMENT TACTICS

The remainder of this reading concerns the problems of measuring responses of limited accessibility, regardless of the accessibility of the environmental events to which they are functionally related. This is not intended to diminish the importance of precisely specifying such stimuli. It is normally assumed that the public stimulus dimensions of the experimental environment under investigation will be adequately described, because this is usually a relatively easy task. If completely inaccessible stimuli must be measured, they can be inferred only from the results of measuring public responses. Thus, considering response measurement tactics becomes both necessary and sufficient for dealing with the limited accessibility of stimuli as well. Moreover, in the event that both stimulus and response are fully inaccessible, the distinction becomes largely theoretical.

Definition of Response Classes

Although defining less accessible response classes requires some special considerations, the basic tactics discussed in chapter 4 of *Strategies and Tactics* with respect to publicly observable responses fully apply here. Additional considerations stem from the fact that, even though the researcher may have some conception of the behavior of interest, satisfactory access to its features and limits cannot be gained. This lack of access will hinder, not only applying proper definitional tactics, but the adequate training of the observer who must also serve as subject.

Although the ultimate solution to these difficulties rests with technological advances that will make such responses public, there are some special tactics that, in the interim, can ameliorate the situations. The first of these is to define the response class as clearly, simply, and thoroughly as possible so that each instance will be maximally obvious to, and detectable by, the subject. For example, a detailed definition of "smiling" will facilitate far more accurate self-observation than will a definition of "presenting a positive self image."

Second, if the experimenter can also define private responses that have some kinds of public behavioral accompaniments, there will be the advantage of a source of corollary evidence about the occurrence of the behavior. For instance, the occurrence of a flatus emission may or may not be aurally detected by others depending on topographical features of the response and the ambient noise level in the surrounding environment. However, there are inevitably malodorous byproducts whose public detectability is attested to by a variety of reactions on the part of those in the immediate vicinity.[2]

A third tactic is to define the inaccessible response class in such a way that the experimenter can arrange some kinds of tests to probe for verification about the definition the subject is using (as well as the occurrences of the behavior itself). To illustrate, a dental patient's personal definition of "cleaning teeth" can easily be evaluated with the use of plaque disclosing tablets that tint any plaque on the teeth so that it is easily detectable by the dentist. Because the dentist has little or no access to the patient's teeth cleaning behavior, it is necessary to arrange a "probe" for the effects of that behavior that will be accessible by both patient and dentist so that communication will have a shared, objective referent. These three general tactics are all means by which society teaches the individual to respond to his or her own private events (Skinner, 1953). The researcher can use the same tactics to provide supplementary information about the definition of the private event that the subject is using.

In all cases in which the target response still remains essentially inaccessible, it becomes necessary to train a publicly observable response and to establish its correspondence with the private event. The characteristics of this public response are of the utmost importance in ensuring that the correlation between private and public responses is high. The general tactic is to arrange the environment of the subject such that the emission of the private response (and no other event) becomes the occasion for the emission of the public response. The tactics here are somewhat different than in the more common case in which one wishes to bring a public response under the control of some public stimulus that precedes the response. Here, the private event that will serve the stimulus function is inaccessible to the experimenter, thus preventing reinforcement of the public response in the presence of the desired stimulus.[3]

Criteria for selecting the public response that will be brought under control of the private event are that it be simple, discrete, clearly defined, and exclusively under the control of the private event. It should also be physically easy to emit with as little cost to the subject as possible. For example, recording responses on paper requires the subject, not only to have a pencil and paper available at all times, but also to get them out and make a notation each time the defined event occurs. On the other hand, pushing a button on a mechanical counter worn on the wrist is comparatively easy. Selecting a public response that involves such mechanical or electrical assists can be important in facilitating development of control by the private event and, ultimately, accurate reporting. The constant presence of a counter worn on the wrist, for example, can

---

[2]For a more thorough discussion of this phenomenon, particularly those aspects bearing on detectability, see Carlin (1973).

[3]The reader should note the strategic communality with the situation discussed earlier in which the stimulus (the inaccessible response event) is private and the response is public.

serve as a stimulus prompting the subject to observe the private events that comprise a part of the functional definition of the public counting response. Furthermore, the topography of the selected recording response should be distinctive, to endow it with an extremely low probability of occurrence except in the presence of the targeted private event. If, by virtue of special history or training, the public response is likely to be made to other events, either public or private, some loss of measurement accuracy is almost inevitable.

Dimensional Quantities and Units

All issues concerning the dimensional quantities of behavior and their corresponding measurement units are fully applicable to behavioral events of limited accessibility. The properties of repeatability, temporal locus, and temporal extent are characteristic of all behavioral events, regardless of how readily they may be observed. Nonetheless, from a tactical perspective, certain dimensional quantities may be preferable in the case of less accessible events because of the general requirements of ease and simplicity of making the corresponding public response. Selecting a temporal dimensional quantity, for example, may require timing devices and procedures that are unjustifiable if simple counting would suffice in meeting experimental needs.

Observing and Recording

The special problems surrounding observing and recording behavioral events of limited accessibility emanate from the fact that the same individual who is to perform observation and recording functions is the author of the behavior as well. The general range of tactics required for good observing and recording are fully relevant in this situation, but there must be special concern that they do not encroach on the individual's role as subject. Because most individuals are accustomed to fulfilling a variety of roles simultaneously, this requirement is not insurmountable if approached knowledgeably and cautiously.

It is imperative to select subjects/observers who have a source and degree of motivation to participate that is compatible with the nature of the project. The researcher should also take great care in arranging the many contingencies that are part of an experiment to maintain this motivation. Some subjects may be inclined to produce the kind of data they think the experimenter wants to see, for example. The initial training and all subsequent interactions with the experimenter must therefore be carefully designed to avoid encouraging any kind of observer bias. Thorough efforts must be made to ensure that all consequences that follow observer behaviors are consistent with the goals of accurate observation and must not be differentially related to any features of the data. For example, the subject should not feel uncomfortable in reporting that she didn't feel like observing one day or that he forgot his counter.

A special consequence of observing and recording that must be carefully managed is the permanent response product of the whole procedure—the data themselves. From the standpoint of maintaining bias-free observation, it is usually necessary to restrict the subject/observer's access to the data in any form. This tactic may even extend to covering the dials on a counter so that information the subject would not otherwise have is not available concerning the day's cumulative performance.

Accuracy, Reliability, and Believability

Having proceeded this far in an investigation of functional relations involving stimuli or responses of less than desirable accessibility, the inevitable question of the accuracy and reliability of measurement must be squarely faced. Assessing these data characteristics unavoidably requires knowledge of the true values of the dimensional quantities being measured so that they can be compared to observed values. Such true values may often be available when the source of the limitations on accessibility is primarily logistical in nature. For example, when response products resulting from the behavior of interest are potentially public but logistically difficult or costly to measure directly, subject self-observation data may be compared to periodically obtained measures of the response products for a proper assessment of accuracy and reliability. There may be many such instances when special, intermittent measurement efforts can be used to determine true values for this purpose.

The limitation on accessibility to the events of interest may be complete, however, precluding any evaluation of accuracy and reliability. The only remaining tactic available to the researcher is to collect supplementary data that will augment the believability of the primary data. That is, data must be gathered that will serve to enhance the confidence of the researcher and others that the subject-collected data constitute acceptably credible representations of the unknown true values. An example of this approach in an actual research program may help illustrate the issues and procedures involved.

The focus of the research program concerned the study tactics college students use in preparing for tests over textbook material (Johnston, O'Neill, Walters, & Rasheed, 1975). One of the reasons for the paucity of empirical information concerning what is probably the single most important behavioral determinant of academic performance is that study behaviors occur at the choice of the individual in a wide variety of physical settings at all hours of the day and night. Even under ideal conditions, only some of what is usually called "studying" is publicly observable. Arranging for frequent public observation would have required using a study hall setting and restricting availability of materials to that room. Not only was this logistically impossible, such an atypical condition would probably have altered the characteristics of normal student study activities. Moreover, most study behaviors remain inaccessible to others regardless of any arrangements for external observation.

These facts necessitated developing a technology for measuring both public and private study behaviors via observing and recording by the individual student. A reporting form was developed over a period of two years. Versions of it were used every academic quarter in a variety of courses with hundreds of students, with major and minor revisions made continually on the basis of the resulting data. Throughout this lengthy process (during which no experiments using this evolving measurement technology were conducted), efforts were made to construct the Study Report Form so that it would occasion accurate reporting responses of both public and private study behaviors.

This effort produced many changes in the form, sometimes of a seemingly subtle and sometimes of a more obvious nature. This process is too lengthy and complex to chronicle here (see Johnston et al., 1975), especially because the Study Report Form was only one component of the eventual technology. The procedures for training students to use the form and the contingencies designed to facilitate their proper use of it were of equal importance to the form itself; these procedures included arranging appropriate consequences simply for completing the form as well as for making errors that were publicly detectable.

During the latter part of this development period, the data were used to augment confidence that the obtained data were valid, indirect measures of study behavior. This assertion was examined by collecting at least four kinds of data (O'Neill, Walters, Rasheed, & Johnston, 1975; Walters, O'Neill, Rasheed, & Johnston, 1975). First, if the form was soliciting valid reports of study behavior, a certain class of possible errors should be seen rarely, if at all. For example, in their successive attempts to meet criterion on each unit, students should never have reported "rereading" the text assignment as a study tactic until they had first reported "reading" the material on the same or a previous attempt. An examination of the data from two academic quarters in one course showed that in 849 instances when "rereading" was reported, it never preceded the reported occurrence of "reading."

Another kind of data required by the asserted validity of the measurement procedure stemmed from the design of the individualized, repeated testing-to-mastery style of the courses serving as a research vehicle (Johnston & Pennypacker, 1971). Given the nature of the teaching methods, it would have been highly unlikely that certain types of study behavior listed on the form would be reported. In these courses, such improbable study behaviors included writing multiple choice questions (all testing was with fill-in questions), rereading and transcribing lecture notes (there were no formal lectures and tests covered only text material), and using audio-visual materials (none were available to the student). The examination of many thousands of Study Report Forms showed that these behaviors were either not reported at all or in less than one-half of 1% of all possible instances.

A third kind of data was available in the patterns of academic performance exhibited by students. If there was a sound relation between test performance and study behavior and if study behavior was being properly reported, this correspondence should be evident in the case of unusual patterns of academic performance. One such pattern that was occasionally observed was termed a reversal; when three or more quizzes were taken in the attempt to meet the 90% correct criterion, sometimes the score on the second (or third) quiz was markedly poorer than on the previous and subsequent attempts. A number of

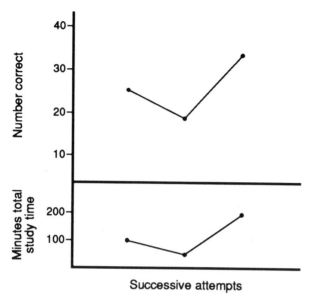

FIG. 6.2.   Corresponding reversal between correct performance and total study time for one student (adapted from Walters et al., 1975).

such patterns were examined along with the corresponding reports of total study time on each quiz attempt. Figure 6.2 shows one such comparison.

A fourth kind of data follows from manipulating academic variables that should exert predictable effects on the reported study data if the students' observations are valid. One experiment that followed the development of the measurement procedure investigated the effects of the size of each unit of course material. Eight successive units in one course were arranged into lengths of 30, 60, or 90 textbook pages. Such major variations in the curriculum should result in corresponding variations in the total time spent studying each unit. Even greater correspondence should be seen in the time reported as spent reading the text material for the first time in each unit (assuming nearly constant reading speeds across all units). This prediction was evaluated in two separate experiments with different unit size sequences and was consistently confirmed. The data for one individual are shown in Fig. 6.3.

It should be clear that these kinds of data did not "prove" the validity of the measurement technology. However, evidence that could have weakened confidence in the validity of the measurement system was shown to be false, thus increasing confidence in the asserted validity by some unspecified degree. Exactly how much data are required to be convincing is, of course, unknown and depends on many influences, such as (a) available literature on the question, (b) the investigator's experience in the area, (c) the details of measurement procedures, (d) the nature of the research question, and (e) the characteristics of the reported data. However, this remains as an extremely useful tactic for building believability in the validity of data resulting from procedures designed to measure events to which accessibility is limited.

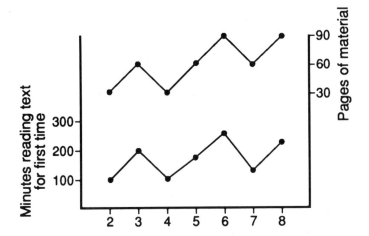

FIG. 6.3.   Time spent reading the text for the first time and pages of material across units for an individual student (adapted from Walters et al., 1975).

The development of this measurement technology permitted for the first time the experimental investigation of, not only those variables directly influencing study behavior, but also the effects of controlled variations in study behavior on subsequent academic performance. The investigation was able to replace the traditional assumptions about the role of study behavior with replicable functional relations, thus opening a new area of educational research to experimental analysis.

The strategies and tactics underlying this research program demonstrated a level of robustness worthy of consideration in other areas of human behavior that are logistically or generically inaccessible. Generally speaking, one gains precise experimental control over those relevant variables that are accessible, and then the inaccessible phenomena reveal themselves, if only by their effects. Canons of parsimony are not violated by a demonstration that a major determinant of experimental variability can be controlled, even if not directly observed.

Once penetrated, the barrier of limited accessibility will yield to careful experimentation. Skinner (1953) reminded us that no description of behavior will be complete without an account of events occurring inside the skin of the organism. The rapidly advancing technology of bioelectronic instrumentation is opening new avenues of experimental access to numerous physiological state variables on which internal behavior surely depends. Our enhanced ability to identify, measure, and control these hitherto inaccessible independent variables permits even greater versatility in isolating the behavioral phenomena that are the result of such processes. As research embodying this strategy becomes commonplace, the traditional inventions of mentalism will lose whatever explanatory utility is now claimed for them. In their place will appear functional explanations of those phenomena that, because of their limited accessibility, have posed problems of interpretation that are more apparent than real.

PART THREE

DESIGN

Traditions of
Experimental Design

INTRODUCTION

The purpose of experimentation is to provide empirical comparisons when naturalistic observation alone is insufficient. By creating special conditions of observation (i.e., an experiment), a scientist may gain access to facts that will support conclusions that may not be supportable in the absence of such conditions. Within the last century, however, the nuances and complexities of methods of experimentation have become the focus of a broad, generic subdiscipline known as *experimental design* or the *design of experiments*.

The subject matter of this specialty has come to depend heavily on inferential statistics and cuts across many areas of scientific endeavor. Especially within the social sciences, it is now accepted that by properly applying the principles of experimental design, anyone can force nature to provide useful information about almost any subject. Concern about the relevance or importance of the experimental question has given way to emphasis on the quality of the formal design through which an experimental attack on the problem is to be mounted. The interdependence of experimental design and methods of statistical data analysis has created a situation in which legions of experts in "research method," with little knowledge of the relevant subject matter, regularly advise both scientists and policy makers on the propriety of proposed experimental agenda.

Our aim in this reading is twofold: We first take a brief historical review of the evolution of experimental method in the natural sciences and then focus more closely on the origins and practices of contemporary approaches to "experimental design," evaluating their applicability to the natural science of behavior.

EARLY HISTORY OF NATURAL SCIENCE EXPERIMENTATION

Formal experimentation is usually traced to the writings of Roger Bacon (1210–1292) and William of Occam (d. 1347), although it is now clear that the Arabians of the Middle Ages performed important experiments sometime earlier. According to Dampier (1942), the Muslim physicist Ibn-al-Haitham (965–1020) accomplished major feats in experimental optics using spherical and parabolic mirrors and even understood atmospheric refraction. The translation of his work into Latin must surely have been a major impetus to Bacon and his contemporary Robert Grosseteste. Nevertheless, intellectual life in the western world was heavily dominated by scholastic theology until the 13th and 14th centuries, and there was little demand or tolerance for natural experimentation under those circumstances.

Probably the single figure most responsible for breaking with theological tradition in the study of nature was Leonardo da Vinci (1452–1519). Unlike his predecessors, Leonardo approached inquiry from a purely practical perspective, investigating and experimenting as necessary to develop solutions to problems in the vast range of topics that interested him—art, biology, engineering, military tactics, physics, physiology, and zoology. Unfortunately, Leonardo published very little, although he was widely known in Renaissance Italy. His notebooks have only been recovered and published in the 20th century. Much of the fundamental science of the 16th and 17th centuries was anticipated by Leonardo, but his work was as unavailable to Galileo and Kepler, as that of Archimedes had been to him.

Throughout the 16th, 17th, 18th, and most of the 19th centuries, scientific experimentation consisted of reasoned demonstration assisted by precise measurement. An interesting illustration of such activity is the work of van Helmont (b. 1577), who according to Dampier (1942):

> planted a willow in a weighted quantity of dry earth, supplied it with water only, and at the end of five years found that it had gained 164 pounds in weight, while the earth had lost only two ounces. This was a very ingenious proof that practically all the new substance of the willow was made of water, indeed quite a convincing proof, until Ingenhousz and Priestly, more than 100 years later, showed that green plants absorb carbon and carbon dioxide from the air. (p. 127)

William Harvey's demonstration of the circulation of the blood (1628) similarly illuminates the type of experimental reasoning on which it depended.

Consider the growth of a single field of inquiry from the standpoint of the critical advances made by experimentation. The study of electromagnetic phenomena provides a convenient example, partly because such phenomena were puzzling and given to misinterpretation by early thinkers. Progress in correcting such misinformation came slowly and only by carefully reasoned experimental analysis. The early work of William Gilbert of Colchester (1540–1603) furnished elegant experimental reasoning. His work with magnets led him to conclude that the earth was a giant magnet whose poles did not quite coincide with the geographic poles. Gilbert also coined the term *electricity* to describe the forces that resulted when various materials, especially amber, were rubbed together.

Oddly enough, the connection between electrical and magnetic phenomena was not made until the work of Farraday in 1831, although it was probably suspected by Franklin and others. The problem was that a controlled source of electricity was not available before the early 1800s. The history of experimental science makes it clear that rapid progress in a field usually awaits discovery of methods of producing the essential phenomena at will. Whereas in 1752, Benjamin Franklin was able to charge a key with a series of Leyden jars and conduct his famous kite experiment, which demonstrated the electrical nature of lightning, it was an observation in 1786 by Luigi Galvani that paved the way for storage batteries. Galvani noticed that if the nerve and muscle of a frog's leg were simultaneously touched by two dissimilar metals and then the metals brought into contact, the leg would twitch. He thought the phenomenon was the result of "animal electricity," but in 1800, Alessandro Volta (1745–1827) showed that no animal was necessary—the electrical charge was the result of chemical action. Volta arranged strips of zinc and copper separated by paper in a salt solution and was able to produce electrical energy from this "pile," as it came to be called. Farraday invented the first electric motor in 1821 and, following Oersted's 1820 observation that a wire leading away from a Volta pile will produce deviations in a compass, verified the existence of electromagnetic phenomena as described.

Over 200 years of effort were required to move from the discovery of magnetism to its understanding as a basic electrical phenomenon. We could easily trace the history of similar scientific odysseys, such as the discovery and classification of gasses, from the efforts of the early Greeks through the work of van Helmont, Priestley (1733–1804), Cavendish (1731–1794), and Lavoisier (1743–1794), or the evolution of mechanics from Galileo through Newton and Einstein.

One fact clearly emerges through any such historical journey, regardless of the discipline in question. Experimentation was arranged to permit a single observation at a time, usually under known or at least controlled conditions. Observations were then repeated a second and a third time to ensure the repeatability of the first. To be sure, the results of any series of observations were not identical. Concern with measurement error can be seen in the work of Leonardo and Galileo, as well as the later, more sophisticated treatment afforded by Legendre. Nowhere, however, do we see experimental method dictated by a concept of chance or random variation in the phenomena under study. The origins of the mode of experimental inquiry that may be called "groups comparisons" are altogether different.

EARLY HISTORY OF GROUPS COMPARISONS

The origins of the distinctly modern practice of using composite group measures as a basis of experimental comparisons are complex and difficult to trace. In an excellent book on the history of statistics, Helen Walker (1929) cited three major, diverse traditions coming together to create the discipline of statistics. To these, we later add a fourth tradition—agricultural experimentation—that joins Walker's three as the essential elements that combine to give the rationale underlying scientific inference on the basis of groups comparisons. Let us first briefly recount the three traditions Walker identifies.

Social Enumeration

The oldest of these traditions can be traced to biblical times when King David is said to have counted his people, sheep, and so forth. Early civilizations, including those of Babylon, Greece, and Rome, apparently made periodic tabulations of people and property, perhaps for tax purposes. In the Middle Ages, Pepin the Short and Charlemagne forced the Church to account, not only for the land it held, but for the serfs who lived on it. In England in 1086, there was the Doomsday Book, which listed the names of landowners and an inventory of their serfs and property.

By the early 14th century, descriptive economic statistics had appeared in the form of records of tariffs and customs duties in Paris markets. The practice of registering marriages and deaths began at that time. Baptisms were added in the 15th century, and all such registrations were the responsibility of the Church. In 16th- and 17th-century England, outbreaks of plague inspired maintaining the Bills of Mortality (a death registry), which was gradually refined to include, not only the sex of the deceased, but the occurrence of any baptisms.

Walker viewed these and similar events as contributing to a tradition of political enumeration, whose full realization occurs in the modern decennial census. Actually, census taking appears to have originated in Canada in 1605, with the Scandinavian countries following soon thereafter. England did not initiate a formal census until 1801, although the practice of keeping birth and mortality data apparently persisted from the time of the plague. The close of the 18th century witnessed many political upheavals, among them the American and French Revolutions. With these came elected forms of government that required political census taking for purposes of apportionment. Thus, the first American census was conducted in 1790, as required by the Constitution. Previous apportionment to the Continental Congress was evidently on the basis of state boundaries alone. At that time, census taking had already been going on in Norway, Sweden, and Denmark for at least 50 years; it became a regular function of the Swedish government in 1756.

Economic Quantification

The second major tradition from which modern statistical practice derives accompanied the rise of the mercantile economies following the Age of Exploration. As the foregoing discussion indicates, this tradition was at first indistinguishable from that of social or political enumeration. Many of the early monarchs required periodic tabulations, not only of their subjects, but of their resources, so that decisions of military strategy could be made on the basis of something other than pure guesswork. We have already mentioned that economic tabulations were made in 14th-century France in terms of transactions, not just holdings. In the late 16th century, there appeared a document entitled *Secret of French Finances*, which Walker believes may represent the first effort to use such data in formulating state policy.

At about this time, people began using such enumerative data for predictive purposes. Walker argues that the first effort to use enumerative data to examine the regularity of social phenomena was Captain John Graunt's *Observations on the London Bills of Mortality* (1662). In 1693, the astronomer Halley published *An Estimate of the Degrees of Mortality of Mankind, Drawn From Curious Tables of the Births and Funerals at the city of Breslaw, With an attempt to ascertain the Price of Annuities*, which marks the first attempt to base annuities upon actuarial data.

Thus the insurance business was born in the modern, actuarial sense. We agree with Walker that it is beyond mere coincidence that astronomers, such as Halley and Legendre, as well as Quetelet over 100 years later, played a role, not only in developing statistical procedures for refining observational data in their laboratories, but in the inductive use of demographic measures as well. This leads us to the third major tradition, probability theory.

Mathematical Statistics

We have already recounted the development of this discipline in some detail in Reading 3. For the present, we remind the reader that by the end of the 18th century, the mathematics of probability had progressed from its origins in the letters of Pascal and Fermat around 1650 concerning gambling problems to the formal statements of the Normal Law of Error furnished by Laplace (1778) and Gauss (1809). With the advent of the formal calculus of probabilities late in the 18th century, the stage was set for using collections of quantitative characteristics of individuals within groups as a basis for inductive generalizations concerning social phenomena. Prior to this time, the practical significance of the theory of probability had not been appreciated beyond its applicability to games of chance.

Much earlier, Abraham De Moivre (1667–1754) developed a close approximation to the normal curve (1738) on purely mathematical grounds, reasoning from the distribution of coefficients in the binomial expansion $(a + b)$. He saw the significance of this as largely theological, supporting a concept of *Great First Cause* (Walker, 1929): "And thus in all cases it will be found, that although Chance produces irregularities, still the Odds will be infinitely great, that in the process of Time, these irregularities will bear no proportion to the recurrency of Order that naturally results from Original Design" (p. 17). Similar thinking is evident in the work of Jacques Bernoulli (1654–1705) and other moral philosophers of the period.

The developments in formal probability theory that occurred at the turn of the 19th century furnished powerful mathematical tools with which to provide quantitative descriptions of various phenomena that seemed to obey the normal distribution, as well as to estimate with astonishing accuracy the likelihood of occurrence of particular instances. As we have seen, the 19th century witnessed vigorous development of this potential in a number of areas, including the invention of measurement practices that seemed to bypass the need for absolute units. Two early 19th-century figures, Augustus De Morgan and Adolphe Quetelet, are at the apex of these developments. It is useful to sketch briefly their contributions apart from the origins of vaganotic measurement.

Augustus De Morgan

Augustus De Morgan (1806–1871) was among the first to grasp the enormous potential of mathematical statistics for addressing complex practical problems in human affairs. In 1838, he published *An Essay of Probabilities and on Their Application to Life Contingencies and Insurance Offices,* in which he presented simplified rules for the mathematically uninitiated that would (as quoted by Walker, 1929): "enable them to obtain at least the results of complicated problems, and which will therefore, permit them to extend their inquiries further than a few simple cases connected with gambling" (p. 26). Around 1838, De Morgan wrote a speculative article on probability theory in which he suggested its applicability to evaluating the truth of testimony, the correctness of jury decisions, and the occurrence of miracles. He even suggested comparing 500 trials for which a jury renders an immediate verdict to 500 in which it deliberates two or more hours to see which set of verdicts displays the smaller percentage of error.

This may very well be the first suggestion of an intergroup experimental comparison and clearly forecasts the reasoning which statistical theory would later serve. Its importance at the time, however, lay in the promise offered for coping with established problems dominated by the ingredient of uncertainty. Of course, the guilt or innocence of a defendant was and continues to be an uncertain matter, which must often be determined by methods of approximation, even though the penalty might be excruciatingly exact.

Adolphe Quetelet

It is clear that the dominant figure of this tradition was Adolphe Quetelet. It was Quetelet more than anyone else who melded the actuarial properties of large collections of data with the mathematics of expectation furnished by the Normal Law of Error. Quetelet clearly saw the value of gathering detailed demographic data on an orderly and regular basis. He was quite naturally convinced of the connection between all manner of social phenomena and the laws of probability by the fact that the bell-shaped distribution kept reappearing. He founded the London Statistical Society in 1834, and the Commission Centrale de Statistique in 1841, and he organized the first International Statistical Congress in 1853. A man of prodigious energy, Quetelet was apparently determined to ensure the availability of an adequate data base for further development and application of statistical techniques.

We mentioned earlier that Quetelet was a wide ranging intellect. He regarded the new statistical method as equally applicable in all fields from agriculture and anthropology to zoology, depending only on the existence of an observational data base. Like his predecessors, he apparently regarded the persistence of the normal curve as evidence of some supraordinate regularity. His concept of the *average man* as a natural ideal is discussed in Reading 3 and came to have a profound effect on anthropologists, physicians, and educators for the next 100 years. From our point of view, however, it was in the area of moral measurement that Quetelet established the most important precedents.

Quetelet delivered a paper entitled "Recherches sur la Penchant au Crime anx Differents Ages" in 1831 in which he related such factors as age, sex, education, climate, and seasons to the incidence of crime. He observed (as quoted by Walker, 1929) that these relations were highly stable from year to year:

> Thus we pass from one year to another with the sad perspective of seeing the same crimes reproduced in the same order and calling down the same punishments in the same proportions. Sad condition of humanity! We might enumerate in advance how many individuals will stain their hands with the blood of their fellows, how many will be forgers, how many will be poisoners, almost we can enumerate in advance the births and deaths that should occur. There is a budget which we pay with frightful regularity; it is that of prisons, chains, and the scaffold. (pp. 40–41)

Aside from the charming manner in which Quetelet states a problem that still persists after 150 years, it is important to note his use of characteristics obtained from successive samples of different individuals to induce a general process presumably characteristic of a single individual. Walker (1929) identified the fatal flaw succinctly: "He suggested that instead of making numerous observations on an individual as he progressed through life, the changes from one age level to another might be studied by making observations on large numbers of people at different ages" (p. 41). This suggestion, and the enormous volume of Quetelet's applications of it, clearly establishes the precedent for drawing inferences concerning the nature of dynamic individual phenomena on the basis of statistical comparisons made between large groups of individuals. The full development of an experimental method based on this practice did not occur until the late 19th and early 20th centuries. It is to the major figures of this period that we now turn our attention.

Francis Galton

The evolution of the statistical method into a foundation for designing experiments was greatly assisted by the work of Francis Galton (1822–1911), whom we encounter in Reading 3. Galton's impact on the modern social sciences is probably largely due to his expansion of the new discipline into the area of education, not only touching the lives of virtually every Englishman until the present day, but also defining a subject matter area that remains a mainstay in psychology—mental measurement. As we indicated earlier, Galton was convinced that mental abilities must obey the Normal Law of Error in much the same fashion as physical characteristics demonstrated by Quetelet. Galton's adoration of the normal curve is nicely captured in the following excerpt from *Natural Inheritance* (1889):

> I know of scarcely anything so apt to impress the imagination as the wonderful form of cosmic order expressed by the "Law of Frequency of Error." The law would have been personified by the Greeks and deified, if they had known of it. It reigns with serenity and complete self-effacement amidst the wildest confusion. The huger the mob and the greater the apparent anarchy, the more perfect is its sway. It is the supreme law of Unreason. Whenever a large sample of chaotic elements are taken in hand and marshalled in the order of their magnitude, an unsuspected and most beautiful form of regularity proves to have been latent all along. (p. 86)

Earlier in the volume, Galton stated:

> I need hardly remind the reader that the Law of Error upon which these Normal Values are based, was excogitated for the use of astronomers and others who are concerned with extreme accuracy of measurement, and without the slightest idea until the time of Quetelet that they might be applicable to human measures. But Errors, Differences, Deviations, Divergencies, Dispersions, and Individual Variations, all spring from the same kind of causes. . . . All persons conversant with statistics are aware that this supposition brings Variability within the grasp of the laws of Chance, with the result that the relative frequency of Deviations of different amounts admits of being calculated, when these amounts are *measured in terms of any self-contained unit of variability* [italics added]. (pp. 54–55)

Here is a clear statement from Galton concerning the utility of what in Reading 3 we call *vaganotic measurement*—the use of units derived from variability in the phenomenon itself.

It was Galton's fascination with variation within and between wide arrays of measures that led him to attempt something not previously undertaken, which was to have a profound effect on the future of experimental reasoning. His observation of co-relation between characteristics (measured in terms of variability) across generations led him to develop the first mathematical expression of *correlation*. We discussed the impact of this invention on the field of mental measurement; however, one point must be emphasized. A general mathematical method of obtaining correlations, regardless of the underlying dimensions of measurement, added to the arsenal of statistics a means of determining *association*, which is of great utility in experimentation. In order to make statements about relations that might exist between variables, it is first necessary to be able to document the existence of such relations. The mathematics of correlation permitted this to be done in the case of the masses of uncontrolled actuarial data that Quetelet, Galton, and others caused to be collected. However, it was not until the genius of Karl Pearson was directed at the problem that the full mathematical and theoretical generality of Galton's invention was realized.

Karl Pearson

Karl Pearson (1857–1936) was probably first attracted to the field of mathematical statistics by the work of Galton and its implications for the scientific study of heredity. He took the problem of correlation from the level of the simple statement that Galton had proposed and the development of the first correlation coefficient by Edgeworth in 1892 and subjected them to full mathematical development. In a series of papers entitled "Mathematical Contributions to the Theory of Evolution," Pearson introduced, not only the mathematics of correlation, but also the idea of moments of any distribution, the term *standard deviation*, and the general mathematics of sampling distributions. In 1898, he developed a general method for determining the sampling error of any moment of a distribution. When it was observed that many sampling distributions were themselves normal, the foundation for experimental inference on the basis of theoretical probability distributions was solidly laid.

Ronald Fisher

The towering edifice that has come to be known as modern experimental design was not constructed by Pearson, but by Ronald Fisher and his students and followers. Fisher was trained as a mathematician and biologist and, like many of his contemporaries, was fascinated by the mathematical issues underlying evolution and heredity. Unlike some contemporaries, however, he turned his attention early to a broad new domain of field research—agriculture. Fisher and his followers developed statistical methods for evaluating agricultural data collected under carefully controlled growing conditions and elaborated the procedures whereby experiments should be conducted in order to permit proper comparisons and reasoning from large sets of data. This is the formal origin of the phrase "experimental design," and it clearly implicates agriculture as the fourth tradition from which modern groups comparison practices emanate.

The pivotal event was the articulation of the test for the significance of hypotheses, a process begun with the publication in 1908 of W. S. Gossett's classic paper, "The Probable Error of a Mean" and effectively concluded by the publication in 1935 of Fisher's *The Design of Experiments*. The great importance of Gossett's work is touched on in Reading 3. He showed that the variance of a sampling distribution of a mean could be estimated from the data in the sample, and he provided a mathematical basis for accommodating the loss of precision that occurs in inverse relation to the size of the sample. Thus, from observed variability in a series of measures, it became possible to establish limits on the probable error of the estimate of the mean of the parent population and, even in the case of small samples, to calculate the likelihood that a particular value could be the true mean of the population from which the given sample was drawn.

The actual form of the sampling distribution of a sample mean varies with the size of the sample, yielding a family of such distributions that approach normality as the sample size increases. Gossett's t-distribution provides the likelihood of a sample mean deviation of any magnitude for any size sample and thus extends the reasoning associated with the normal curve. This procedure was quickly extended to differences between sample means, and the well-known test of the null hypothesis that the means of the parent populations are equivalent was then available to researchers. Fisher extended the reasoning to groups of means when he introduced the analysis of variance (Fisher, 1925). The techniques were greatly elaborated, both practically (Cochran & Cox, 1950; Snedecor, 1937) and theoretically (Mann, 1949; Mood, 1950; and many others) over the next three decades.

In the time since Fisher's original work, there have been both disputes and refinements of the basic techniques of statistical inference and hypothesis testing. In particular, J. Neyman and E. S. Pearson introduced the Likelihood Ratio Test, which is a mathematical technique for deciding which statistic will give the most powerful test of a particular hypothesis (i.e., correctly allow rejection of a false null hypothesis). From this point of departure (with which Fisher essentially disagreed on the grounds that it is experimentally illogical) have come a large number of statistical procedures, including the so-called nonparametric methods that require fewer assumptions concerning the nature of the hypothesized parent population.

We find the reasoning underlying all such procedures alien to both the subject matter and goals of a natural science of behavior and regard the utility of group comparisons as extremely limited, no matter how elegant the mathematical treatment of data they afford. We should note, however, that these methods have enjoyed almost unchallenged acceptance in psychology, education, and other disciplines that purport to be concerned with behavior. The origins of this acceptance clearly coincide with the influence of Quetelet and Galton on the social sciences and on the apparent utility of their methods for mental testing and educational classification.

More recently, the work of Fisher and his followers has been adapted to virtually all efforts at experimentation in these disciplines. David A. Grant was among the first to use the model of the analysis of variance in 1945 as a basis for experimental design and subsequent reasoning in experimental psychology. Soon after, standard textbooks (e.g., Lindquist, 1953; McNemar, 1949) presented these models along with simplified computational procedures as the basis for controlled experimentation in psychology and education.

Today, students in these disciplines have available a wide array of "cookbooks" that present the problems of experimental design almost exclusively in terms of the statistical models by which data may be analyzed, rather than from the perspective of arranging opportunities to make comparative observations under conditions not readily found in natural contexts. As a result, students learn a process of scientific inquiry that is almost totally inverted. Instead of using questions about natural phenomena to guide decisions about experimental design, models of design are allowed to dictate both the form and content of the questions asked. Not only is this antithetical to the established role of experimentation in science, but the types of questions allowed by groups comparisons designs are often inappropriate or irrelevant to gaining an understanding of the determinants of behavior.

EXPERIMENTAL DESIGN IN THE SCIENCE OF BEHAVIOR

The tradition of designing experiments in accordance with the requirements of tests of statistical hypotheses has ossified into the methodological backbone of the social sciences in this century. With the exception of certain applications in the applied life sciences, however, the natural sciences have largely ignored these prescriptions, much as they have ignored the parallel development of vaganotic measurement discussed in Reading 3. In particular, those major contributors to a natural science of behavior who could have adopted groups comparison methods of experimentation have been conspicuous by their failure to do so. Pavlov (1927) reported no correlation coefficients or F-ratios in *Conditioned Reflexes*, although that research was contemporaneous with Pearson's and Gossett's work, with which Pavlov was almost certainly aware.

More recently, the writings of B. F. Skinner, Murray Sidman, and others have attempted to clarify the many reasons for their steadfast adherence to the strategies of natural scientific experimentation in the study of behavior. We present the alternatives to groups comparison designs in Part III of *Strategies and Tactics* and in other readings of this volume. However, it is important to examine here the two most fundamental reasons for our concurrence with the views of Pavlov and Skinner concerning the inappropriateness of groups comparison design tactics in the study of behavior.

Behavior as an Individual Phenomenon

Behavior is defined as a part of the interaction between organism and environment. As such, its occurrence is always peculiar to individual organisms and it is only those peculiarities that are of scientific interest if our subject matter is behavior. Our extended discussion of the history of group statistical techniques should have made it clear that these methods were inspired by an entirely different set of problems, ranging from census enumeration to predicting the relative frequency of occurrence of events in large populations. For such purposes, these methods are beautifully suited and highly effective.

The methods of experimental design and analysis introduced by Fisher are equally suited to the purposes for which they were developed—population genetics, agricultural research, and industrial quality control. In these and similar areas, the individual case—be it fruit fly, ear of corn, or light bulb—is of little concern, and descriptions of population characteristics in terms of means and standard deviations are more than adequate for the inferences that group experimentation permits. Fisher himself carefully explained that the types of valid inductive inference were from samples to populations, not from samples to the single case (Fisher, 1956).

To be sure, there are also valid applications of these procedures to certain problems in psychology and education. Large-scale educational evaluation, for example, is not concerned with whether and why a particular procedure is effective with a particular child, only with its effects on a population of children taken as a whole. The former is a behavioral question, whereas the latter is an actuarial one. It should not be expected that methods appropriate for one class of questions would apply to the other. The popular volume by Campbell and Stanley (1966) is an excellent reference for workers in the area of evaluation research. Its applicability to the study of behavior, however, is another matter.

The problem lies in the generality of groups comparisons to the individual case. Because behavior is a phenomenon that occurs only at the individual level, the science of behavior must have as its goal the understanding of the individual organism's interaction with its environment. Once that is accomplished, the question of generalizing the results from one or a few individuals to a larger number can be properly addressed. However, as we detail throughout this volume, beginning at the group level and attempting to generalize to the individual case is ultimately impossible, in spite of Quetelet's contrary conviction.

Even if it were possible, it is surely not the best approach because error is introduced to whatever extent a given individual deviates from the group norm. As Dunlap pointed out in 1932 (Herson & Barlow, 1976), there is no such thing as an average rat. In making this observation, he was echoing the assessment of the futility of statistical procedures in the study of physiology made by Claude Bernard (1865/1957). Methods for studying behavior must isolate and identify the determinants of the individual's behavior and experimental comparisons based on groups are inappropriate by definition. If valid generalizations to the individual case could be made on the basis of group data, scientists concerned with behavior would probably have adopted the methods with enthusiasm, particularly because they are very often experimentally economical. Unfortunately, our need for a scientific understanding of the determinants of human behavior has been almost totally unfilled during the last 150 years in research in which groups have served as the basis for experimental comparisons.

Behavior as a Continuous Phenomenon

The second problem with the use of groups comparison techniques in the experimental study of behavior is a variation on the problem of representative sampling. Behavior is a continuous process, changing through time as a function of the influence of its determining variables. Mathematical methods for describing such processes have been developed. Quantitative description of behavior, which must precede experimental analysis as measurement always precedes experimentation, must be sensitive to this dynamic property and must be essentially continuous. Furthermore, a crucial facet of the subject matter of the science of behavior concerns the nature of this change over time, and that nature cannot be understood unless the phenomenon is tracked through time. Unfortunately, the bulk of the design models that have evolved from the groups comparison tradition become awkward and unmanageable in the face of continuous measurement, as well they should.

The validity of these models for groups comparisons partly rests on the extent to which the underlying data conform to certain assumptions of independence, so that the collections of discrete measures necessary for performing the analytical techniques must be corrected for any correlation. But collecting discrete measures of a continuous process necessarily presupposes a sampling procedure, and this requires assumptions about the representativeness of the sampling. In order to satisfy those assumptions, one must know the nature of the universe from which the sampling is done, and this is precisely the question the science is seeking to address.

In other words, using groups comparison methods of experimentation forces one to second guess by assumption the very phenomenon under investigation. This strategic defect has evidently been overlooked by a number of well-intentioned individuals who are laboring mightily to reconcile the requirements of a science of individual behavior with the tactics of data analysis and experimental inference provided by the tradition of groups comparison. Meanwhile, others practice methods of science that foster comparison based on observation, not assumption, and inference based on replication, not speculation.

Pure Versus
Quasi-Behavioral Research

BEHAVIOR AS A SCIENTIFIC SUBJECT MATTER

Introduction

Among the many struggles that have constituted psychology's attempts to study human activity, the conception of exactly what it is about human beings that should be the object of our investigations has been, and continues to be, a mighty one. This struggle is certainly appropriate. There can be no more central and pervasive an issue in psychological research than the definition of the phenomenon to be addressed by experimental methods. One of the reasons why an unambiguous definition of the subject matter is critical is so that the details of research method can be properly suited to the task of preserving the subject matter in the processes of definition, measurement, design, analysis, and experimental inference in undiluted and uncontaminated form. Failures to maintain such purity depreciate to some degree (perhaps beyond any scientific value) the legitimacy of experimental conclusions, such "bastardy" taking the form of inferior reliability and generality of effects. These limitations on experimental data eventually come to characterize entire literatures, thereby retarding the development of a human science and stunting its technological progeny.

Although it is by no means universally agreed upon, many in psychology and the social sciences describe behavior as the focus of their scientific efforts. Of this population, some refine their mission even further to the study of behavior as a natural phenomenon in its own right, rather than as an epiphenomenal means of investigating putative events inside the organism. However, even within this hearty minority, there is often considerable discrepancy between the intended subject matter and the subject matter that survives experimental methods. That is, the conception of behavior that guides the investigator's creation of the experiment and eventual inferences is often far from congruent with the subject matter defined by research methods and represented by the data. (Of course, nature speaks only through experimental procedures and without regard for the intentions of the investigator). This kind of slippage seems to issue partly from an inadequate understanding of what the biological phenomenon of behavior is, thereby ensuring insensitivity to the consequences of its characteristics for the selection of methods for studying behavior.

A Definition and Some Methodological Consequences

Chapter 3 in *Strategies and Tactics* offers the following biologically and empirically functional definition of behavior:

> The behavior of an organism is that portion of the organism's interaction with its environment that is characterized by detectable displacement in space through time of some part of the organism and results in a measurable change in at least one aspect of the environment. (p. 23)

Certain facets of this definition carry a major responsibility in guiding experimental investigation of the subsumed subject matter. Certainly, the stipulation that behavior is characteristic only of individual organisms is fundamental. Behavior is an intraorganism phenomenon, a result that can exist only when an interactive condition prevails between a single creature and some part of its environment. That environment may sometimes include other organisms, but it is still each individual that is behaving, not collections of individuals. In other words, there is no such phenomenon as group behavior, just as there is no such biological organism as a group. It is only our linguistic traditions and statistical machinations that create such illusions.

Although this argument could be pursued at far greater length, it should already be clear that one of its methodological consequences is that the fundamental features of behavior can be clearly detected only at the level that they exist. A scientific effort to understand organism–environment interactions (behavior) must examine the effects of independent variables on those interactions. Given the uniqueness of individual organisms and their past and present environmental interactions, any attempt to abbreviate the search for empirical generalities by collating the effects of the independent variable on the behavior of different subjects can only obfuscate rather than extend the relations of interest.

Another methodological implication of this definition emerges from the reference to "the organism's interaction with its environment" and to "detectable displacement in space." The first phrase denotes behavior as the interface between the organism and the environment, not a property or attribute of the organism. Behavior is not possessed by the organism and is not something that the organism does. It is the result of a relational condition between the separate entities of organism and environment. The requirement for an interaction means that real or hypothetical states of the subject (being hungry or anxious) does not constitute behavioral events and that neither do independent conditions or changes in the environment (e.g., if you walk in the rain you will get wet, but getting wet is not behavior). The reference to "detectable displacement in space" removes any confusion by requiring movement, however gross or minute.

Furthermore, the last phrase of the definition—"that results in a measurable change in some aspect of the environment"—dictates that the movement of interest be detected and measured by its effects on the environment. This is not an unreasonable requirement. Because behavior refers to organism–environment relations, there will unavoidably be relevant environmental changes to serve this definitional and measurement function. It is also a useful restriction because it tends to insure that the phenomenon being measured is indeed behavior.

A further methodological consequence of this definition stems from the requirement of organism–environment interaction and the reference to this process taking place through time. These elements define behavior as a dynamic, continuous, interactive process occurring through time; not as a discrete, static event or state. It follows that attempts to study such a phenomenon must strive to capture these qualities through the tactics of measurement and design that are selected.

In summary, behavior is first a phenomenon that exists only between individual organisms and their environments. Second, behavior involves some movement that is an interaction between the behavior organism and its environment. Third, such movements constitute a dynamic and continuous process through time. Whatever else may be true about behavior, it would seem difficult to deny the validity of these fundamental qualities. That this definition was crafted primarily for methodological uses is clear by its requirement for detectable movement. This should not be taken to mean that events whose reality and nature are uncertain and that cannot now be directly measured may not satisfy the remainder of the definition and otherwise qualify. Consistent with the tenets of radical behaviorism, it does mean that the experimental study of such supposed events is relatively difficult and risky and that we must question very carefully the nature of the data and our interpretations.

It may be important to remind ourselves that although we may debate the details of a definition of behavior, the process itself is a real, natural, biological phenomenon whose existence and features will be no more affected by our convictions than lead was turned into gold by alchemists. To the extent that our conception of behavior and the ways in which we go about studying it are not concordant with its actual features, our experimental data and subsequent conclusions will suffer from insufficient reliability and inadequate generality.

PURE BEHAVIORAL RESEARCH METHODS

Introduction

Experiments embodying methodological practices that preserve the fundamental qualities of this subject matter in undisturbed and uncontaminated form constitute pure behavioral research. What is pure is the representation of the complete array of fundamental qualities of behavior in the experimental data. Pure behavioral research is created by measurement, design, and inferential procedures that respect these qualities by doing nothing to abridge, dilute, or distort their manifestation in the data. Although this hardly guarantees correct inferences, it at least affords them a proper basis in fact.

The standards for pure behavioral research are as uncompromising as the behavioral nature that dictates them. As with the phenomenon itself, we have no say in their specifications. Their violation may not doom an experiment to utter worthlessness, but it must suffer in direct proportion to the trespass. Of course, the limitations exist whether or not they are recognized, and therein lies nature's contingency for the scientist. What, then, are these requirements?

Unit of Analysis

Although important strategically, the formal definition of behavior only describes the general phenomenon of interest. The experimenter must select and define a particular piece of behavior for study, instances of which can then be repeatedly and accurately measured. In other words, out of this continuous stream of behaviors the experimenter must define the limits of a single class of behavioral instances that are homogeneous along certain dimensions. Because each unique instance of behavior is a relation between some part of the organism and some part of its environment, it should not be surprising that a class of responses must be defined in terms of the classes of surrounding environmental events (stimuli) to which its members are functionally related.

Defining a response class with references to antecedent and consequent environmental stimulus classes insures a class of responses that is homogeneous in the functional relations that each response has with its controlling influences in the environment. This functional homogeneity avoids using topographical similarity or idiosyncratic verbal history as a basis for defining a class that might then include responses having different sources of environmental influences and that might therefore be differently affected by the independent variable. Functional response class definitions thereby facilitate realizing experimental inferences about treatment effects that can be reproduced by others and that may hold for additional response classes as well.

Dimensional Quantities and Units of Measurement

Another aspect of experimental method that is central to preserving the characteristics of behavior as a subject matter concerns the dimensions of responding that are quantified through observation and the ways in which the amounts of those dimensions are described. The fundamental properties of behavior dictate a number of those dimensional quantities. Duration, latency, and frequency are probably most commonly used, although there are many others, including those characteristic of a body in motion (velocity, acceleration, etc.). Selecting for measurement dimensions of responding that are real, quantifiable, and likely to show variability of experimental interest is required if the data are to reflect orderly and useful relations between responding and experimental conditions.

The proper use of dimensional quantities depends on the units of measurement used to describe the amount of the dimension being measured. These units must be absolute or unvarying in their meaning and that meaning must be standard for all users. Temporal dimensions are readily quantified with the units of time (seconds, minutes, etc.) whose meanings have long been absolute and standard. In the case of frequency, the compound unit, cycles/unit time, reflects the reference that the compound dimension of frequency makes to two different properties of behavior. The importance of absolute and standard units of measurement stems from the encouragement they lend to measuring real qualities of behavior, the facilitation of measurement accuracy that they provide, and the resulting clarity that is attached to the data from observation through design, analysis, and interpretation. The natural sciences have long enjoyed these benefits.

Observing and Recording

The observational practices necessary to preserve the characteristics of behavior are probably more obvious than dimensional issues. Certainly, observation must be of the defined responding of a single subject. If multiple subjects are used, each must be observed independently and their data maintained separately in recording and analytical processes. Because behavior is the interaction between the individual and the environment, attempting to analyze the influence of some independent variable on that interaction would be fatally complicated by mixing that result with the different effects from other subjects.

The dynamic and continuous nature of behavior must be acknowledged by scheduling periods of observation that are as long as possible and that occur as frequently as possible. Furthermore, it is even more important that the target response class be measured continuously while observational sessions are in progress, not only because this is generally required by the nature of the subject matter, but because discontinuous measurement assures some degree of inaccuracy. Of course, these decisions depend on a great many factors that are sometimes difficult or impossible to turn to the service of experimentation. Nevertheless, the reasons for the importance of these tactics will remain influences in the data, whether or not the tactics are accommodated.

Finally, the quality of the data yielded by the measurement process must be regularly assessed. The standard here is not validity or interobserver agreement, but accuracy, and the researcher's task is not to evaluate it passively but to guarantee it. Pure behavioral research requires that the data approximate the true state of nature, a condition that can be determined and certified only by examining the correspondence between obtained and true values and adjusting the transducer as necessary. This process is called *calibration*, and it is required whether the transducer is machine or human.

Experimental Design

Although there are many details that must be carefully considered in arranging an experimental design, there are a few elements that are mandatory if the characteristics of behavior as a subject matter are to be preserved. One of these characteristics—the dynamic nature of organism–environment interactions through time—dictates that measurement must be scheduled to occur repeatedly over some period of time under each different set of experimental conditions. The purpose of these repeated observations of responding is to allow the complete and stable effects of each condition on the measured dimensions of the target response class to be clearly seen. This is called the steady state strategy, and it has a number of invaluable benefits, but clarifying the nature of responding under each condition is certainly the most important because these data will be the foundation on which experimental inferences are constructed.

However, a prerequisite to this benefit is that the data accumulated through repeated observations under each condition separately represent the responding of individual subjects. Any attempt to address prematurely the issue of intersubject generality by creating some amalgam of the behavior of different subjects under the same conditions only insures that the purity of the subject matter will be destroyed by mixing treatment-induced variability with intersubject variability, an extraneous artifact that has nothing to do with the description of, and cannot ever be used to explain, the behavior of a single organism.

Quantification and Display

The data that guide experimental inferences have usually been subjected to various quantifying operations and displayed in accordance with different graphic formats, and these manipulations can substantially influence the reliability and generality of interpretations. In order for this influence to be favorable, any treatments of the data must conform to strategies dictated by the nature of the phenomenon. That is, the data representing the behavior of a single subject must not be tainted with that from other subjects, and their temporal continuity must be respected. Although these strategies leave a useful variety of quantification and display options, other popular manipulations are relegated to only a supplementary analytical role.

Experimental Inference

Experimental inference refers to the translation the scientist makes from the language of nature to the language of the culture. Nature speaks through variations in behavior that are correlated with variations in experimental procedures. As interpreters, our scientific verbal behavior functions to direct others not having these experiences to act successfully. The reliability and generality of our inferences depends on their being properly tempered by the details of experimental method and the characteristics of variation in the subject's behavior as represented by the data. However, if the data do not properly represent the phenomenon that is the focus of our inferences, the reliability and the generality of those inferences must unavoidably suffer. In turn, the progress of the science will suffer.

Such progress can come only in the form of veridical descriptions of the relations between behavior and those variables that influence it, these relations being repeatedly verifiable (reliability) and having some meaning or effectiveness beyond the circumstances of their origin (generality). These characteristics will be attained only if our interpretive verbal behavior is adequately controlled by the details of both experimental procedure as well as the resulting data. This challenge can be met only if the foregoing strategies have been followed so that the basic characteristics of behavior have survived the vicissitudes of experimentation intact and untainted.

Uses and Limitations

It should be clear that pure behavioral research methods are required whenever it is necessary to make inferences about behavior in its phenomenal sense. In other words, if the overall research goal is to identify behavioral facts that will eventually accumulate into well-understood behavioral laws of broad generality, experimental inferences must be based on data that fully represent the qualities of the phenomenon and nothing else.

Another way of saying this is that these methods are required whenever the researcher's immediate inferences are to the level of the individual rather than the population. However, the phrase "the level of the individual" may need some definition. An obvious referent is to the individual subject. These methods are mandatory if there is to be discussion about the effects of experimental procedures on each separate subject. This interpretive preference does not mean that the researcher has no interest in the population of individuals from which the subject is drawn; indeed, one of the subject's functions may be to represent that population. But if the researcher's goal is to learn something about the subject's behavior whose generality to other individuals in the population can then be experimentally pursued, pure behavioral research methods are obligatory. In other words, the researcher's desire to identify behavioral relations that hold for certain populations does not mean that the immediate experimental inferences should be to the population level. In fact, generality across individuals cannot be established or even reasonably guessed at on the basis of the data from a few or even a large number of subjects in a single study. This and the other dimensions of generality can be established only through many experiments that identify and explain the variables that influence the relation of interest.

In spite of this argument, some might still be tempted to insist that they do not want to discuss the effects of the independent variable on the basic laws of behavior that they embody, but because adequate effectiveness and reliability can only be attained by establishing the exact behavioral (individual) effects of procedural variables. The development of a procedure is not completed until it is understood why it works and what the variables are that influence its effectiveness, and these research goals are unambiguously and thoroughly behavioral in nature, requiring experimental methods that respect the integrity of that subject matter.

The possible exception to this requirement concerns that portion of technological research that evaluates a procedure' s effectiveness and reliability under realistic field conditions. In some of these studies, it may be sufficient to merely describe the resulting behavioral effects, given that their relation to the procedures has long since been experimentally established. In fact, some of the effects of interest may be only indirectly behavioral, such as logistical and economic results. Although certain features of pure behavioral research are always advisable (standard and absolute units of measurement, for instance), other elements may be unnecessary or even inappropriate, especially if any inferences are to the level of the population rather than the individual.

QUASI-BEHAVIORAL RESEARCH METHODS

Introduction

Experiments whose data originated with observations of behavior but whose methods prevent the data from representing its fundamental qualities fully and without distortion or contamination may be termed *quasi-behavioral research*. The prefix denotes the potential problem: Such research seems to be behavioral although it is not by the standards of the phenomenon itself. Even though the data in quasi-behavioral research may indeed be based on observations of behavior, at least one or, more commonly, many features of its method have in some way limited the representation in the data of the fundamental qualities of behavior that must be present if the research is to serve successfully as a basis for inferences about behavior. The problem is not that the methodological practices that create quasi-behavioral research are inherently improper; they can be quite appropriate in the service of many kinds of experimental questions. The problem lies in the risk of deception, of assuming that procedures and data allow inferences about behavior when they do not. Understanding those methodological practices that make research quasi-behavioral will diminish this risk.

Unit of Analysis

Beginning an experiment with a good understanding of behavior's properties is not sufficient to guarantee an adequate basis for eventual inferences about behavior. Each individual's behavior is made up of a myriad of different and continuously changing classes of responses, each class being determined by the surrounding environmental events that simultaneously define its existence. Failing to acknowledge these natural influences when defining the unit of analysis means that the designated class will actually be made up of multiple classes, each having differing environmental determinants and, possibly, differing susceptibility to the independent variable in the study. Thus, the changes observed in the designated class will be some mixture of the treatment variable's effects on the various natural or functional classes. This will not be detectable in any obvious way in the data (although they will probably be more variable than would otherwise be the case), but inferences drawn about the relation between the independent variable and the designated response class will have poorer reliability and generality than a properly defined response class would have afforded. A powerful treatment variable may minimize the damage, but this is hardly an auspicious way to begin an experiment.

There are a great many ways to avoid proper functional response class definitions. One of the most common is to define responses into a class on the basis of their topography or form in three-dimensional space. Sometimes topographical features are not substantially divergent from functional considerations, but often such designated classes are aggregates of functional classes whose responses may have different environmental determinants.

The popularity of this kind of criteria may be because form is easier to see and describe than function and (perhaps as a result) because common language descriptors tend to be based on form. We often decide how to isolate some part of a subject's behavior on the basis of our verbal history. This history is manifest in coding systems, which parcel pieces of behavior into large multiclass categories. One such system breaks all human behavior into 29 classes, but the most absurd version of this practice has only two categories: positive or appropriate behavior and negative or inappropriate behavior. Sometimes interest in the popular artifact called "group behavior" is expressed early in the experimental process by defining the response class in such a way that the behavior of different individuals must be collectively observed in order to meet definitional requirements.

All of these and the many other ways of defining response classes that ignore the natural classes defined by environmental relations must pay some penalty, whether large or small, in the reliability and generality of any behavioral inferences. This is because the functional response class is the unit of analysis, the level at which individual behavioral effects occur and at which order is most clearly seen. Definitional procedures that violate this fact make the data and, thus, the research, quasi-behavioral.

Dimensional Quantities and Units of Measurement

Another means of constraining the basis for making inferences about behavior concerns the dimensions of behavior that are observed and the ways in which those dimensions are quantified. There is often no behavioral dimension clearly referred to by the measurement process. The ubiquitous questionnaire in psychological research is plagued with this problem. Even when there is a clear behavioral dimension, two like dimensional quantities are frequently put in ratio in order to form a relative quantity that may be expressed as a percentage. One difficulty with this practice is that the dimensional referents cancel with division. Another is that variation in the percentages across sessions may be the result of changes in the numerator, the denominator, or both, but the quotients hide the exact nature of behavioral variability.

The justification of inferences about behavior is further weakened when units are used whose definitions are vaganotic (based on variation in a set of underlying observations of behavior; see Reading 3). Thus, the meaning of the unit varies from application to application both within and across experiments. Most standardized tests involve such variable units, although the units (such as the IQ point) are not usually given a formal name. Often the underlying variability is only assumed and does not actually enter into the calculation of scale values or unit definition; rating scales typify this practice. Whatever the details, not quantifying the amount of the observed dimension of behavior with units of measurement whose meaning is absolute and standard insures that the representation of behavioral qualities in the data is not what it seems.

Observing and Recording

The most obvious threat to a sound basis for inferences about behavior that emerges from observing and recording practices involves mixing observations of the responding of different subjects in some fashion. This may occur through actually observing a number of different subjects simultaneously and treating the data as if they were from a single subject; or, the collating may occur at the recording stage, when separate observations of different subjects are transcribed into some aggregate form, such as a mean or a median. The effect in either case is the same—the orderly relations that might exist in the individual data are hidden when contaminated with intersubject variability, and the experimenter and anyone else is prevented from seeing behavioral effects in pure form. Basing primary experimental inferences on grouped data from different subjects automatically defines the research as quasi-behavioral.

Another barrier to sound behavioral inference may come from inadequacies in the amount and distribution of periods of observation. If observational periods are very brief, occur intermittently or infrequently, or are few in number under each condition, or if observation is not continuous during each session, the data base for eventual interpretation will be insufficient, regardless of the propriety of other methodological decisions. These are routine sampling issues, but when the subject matter is behavior with its dynamic and continuous character, they take on primary significance. Without a complete representation of the ebb and flow of responding as the experiment proceeds through one phase to another, the risk that inferences will not be congruent with what really happened becomes unacceptably high.

Experimental Design

One of the reasons for the repeated observations already discussed has as much to do with the determinants of the inferential behavior of the experimenter as it does with the nature of behavior as a subject matter. The steady state strategy referred to earlier draws its justification in part from the effort to study individual subjects intensively over time. This necessitates making experimental comparisons using the data from two different conditions to which a single subject was sequentially exposed, rather than using the data from two different subjects, each exposed to only one of the conditions. In order to accomplish this within-subject comparison, it is important to be certain that the data taken as representative of the effects of each of the two conditions are fully characteristic of the subject's responding under each condition. If for whatever reason the data do not fully represent the actual relations between experimental variables and behavior, inferences regarding those effects cannot be complete and accurate.

Certainly, the most common design practice that successfully misrepresents and contaminates the fundamental qualities of behavior is making inferences about the effects of an independent variable on behavior on the basis of data that represent the aggregate of its separate effects on the behavior of each of a number of different subjects, with any one subject having been exposed to only one of the two conditions being compared. This example of groups comparison design inferences is useful because it highlights the flaw that makes it a quasi-behavioral research practice—the use of grouped data across subjects but within conditions or, conversely, the absence of inference based on the data of individual subjects obtained under repeated exposure to both conditions.

Quantification and Display

One of the unfortunate side effects of groups comparison designs is their inextricable relation to inferential statistics, whose rules completely determine quantification and display practices. The consequences of inferential statistics for experimental method are sufficiently substantial and pervasive that they will be treated in a separate section. However, it should be clear that they require the data from many different subjects be thoroughly homogenized and processed in a way that greatly limits access to pure behavioral data at the individual level, if they even exist. The rules for quantifying operations are extensive and rigid, and graphic displays tend to be preempted, in spite of their ability to highlight detailed relations between two variables. Because of their dominant influence on inferential behavior, quantifying and display practices alone can make research quasi-behavioral, even if all of the preceding elements of method supply pure behavioral data.

Experimental Inference

As suggested by its definition, quasi-behavioral research is created by any methodological practices that result in experimental inferences that are not under the control of all of the fundamental qualities of the phenomenon of behavior. Aside from their other methodological consequences, the interpretive process required by all inferential statistical models guarantees this final limitation, and the following section details the reasons for this and the many other effects of statistical practices on the subject matter.

In summary, then, quasi-behavioral research methods can be said to create a qualitatively different subject matter from that of pure behavioral research. This subject matter is composed of both pure behavioral qualities and artifactual qualities created by elements of research method, the exact proportions of each varying from one study to another depending on particular methodological practices. However, the scientist's mission is not to create subject matters but to understand natural phenomena. In order to accomplish this mission, experimental methods must do no more and no less than represent the natural phenomenon fully and without distortion or contamination. They must not create any discrepancies between the raw phenomenon and the experimental subject matter. When this occurs, the research may appear to be about something that it not quite *is*, and inferences about the phenomenon innocently based on a subject matter that is slightly or substantially different must suffer slightly or substantially weakened reliability and generality, whether or not we like it (or even know it).

TRADITIONS AND PRACTICES
OF INFERENTIAL STATISTICS

History of Application in Psychology

Psychology and the social sciences have a kind of familial relationship with statistics; to a great extent they grew up together—like cousins. Their lineage actually goes back to biblical times when the first efforts at social enumeration were made, and by the 17th and 18th centuries, formal censuses were conducted with the support of simple descriptive statistics. The utility of this technology to the business and financial world was obvious, and the need for economic quantification spurred statistical applications. The need to make predictions based on economic and other data was served by developments in the mathematics of probability, and by the turn of the 19th century it was possible to estimate with serviceable accuracy the likelihood of occurrence of particular instances.

It is not clear just when the notion emerged of using mathematical statistics and the new developments in probability theory to assist in making intergroup experimental comparisons. Augustus DeMorgan (1806–1871) may be able to lay claim to that accomplishment, but it was clearly Adolphe Quetelet (1796–1874) who became the dominant figure in this history. This Belgian statistician and astronomer is widely regarded as the founder of the social sciences (Woolf, 1961). He saw with his wide-ranging intellect the possibility of applying the calculus of probability to detailed demographic data cataloging all aspects of human affairs so as to estimate the ideals of human qualities.

Like others of his time, he viewed the normal law of error as evidence of some supraordinate regularity, and his concept of the average man as a natural ideal was a major influence on 19th century concepts of behavior. It was Quetelet who suggested and popularized the practice of drawing inferences about dynamic individual phenomena on the basis of statistical comparisons between large groups of individuals (Walker, 1929).

Francis Galton (1822–1911) greatly assisted this practice by applying it to the task of mental measurement and the field of education. His development of the mathematical expression of correlation was an important advance that attracted the attention of Karl Pearson (1857–1936). Pearson not only developed fully the mathematics of correlation but also the idea of moments of any distribution, the term standard deviation, and the general mathematics of sampling distributions.

However, the modern concepts of experimental design were constructed by Ronald Fisher and his students. Like Pearson, he was interested in biological issues, and he turned his attention to the new field of agricultural research. Out of this work came the concept of experimental design in the sense of creating experimental conditions that allow statistical reasoning from large sets of data collected so as to permit comparisons between groups.

Meanwhile, the emerging disciplines of the social sciences needed an experimental method, and the new inferential statistical practices and reasoning were not only historically familiar, they brought with them a needed aura of scientific respectability. The ensuing decades have seen the practice of designing experiments in accordance with the requirements of tests of statistical significance ossify into the methodological backbone of the social sciences. This tradition has grown so secure that any other experimental procedures are called quasi-experimental (Campbell & Stanley, 1966).

Consequences for the Study of Behavior

Experimental Question.   The effects of this tradition never were narrowly limited to experimental interpretation, and over the years they have pervaded all aspects of scientific method. Some of these methodological consequences are rigidly dictated by the mathematical model, but they often strongly encourage still other practices until the invasion is complete.

These effects begin at the beginning with the experimental question. Its form is thoroughly subservient to the logic of inferential statistics, which is required by the underlying mathematical procedures. The technique requires calculating the probability of obtaining the observed difference between two sample group means given the assumption that there are no differences in the populations. Aside from the sham of the null hypothesis (which is a bit of logical sleight-of-hand necessary to give the reasoning the appearance of deductive validity), the real experimental question only asks, "Is there a difference [between the measures of central tendency for the different groups being compared]?"

This is a frustratingly crude question. It turns science into an inefficient game of 20 questions, in which questions must be phrased so that they can be answered only by *yes* or *no*. The chafing of this restriction is easily seen in discussion sections, where the experimenters routinely exceed their inferential limits by waxing poetic about the nature of the difference—the true theme of interest.

However, the effects of inferential statistical traditions on question asking are even more serious than the formalities of interrogatory form. They go to the very depths of our wonderings about behavior. They encourage a curiosity about differences, about whether "this" makes a difference or whether "this" is different from "that." Of course, it is not that observed differences are uninformative, but they are inevitably easy to find. Their availability may be experimentally gratifying, but their accumulation in the literature may improperly comfort us about our progress. For science advances by pursing similarities, and similarities are discovered by asking about the detailed nature of the relations between independent and dependent variables.

Measurement.   The impact of inferential statistics on measurement is relatively indirect, though still powerful. For example, there is nothing about inferential statistics that specifies the means by which response classes are defined. However, the mathematical requirement for adequate sample size has the indirect effect of encouraging response class definitional practices that are compatible with a large number of subjects. This is especially true when their performances are measured simultaneously; but even when they are observed one at a time, definitional niceties are deemphasized by observational logistics. As a result, the rigors of functional definitional strategies tend to be avoided in favor of simplicity, which usually means broad categorical labeling guided by cultural linguistic history and its topographical foundation.

Observational procedures become similarly subservient to large-N logistics. The perceived need to sample from a large number of individuals in a population indirectly though strongly encourages observational procedures that sample only a small portion of the occurrences in the response class's population. In other words, the tendency is to observe the behavior of each subject relatively few times, usually only once. The obvious consequence is data that depict an incomplete and possibly misrepresentative picture of the true effects of experimental conditions. The dynamic character of behavior is lost to a static illusion that is comforting only if variability is viewed as an inconvenience useful for no more than algebraic manipulation in the service of the statistical model.

Experimental Design.   This style of observational sampling creates part of experimental design as well. In its narrowest sense, experimental design refers to the arrangement of the independent variable (and, by implication, the scheduling of dependent variable measurement) throughout the entire course of the experiment. When large-N logistics encourage relatively few measurements, there is further encouragement for relatively limited exposure of each subject to experimental conditions. Of course, the number and duration of exposures to the independent variable varies greatly depending on its nature, but the contrast to repeated-measures designs with their repeated contacts with the treatment condition is easily drawn. Furthermore, whereas to the statistician the difference is simply a matter of the number of contacts, to the behaviorist one exposure each with many subjects is very different from many exposures with one subject. Only the later can fully illuminate the nature of the phenomenon.

A more subtle effect of statistical traditions on experimental design is to make it a static and rigidly rule-bound set of practices, whose requirements in any one application are set down by an underlying mathematical model that has nothing to do with the nature of the phenomenon and the needs of the independent variable. The experiment then becomes a somewhat secondary process of filling cells with empirically derived numbers; and once begun, it must be completed regardless of how clearly the numbers suggest a better design or the futility of the effort because the results cannot be clearly known until the statistic is finally computed. This static perspective thus forces the investigator to guess the results in advance in order to predict all of their experimental needs. In effect, it attempts to coerce nature to adapt to the design rather than the other way around.

Interpretation.   Not surprisingly, the consequences of inferential statistics for experimental interpretation are direct, clear, and encompassing. They begin with detailed rules for quantifying the results of observation, and the most unfortunate one is the common requirement for aggregating data across subjects into various groups. However, the quantitative digestion of the data by statistical formulae continues by specifying the entire quantitative basis for experimental comparisons, regardless of the nature of the data. Along the way, intersubject variability and treatment-induced variability are thoroughly homogenized, and any chance of describing pure behavioral effects is lost.

Although they are not specifically precluded, any meaningful graphic traditions are typically preempted by these quantitative traditions. In fact, descriptions of statistical outcomes do not tend to be regularly accompanied by graphic displays that relate even group responding to treatment conditions over time, and the displays that are used are usually highly summarized with few data points.

The results of all of this quantification is a rigid inferential process that is narrowly aimed at a probability-bound decision about the existence of differences between groups. It is not a searching and inquisitive process, looking anywhere in the data where nature may have left a message. It is more like a blindered old workhorse following the same route each time.

The destination is equally predictable. As already discussed, the "official" inferential statement allows only acceptance or rejection of the null hypothesis. In the latter case, this then allows arguments about why an alternative hypothesis (the real one) might be responsible for the obtained difference. However, because data analysis procedures have usually focused solely on the mere existence of a difference, there is little if any formal basis for discussing the degree of the difference or its nature. This raises the issue of the source of control over the inevitable inferential discussions that exceed these bounds.

Unfortunately, the legitimacy of their statements further depends on the correctness of a number of assumptions. This requirement is unfortunate because the assumptions are rarely viable on their face in the case of a behavioral subject matter. For example, these assumptions usually derive from the normal law of error, which asserts that, as a result of random determination, errors will be distributed evenly around a central value and tend to cancel. Furthermore, it is also often required that multiple distributions of such errors be roughly equivalent so that they can be pooled.

The problem is that these assumptions are rarely met by behavioral data. The effects of uncontrolled variables on behavior cannot be assumed to resemble independent, random occurrences because behavior is a continuous process. The effects of any variable (extraneous or independent) are most likely to exhibit serial dependence. It is simply the nature of the phenomenon that every moment of our experience may influence subsequent actions. These assumptions are easily made and verified if ears of corn are the subject matter, but when the subject matter is behavior, the assumptions are only easily made.

Many of these and other shortcomings of inferential statistics are no longer novel, and a battery of further quantitative operations are often called on for resuscitation or justification of the data. Such efforts suggest notions of statistical control that diverge sharply from the contrary tradition of experimental control. Experimental control refers to actual manipulation of real events in order to modulate their influence on the dependent variable. However, quantitative operations manipulate only numbers and have no impact on what they actually represent. In other words, statistics control no more than the verbal behavior of the investigator.

Generality.   The great paradox of inferential statistics is that their use kills almost all hope of achieving one of their primary goals. Probably the most frequently articulated need motivating their use is to establish the generality of the results across subjects. To understand why this is ultimately impossible with these methods, it is important to understand that cross-subject generality (there are other "flavors") first depends on the existence of a reliable behavioral relation or effect whose generality can then be queried. Knowledge about how well that effect holds for different members of some population comes from understanding how certain variables influence it. This understanding can be obtained only through experimental analysis of the relation and its controlling variables, and the experimental methods must accommodate their behavioral nature.

The statistical tradition misunderstands the task by, instead, attempting to make it an interpretive process. Whereas inferences from the sample to the population are indeed proper statistically, they are not meaningful behaviorally because of the nature of the phenomenon. The grouped data supporting inferences to the population cannot properly describe the heterogeneity of

actual individual effects. In other words, the group "effect" whose generality
is being argued is not a behavioral phenomenon but a mathematical artifact.
In fact, there are usually many different behavioral effects among the sampled
subjects, and such variety suggests a fair amount of proper experimental spade
work before enough will be known to produce a reliable (individual) effect
whose generality can then be pursued. Of course, that accomplishment will
inevitably identify a number of controlling variables that influence cross-subject
generality.

Summary.   Some have countered these limitations of inferential statistics
by proposing nonparametric alternatives (e.g., Kazdin, 1976; Levin, Marascuilo,
& Hubert, 1978). Although the substitution may be well intentioned, it should
be clear that nonparametric statistics suffer a sufficient number of the same
problems to guarantee their quasi-behavioral status. They may avoid the plague
of intersubject variability and assumptions about the nature of the hypothesized parent population, but they require or encourage many practices that
compromise pure behavioral qualities. For example, their inferential focus on
a single significance statement instead of detailed descriptions of responding
under repeated exposures to experimental phases that are themselves repeated still discourages proper attention to measurement practices and the steady
state strategy. Furthermore, even though they avoid intersubject variability,
their quantification rules can easily obscure pure behavioral effects as successfully as their large-N relatives.

For that matter, descriptive statistical procedures must be applied with care
lest they too "befoul" behavioral data. However, when descriptive quantitative methods are properly used to supplement graphic displays by adding a
degree of descriptive precision about aspects of pure behavioral relations, these
methods can be quite valuable (see Reading 10).

In other words, the concerns expressed here about various statistical traditions and practices should not be misconstrued as a condemnation of the quantitative operations themselves. Statistics, inferential and descriptive, are
perfectly valid and valuable methods for particular tasks, but methods and tasks
must be properly matched. Given their tradition and sophistication, it is indeed unfortunate that inferential statistics and the study of behavior are such
a poor match.

The social scientist's attempts to force the fit by adapting the subject matter to the method has furthered naive, culturally based conceptions of behavior
instead of loosening these bonds. Inferential statistical traditions have encouraged the view that behavior is an intrinsically variable and autonomously
inspired phenomenon that is complex beyond the capabilities of science. It
has done this, not only by obfuscating the orderliness of behavioral relations,
but by requiring, generating, and using behavioral variability instead of explaining it. Variability is thus viewed as inevitable and beyond reasonable, if not
ultimate, explanation. Not surprisingly, this perspective provides limited experimental motivation to control variables and explain their influence, and

the relative paucity of such evidence is only taken to affirm the consequence. It is a tragic circle.

LIMITATIONS AND USES OF QUASI-BEHAVIORAL RESEARCH METHODS

Where does this assessment of quasi-behavioral research methods leave us? It should be clear that they are poorly suited to the task of learning things about behavior. When our experimental questions require inferences about behavior (as a phenomenon, not in the general and vague cultural sense), we must use methods that generate data that retain all of the qualities of behavior intact and undiluted so that our inferences will be successfully reliable and general. Quasi-behavioral research methods fail to meet this requirement and, therefore, should not be used to support inferences about behavior or to the individual. It has already been pointed out that this is the type of inference required by all basic research and most technological research, and quasi-behavioral research methods are thus inappropriate in these areas of investigation.

Lest this seem too extreme an indictment, it should be acknowledged that it is not that quasi-behavioral research methods can tell us nothing at all about behavior. If a treatment effect is unusually powerful, it may survive such methodological mishandling with useful reliability and generality. The ancients learned much about the world without the niceties of scientific method, but they were often wrong, and what little they did learn pales into insignificance compared to the fruits of even a few years of modern science. At the most generous, quasi-behavioral research methods are a highly inefficient way to go about discovering the laws of behavioral nature, and the costs to our field and our culture are certainly more than we can afford.

These constraints may be difficult to accept in those cases where we can plainly see that quasi-behavioral research data originated from the subject's behavior. It looks like the data represent behavior—in the vague lay sense of behavior, they do—but we do not see or appreciate the gravity of their shortcomings. The problem lies in the strength of our culturally based linguistic practices about behavior and the relative weakness of our professional vocabulary, which should be under the control of the experimental facts about the phenomenon and their methodological implications. It may help to remember that the cost comes when we succumb to improper inferential temptations that are then published and become literature. Then, their value to others who wish to act successfully based on our findings is limited (if not worthless or possibly harmful), and they discover that they cannot be effective. This is the real meaning of poor reliability and inadequate generality. When entire areas of behavioral literature are constituted predominantly of quasi-behavioral research, we are likely to find little progress in our understanding of behavior in such areas and meager technological benefits to society.

If analytical behavioral research (experimental or applied) is an improper use for quasi-behavioral research methods, are there any experimental functions that they can successfully serve? The answer is certainly affirmative and does not conflict with all of the foregoing criticisms. The propriety of these procedures is not at issue in the abstract; they can only be evaluated in particular applications. Generically speaking, we can say that the appropriate behavioral applications are those in which the experimental question does not require inferences about behavior, even though the data may be behavioral. There are many occasions for such questions, although they collectively constitute a relatively small portion of our field's technological research efforts.

Some of these questions may indeed require a behavioral data base but only to support inferences to the population level. Much evaluation research is of this sort. When the problem clearly calls for comparing the aggregate performances of groups of individuals and drawing conclusions about the populations that the sampled individuals represent, inferential statistical procedures are appropriate. For example, when the experimental question demands a comparison between the behavioral effects of two different procedures, a groups-comparison design accompanied by statistical analysis is proper.

However, this type of question is far less often appropriate than its prevalence in the literature might suggest. It should only follow a program of research in which each of the two procedures has been experimentally developed, analyzed, and refined so that exactly how and why each works is fully understood. Furthermore, the two procedures must be exactly equivalent in their goals and functions, as well as in the characteristics of their target populations. In other words, they must be fully and meaningfully comparable, and it takes a fairly extensive program of research to reach this point. Absent this comparability, such comparisons serve political rather than technological interests.

Other questions may require that experimental comparisons be within-group rather than between groups. Here inferential statistics might be inappropriate, but collating data across individuals would be necessary to describe and draw conclusions about collective effects. Such studies are only needed when there is no interest or value in understanding the nature and mechanism of behavioral effects for the individual. Many technological efforts designed to manage the behavior of large numbers of people with procedures that are not designed, selected, or managed for individuals may fall into this category. For instance, efforts to control the use of natural resources or to manage behavior in public settings often takes this form (e.g., Geller, Winett, & Everett, 1982). In these instances, the goal is to influence the behavior of individuals but only as members of a large population. However, the fact that the procedure's effects occur for each individual means that these technologies must first be developed with research conducted at the individual level. Nevertheless, the research program will eventually require group data, though the comparisons may be within rather than between groups.

Still other questions may examine logistical aspects of technological procedures. Here, behavioral data may be used to answer financial, personnel, and administrative questions in which inferences need not be made about the individual effects of behavior-change procedures. These types of investigations also come only at the later stages of a technological research program, after the proper development and analysis, using pure behavioral research methods. In these kinds of studies, the behavior of the procedure's target individuals is of interest only insofar as it provides aggregate data that can be used for calculating administrative needs or consequences. For example, such studies may use behavioral data from target individuals to determine the amount and distribution of staff time that must be provided. Of course, this answer would only be useful if the form of the procedures being used was already known to be maximally effective.

These examples of different types of questions that properly call for quasi-behavioral research methods should suggest that they cannot be so easily treated as a single method or even a related set of methodological procedures as the previous discussion may have implied. For instance, of two studies calling for grouped data, one may require between groups comparisons whereas another may necessitate within group comparisons, thus leading to very different quantitative and inferential procedures.

Furthermore, many of these studies may require pure behavioral measurement procedures, regardless of the nature of their design or interpretation. Indeed, pure behavioral measurement methods are probably rarely inappropriate, even though they may not be required. For example, there are no inferential disadvantages to proper response class definition, standard and absolute units of measurement, and continuous and complete observation. The only constraints that may preclude these procedures are logistical, and even then they may be avoided only, if the inferences allow it.

METHODOLOGICAL CONTINGENCIES

In addition to the phenomenon, the nature of the experimental question and the inferences necessary to answer it thus emerge as the criteria for all these methodological decisions. Properly read, they specify even the most detailed methodological features necessary for attaining experimental goals. Of course, the risk is that their dictates may be improperly interpreted. Investigators may be tempted to presume that their experiments do not require inferences about behavior or to the individual when, in fact, they do.

The quality of our research method (and thus our research) therefore seems to rest in part on how well we understand the nature of our subject matter, our questions, and our inferential verbal behavior. Somewhat more behaviorally, the critical issue is how well we can identify the natural contingencies between our experimental behavior and our subject's behavior. Those contingencies are the essence of scientific method. They are the means by which we come under control of the laws of nature, not only as individual scientists but as a culture.

Recognizing the behavioral relations that constitute research methods is important because it helps us realize that they are irrevocable. We learn about nature (behavioral or otherwise) by arranging conditions so that our behavior (nonverbal and verbal) is effectively controlled by some aspect of our natural subject matter. If our arrangements are improper, our resulting behavior will not be effectively controlled by the facts of our subject matter, and other influences (theory, culturally based preconceptions, extraexperimental contingencies, etc.) are likely to be dominant. In other words, there is no short cut, no alternative way of discovering the facts and laws of nature. If the conditions we arrange do not exactly suit our subject matter and the particular facets of it that are of interest, our subsequent behavior will not be exactly under its control. In other words, although we may have some choice about our experimental methods, we have no choice about their effects.

This assessment should suggest that our intentions and excuses have no bearing on what we learn. Whether we view a particular methodological procedure as troublesome, logistically inconvenient, practically impossible, or unnecessary is completely irrelevant. We will learn what our methods allow us to learn and no more. If we use measurement procedures that have been described here as quasi-behavioral, then we will see an incomplete and distorted picture of the dependent variable that will limit the reliability and generality of our (and everybody else's) inferences. This will be the case whether we are aware of the shortcomings of the measurement procedures or even whether they were the best procedures that were possible under the circumstances.

In conclusion, it would seem beneficial to approach our research in a thoroughly behavioral manner. Our own behavior thus becomes fully as much the target of analysis as that of our subjects, and the goal is to insure that our behavior is effectively under the control of our subject's behavior.

Strategic and Tactical Limits of Comparison Studies

For purposes of this discussion, a *comparison study* is defined as an experiment whose primary purpose, regardless of other methodological features, is to compare directly at least two different procedures for changing behavior or two or more components of such a procedure. Although it is true that all types of experiments necessarily involve comparisons at a tactical level, comparison studies (unlike analytically oriented experiments) also have that focus at a strategic level. In other words, comparisons between whole procedures or between components of procedures are the central reason that comparison studies are conducted, whereas analytical studies are generally designed to identify and understand the nature of controlling variables, even though both types of experiments necessarily make comparisons between responding under treatment versus no-treatment conditions.

The typical experimental format for comparison studies involves running each procedure through its paces while measuring some sort of behavioral outcome, and this comparison focus can be pursued with either between-group or within-subject designs. (In fact, the type of experimental design used has little to do with the arguments in this reading, although between-groups designs do create special difficulties that are noted.) If the arrangement of conditions to be compared is sequential, the two procedures may sometimes use the same subjects. Otherwise, a different, though presumably similar, sample from the population of interest is usually used for each procedure. The ostensible reason for the comparison is to see which procedure (or procedural component) is better or more effective along some dimension for some usually very general set of applied circumstances, and the conclusion customarily attempts to announce a clear winner.

Examples of this experimental approach are easily found in any area of the literature devoted to developing and evaluating methods for changing behavior. For instance, Mosk and Bucher (1984) compared stimulus shaping to traditional prompting procedures for teaching visual–motor skills to retarded children; Barrera and Sulzer-Azaroff (1983) compared oral and total communication training programs with echolalic autistic children; and Repp, Barton, and Brulle (1983) compared two procedures for programming differential reinforcement on other behaviors.

The comparison study has always been a popular type of experimental strategy, especially in the applied literature. It appears to be a relatively easy type of experiment to design and conduct, it has intuitive appeal to nonprofessionals who may be interested in the results, and it is often selected when there is some need to evaluate a program's effectiveness. There may also be a general tendency to think of experimentation in a comparison framework because of the history with groups comparison designs and inferential statistics that we in the social sciences all share. The important methodological issues that comparison studies raise are relevant for both between groups and within subject designs, however.

These tests are a professional version of the popular technological "shoot-out," not unlike those conducted to compare consumer goods like toaster ovens, washing machines, or cars, and they have a face validity that makes them appealing to both consumers and investigators. Although toaster ovens and behavior change methods are both technological products marketed to certain consumer groups, however, the appropriateness of comparison studies in their development, evaluation, and advertising is often quite different.

In fact, it is the thesis of this paper that comparison studies as discussed here are the bane of the applied literature. They often lead to inappropriate inferences with poor generality, based on improper evidence gathered in support of the wrong question, thus wasting the field's limited experimental resources. This is a strong indictment for so common an experimental format, but the problems with comparison studies are fundamental. These problems involve the nature of the experimental question, the nature of the comparison, and constraints on the generality (and thus the utility) of the conclusions. Furthermore, this list assumes that all other aspects of experimental method, such as measurement and experimental design, are properly treated so that they do not exacerbate these problems (in other words, that such studies are internally valid in the terms of Campbell & Stanley, 1963). The problems that plague comparison studies are considered in the following sections.

FUNCTION OF THE EXPERIMENT

First, consider the difficulties surrounding the experimental question, the basic reason for doing the study. In the most fundamental sense, the guiding question in comparison studies is often not really about behavior. Although behavior seems to be a rather obvious focus, the question is usually about methods of controlling behavior. There is nothing wrong with this, of course; most applied research is about methods or procedures, and, in some ultimate sense, it must be. Nevertheless, there is a subtle but very significant difference in focus between applied studies that investigate behavior versus studies that investigate procedures for controlling behavior, even though both are aimed at the same result—effective technology. (Although all experiments "use" procedures, an important strategic distinction may be made between using them to study behavior or using them to study the procedures themselves.)

This point is explored further, but it is important here to appreciate that, among all kinds of applied studies, comparison studies are especially procedural in nature. They simply ask which of two procedures is more effective in producing some kind of behavior change. There is usually little central interest in learning much else about behavior, although it is always possible as a bonus if the experimenter cares to analyze the data in that light.

There is another sense in which at least some comparison studies are not really asking about behavior, and this has to do with the routine details of experimental methods (measurement, data processing, etc.). Behavior exists only between individual organisms and their environments, and in order to be effective, experimental methods must respect this biological fact (see Sidman, 1960, chapter 2). This means that if experimenters do anything that contaminates, dilutes, or otherwise distorts measures of behavior change, there is likely to be some deleterious effect on the inferences that can be drawn from the data. Among other actions, this caveat clearly includes the variety of measurement and data-processing techniques that result in collating individual data into some group amalgam.

Many comparison studies (virtually all that use groups comparison designs and even many that use within subject designs) run afoul of this prohibition in one way or another. Although the consequences do not necessarily hinder conclusions about behavior change procedures, they are quite threatening to inferences about behavior. In fact, based on the extent to which experimental methods respect the fundamental nature of behavior, an important distinction can be made between pure versus quasi-behavioral research (Johnston & Pennypacker, 1986). A large proportion of comparison studies seem to be quasi-behavioral in nature (although analytical studies are hardly immune to these problems). That is, comparison studies look as if they are about behavior (after all, their data-base originated with observations of behaving individuals), but in the required methodological sense they often are not. Thus, the label *quasi-behavioral* may be appropriate.

It may be easier to view most comparison studies as actuarial in nature. Although the formal processes may.deviate somewhat from those of the insurance industry, the general interest seems the same—to estimate dividends and risks for general categories based on statistical records alone; that is, without attempting to understand the reasons for each event so as to allow prediction in a more individualized fashion. This often seems the real reason why comparison studies are conducted—to give the user an experimental basis for predicting that one procedure will yield more or better changes in behavior than another for a typically broad class of individuals. When that experimental justification comes from studies that focus on merely measuring the degree or extent of effect on a sample rather than attempting to identify and understand the variables that make a procedure succeed or fail in each case, it is more an actuarial than a behavior analytic study.

Even this clarification of motives may sometimes be generous. Too often, the real agenda may be political; in other words, advocacy of a prior conviction about the procedures being evaluated. The researcher's interest frequently seems to be primarily aligned with only one of the procedures and it may even be equally strongly in opposition to the competing procedure. The focus of the researcher's interest is usually unmistakably clear from his or her prose alone, but the selection and implementation of the competing procedure often removes any doubt. Not only is the comparison procedure sometimes chosen partly to make the procedure of primary interest look good (by choosing a "traditional" or a "no-treatment" procedure, for example), its implementation may not receive the same degree of attention as does the primary procedure. If this is not enough, it is characteristic of advocacy style research that various features of experimental method (such as measurement procedures) are knowingly or unknowingly bent in favor of the researcher's convictions, further compromising the veracity of any conclusions (see Box 3.7 in *Strategies and Tactics*).

NATURE OF THE COMPARISON

Although all of these problems are certainly worthy of concern, they can in principle be either tolerated or remedied in one way or another. Unfortunately, the remaining problems with comparison studies are more serious and bring into question the general propriety of this type of experimental strategy. One such difficulty concerns how the nature of the two or more conditions chosen for comparison often raises the knotty questions of fairness and meaningfulness.

Because each procedure tested becomes the standard by which the other's effects are measured, selecting the proper procedures for comparison is critical. Certainly there must be a fair and meaningful basis for comparing two or more procedures. Usually the similarity of their intended function is the rationale; however, even this obvious selection criterion may be misleading. Although two procedures may address the same general behavioral goal, a number of detailed differences between them may often make each an inappropriate metric for the other. These differences may include (a) the exact characteristics of the populations and settings with which each works best, (b) the target behaviors and their controlling influences, or (c) a variety of more administrative considerations such as the characteristics of the personnel conducting each procedure. If any of these or other critical features are not optimal for each procedure being compared, it inevitably places each procedure at an absolute disadvantage in producing its best effects, and it probably places one of the two procedures at a relative disadvantage as well (a point also made by Van Houten, 1987).

For example, two programs designed to teach young children to read might not be meaningfully compared because they are unknowingly appropriate for children with different prerequisite skill levels. Contrasting them using the same population of subjects may imply that one program is more effective than the other, whereas each may work equally well when properly applied to slightly different subsets of the young, illiterate population. Although it might be argued that there can always be such differences that affect the results of compared procedures, studies with the comparison focus described here are less likely to discover such critical factors than are analytical studies aimed at identifying controlling variables, thus permitting erroneous conclusions to be made without qualification. In other words, if anything about the task or each's application makes one procedure more appropriate than the other, any comparison is at least misleading or, in the worst case, entirely meaningless. For instance, you can compare a word processor to a typewriter for the task of writing a paper, but it is meaningless and unfair to compare a word processor to a calculator because they are not fully and equally appropriate for that purpose.

Understanding enough about two procedures to select them for a comparison study clearly requires each to have a considerable experimental history with which the prospective researcher is quite familiar. These literatures should identify through experimental analysis at least most if not all of the important variables and any of their critical parameters required for each procedure to produce optimal effects. Any comparison conducted before such a literature is available is likely to misrepresent the procedure to some degree by not being able to implement the procedure in its most effective form. The rigors of this obligation may contribute to the popularity of comparison conditions about which relatively little is known. These are the procedures usually labeled *traditional* and *no treatment*, and they are almost inevitably a weak choice as a standard by which to evaluate some other procedure, however obvious the political benefits of the test.

A no-treatment condition is a blatantly inappropriate standard on at least two counts. First, such conditions do not represent the effects of a condition of nothingness—an environmental void. Whatever the no-treatment subjects are exposed to is simply not specified, usually because the degree to which the competing procedure can be described is not known. This can hardly be a meaningful standard of comparison. Second, even if such a condition can be reasonably described, it is still a weak basis for comparison because it is likely to be the easiest possible criterion. All the procedure of primary interest has to do in order to be judged effective is to produce an appropriate disturbance of the status quo, hardly a crowning technological achievement. If at least this much has not been learned about a procedure through its experimental development, it seems pointless to attempt to certify its utility with such a bogus contest. Furthermore, the use of no-treatment comparison conditions tends to encourage concerns about the advocacy nature of the proceedings, there being less than equivalent procedural interest in the no-treatment condition.

Using some traditional procedure as the standard of comparison runs afoul of the same two difficulties to only a slightly lesser degree. Although the status of some condition as traditional may be unimpeachable, exactly what constitutes that procedure is usually unclear, partly because its popularity insures considerable procedural variety from case to case and partly because it usually lacks a serious, analytical, experimental history. Procedures that have been around long enough and please enough users to be called traditional may also be less effective than most prefer, which makes them a weak comparative standard and thus an easy way to demonstrate the relative effectiveness of some other procedure. Indeed, it is the general ineffectiveness of traditional procedures that often motivates the development of the technologies that they are then called on to assess.

A good example of such tactics is in the literature on individualized methods of college-level instruction. A sizeable portion of that literature is devoted to comparisons of various more or less individualized teaching procedures (such as the Personalized System of Instruction) with the traditional lecture method, clearly for the purpose of demonstrating or, more neutrally, assessing the relative effectiveness of the individualized methods. Given the evidence, conclusions have regularly been drawn about the superiority of individualized methods over the conventional lecture method (e.g., Hursch, 1976; Johnson & Ruskin, 1977; Lloyd, 1978). However, as any experienced college teacher knows, there is no such teaching procedure as the lecture method. Although most teachers do indeed talk in front of legions of adoring students a few times each week, it strains the denotation of the word "lecture" to apply it to all that goes on in these classes. More importantly, there is even less commonality in all of the other features of these lecture method courses, such as with critical variables like testing procedures and course contingencies. However, the popularity of the lecture method as a comparison condition for new teaching procedures is understandable because it is apparently easily beaten by other methods, a fact that may be contributed to by each researcher's freedom in using whatever arrangement of the lecture procedure that seems to be appropriate in each case. Any value in this victory seems more political than technological (Johnston, 1975).

In summary, the requirement that the two or more procedures in question be meaningfully and fairly comparable is not always easy to satisfy. The only way to address it properly leads experimentation away from comparison studies and in the direction of analyses of sources of control over a procedure's effects. Understanding what makes a procedure more or less effective requires a program of experimental analysis that identifies (a) those features of the target behaviors and their histories that can interact with procedural components in some way, (b) those features of the circumstances under which the procedure is applied that can modulate its behavioral effects, and (c) those procedural options and their parameters that can influence behavioral outcomes. This considerable requirement should suggest that comparison studies (and, for that matter, evaluation studies) are often premature, at best. The proper question is not "Which is better?" but "What are the variables that each requires to produce optimal effects?"

GENERALITY

Aside from the appropriateness of the comparison, there is another major problem that depreciates the value of conclusions from comparison studies, and it concerns their generality or, in the terms of Campbell and Stanley (1966) and Cook and Campbell (1979), external validity.[1] In spite of the fact that the motivation underlying comparison studies is primarily to reach a conclusion that one of the procedures is "better" across the broadest of circumstances, the generality of most comparison studies must be evaluated as "poor." The reasons are especially obvious when traditional and no-treatment conditions are used as comparisons, but they plague most behavioral procedures that show up in comparison studies, even those with impressive research histories.

In order for conclusions about the relative effectiveness of two procedures to have good generality to other applications of each procedure, the critical features of each (including procedural elements, parameters of important variables, required characteristics of target behavior and clients, and the necessary degree of control over setting features) must be known and then held constant across all routine applications. Because the first requirement is infrequently accomplished, the second is infrequently possible. In other words, unless the critical variables that actually make a procedure work have already been identified and publicized in the existing literature, they cannot be properly and consistently managed across its many applications. These admittedly challenging requirements make any effort to establish one procedure as "better" than another (or, worse yet, "best" with regard to some broad range of circumstances), an improper and unattainable goal in the absence of such a literature. Furthermore, whether we find such requirements reasonable or attainable for the present state of the field has no bearing on their importance, which stems from the nature of behavior.

Even if one tried to implement a procedure in the same way across repeated applications, it would be difficult to avoid accidentally changing some important variables. However, in practice, each time a procedure is applied, numerous variations in its components and their circumstances are unknowingly made, willingly accepted, and intentionally incorporated (see Barber, 1976, chapters 3 and 7, for a discussion of this problem in research contexts). When this reality is combined with the substantial lack of an adequate experimental rationale for these changes or any evidence in the literature about their different effects, there may be little basis for even describing all such applications with the same label. The result is the emergence of very large, amorphous, and overlapping categories of procedures. The use of simple procedural labels is clearly gratuitous and implies a uniformity that is quite misleading.

For instance, applications labeled *Personalized System of Instruction* collectively include an impressive variety of components, although each instance often does not even incorporate all of the five defining features specified by Keller (1968). This same variety maybe seen for almost all of the field's most

---

[1]Portions of this argument were included in Johnston (1985).

common procedures, ranging from the simple (e.g., differential reinforcement of other behavior) to the complex (e.g., token economies). Many such labels have become rather crude categorical references with no more than the general conversational value of other abstractions.

Of course, there is nothing wrong with variations on a particular procedural theme. In fact, variations that have been examined by analytical research programs and that allow the practitioner to adjust a procedure to accommodate unique circumstances in the field without damaging its effectiveness are extremely valuable. For instance, an analytical program of research concerning rumination in retarded individuals shows that feeding satiation quantities of food at meals will greatly decrease ruminating (although it is clear that this is an inappropriate technique when the resident is at or above his or her normal body weight). However, this research also shows how satiation feeding can be modified or dropped entirely while achieving the same effect by incorporating a number of procedural variations (Rast & Johnston, 1988; Rast, Johnston, Allen, & Drum, 1985; Rast, Johnston, & Drum, 1984; Rast, Johnston, Drum, & Conrin, 1981).

Unfortunately, the lack of such experimental analyses for most procedural applications and their labels means that there is insufficient evidence that each application is effective by virtue of specified critical features. The procedural variety instead suggests that any effectiveness is due to unique combinations of at least partly unknown influences that probably go beyond those uniformly recognized as defining the procedural label.

Poor generality of comparison studies is likely, then, for two reasons: (a) Each of the procedures being compared may be a naively unique arrangement of variables, and (b) Every subsequent application may also be unique with regard to its own arrangement of functional variables. Generality of method accrues not to labels, but only to the particular combination of variables that makes each procedure effective and that will guarantee its repeated effectiveness as often as those elements are brought together. To the extent that those elements are unknown or only suspected, each application risks violating the conditions that define the version used in the comparison study, thus constraining the correctness of the prediction suggested by the comparison study. Generality of method is effectively gained only by discovering and understanding the role of critical variables whose status in particular applications can then be used to predict the effects of the version of the procedure being planned (see *Strategies and Tactics*, chapter 13).

In the terms of Cook and Campbell (1979), the differences between the features of the procedures being compared and the different versions of them subsequently used in other studies or in clinical settings are the source of threats to the external validity of such studies (although the extensions by Judd & Kenny, 1981, of the concept of construct validity originated by Cronbach & Meehl, 1955, should also be noted). However, the present points about generality differ from the usual discussions of external validity (see, for instance, Kazdin, 1982).

The argument here is that there may be no way to sufficiently specify subject, setting, and procedural characteristics to insure reliable generality of comparison study conclusions because the critical variables responsible for the effects of each procedure are unlikely to be thoroughly identified in this style of research (in part, because it is not designed to do so). In such cases, this knowledge is therefore not available to guide or limit either statements of generality or efforts to engineer generality by carefully arranging those features of any application of a study's findings.

LIMITED ROLE OF COMPARISON STUDIES

The indictment has thus far characterized comparison studies as generally being not fundamentally behavioral, not meaningfully comparative, not fairly conducted, not productively evaluative, not very general in their findings, and not very high on the list of research priorities. Perhaps the only remaining question is, "Is there any hope for them?"

The answer is a qualified "yes," but first it is important to distinguish comparison from evaluation. If there is a need to evaluate or assess the effects of a procedure, this need in no way requires or encourages comparison with another procedure. Evaluation only asks about the effects of a procedure under certain field conditions, and simple description is all that is called for. Whether a program works can be measured against standards specified by carefully defined goals that the target behavior, setting, and cultural context supply. This is the only comparison that is meaningful if the purpose of the effort is simply to evaluate the applied effectiveness of a newly developed or differently applied procedure.

What, then, is left for comparison studies to do? To compare, obviously, but only after acknowledging that such studies are not really for asking about behavior or evaluation. Instead, they are primarily appropriate for answering questions about the relative effects of two or more procedures for a particular combination of target behavior, client, and setting variables for relatively narrow or parochial purposes. Furthermore, although comparison studies can certainly be conducted for only one or a very small number of subjects, more often they are justified by the need to make a procedural selection for a larger population, such as all children in a school system. However, the motivating interests should be more practical or even logistical than generic; concern should focus on which of two alternatives is the more applicable and effective choice rather than which is the best in some overall or general sense.

As argued, answering the question about which of some group of procedures is generally superlative is often impossible because it is frequently not really a meaningful question. In addition, there may be fully as much interest in the requirements of the procedures from an administrative perspective as in their relative behavioral effectiveness (see Hopkins, 1987). For instance, Procedure A may be somewhat more effective, whereas Procedure B may require fewer personnel, or less skilled personnel, or less money, or easier scheduling, or any of a number of other practical considerations. Such matters are often no less important than the procedures' behavioral effects because the best choice in terms of behavioral effectiveness may be less effective than its competitor if its administrative requirements cannot be met when it is routinely applied.

Because of this parochial focus that eschews interest in conclusions with general applicability, comparison studies as approached here are unlikely to be conducted for the purpose of being published as statements of the generality of a procedure, and the availability of such data is not likely to encourage a post hoc decision to write a paper that could offer only conclusions of intentionally narrow and local import. This may be why most of the literature that makes comparisons generally does so in the traditional style critiqued in this paper. As a result, actual examples of the alternative style proposed here are not readily available in the archival literature.

Fully as important as understanding the proper role of comparison studies is understanding their priority or place in a procedure's experimental history. They should be the very last type of investigation that a procedure encounters. They are appropriate only after the proper course of experimental development, analysis, refinement, and evaluation has been completed, and this means an experimental history that is more thematic and analytically sophisticated than is customary in today's applied literature. Meeting this challenge requires a rather lengthy and integrated series of experiments that analyze behavior more than procedures by focusing on identifying the variables that do or can control behavior and examining the ways in which those variables can most effectively be arranged in practical form. With such a history, the constraints of comparison studies are not disappointing because all of the other questions concerning the identification of critical procedural, subject, and setting variables, the administrative requirements, and the nature of behavioral effects have already been answered.

With this kind of experimental lineage, the question of which of two procedures is better for a particular type of behavioral problem under a particular set of circumstances simply should not come up very often. The reason is that, when enough is known about the critical variables required for each procedure's maximally effective application, it will usually be clear that one procedure is more appropriate than another for the particular combination of features that characterize the behavioral problem and its attendant circumstances. When this is the case, there is no meaningful and fair comparison that can or will need to be made.

Unfortunately, such a literature is not typically available in any of the many areas in which we are now called upon to provide behavior change services, and the final defense of comparison studies is that they are at least needed to guide programmatic decision-making, how ever crudely, until this more sophisticated database is available. It is true, of course, that even with their limitations, comparison studies are better than no studies at all. However, this argument runs into another serious problem in the applied field—the terribly small proportion of its participants who are interested in conducting or employed to conduct any kind of research at all. Although no figures are available, it would seem that only a precious few of those earning graduate degrees from behavior analysis programs are primarily interested in research careers, and only some fraction of them are interested in an experimental focus on applied problems. Of these, only a small minority wind up being employed under circumstances in which research is even possible or encouraged, and only some of these circumstances are conducive to conducting sound behavioral research, whatever its style. To propose devoting any portion of this tragically small pool of scientific resources to continuing an experimental tradition characterized more by its limitations than by its strengths seems shortsighted, especially when the experimental alterative is so rich with immediate potential for improving our technological abilities.

PART FOUR

INTERPRETATION

Measurement Scales and the Description of Behavioral Variability

THE NATURE OF BEHAVIORAL VARIABILITY

As do other natural scientists, behavior analysts assume that, given sufficiently precise and complete measurement, it can be shown that no two events in its subject matter are ever exactly alike. Identifying and explaining such differences and searching for the similarities that will constitute general laws is the goal of science. This responsibility is discharged through an enormous variety of techniques that have evolved across scientific disciplines by adherence to the twin criteria of orderliness and generality of data. Whatever the methods, the goal is always to account for variability in one observed phenomenon in terms of other observed phenomena.

Chapter 8 in *Strategies and Tactics* discussed the nature of behavioral variability, its sources in the environment and the organism, and the superordinate methodological strategy of bringing the experimenter's verbal behavior under control of those aspects of variability in the data that will augment the opportunity for effective interpretations. Given these arguments, the challenge becomes one of capturing and preserving those aspects of variability through measurement and analytical procedures in such a way as to facilitate this strategic goal. An important step in this process is therefore to understand the consequences of various measurement and analytical tactics. Some of the most pervasive of these concerns are the mathematical rules that relate the nature of the events being studied to the measurement techniques used. This is the topic of measurement scales.

CLASSIFICATION OF MEASUREMENT SCALES

Classification systems in measurement provide coherent methods of categorizing groups of phenomena and generally determine the kinds of descriptive statements that may be made. There are two dominant systems for classifying scales for measuring behavioral phenomena. Campbell (1920) proposed a system that relies on measurement procedures, and Stevens (1946) argued that classification should be done on the basis of mathematical properties of measurement scales. Both approaches have their advantages. Campbell's system indicates the extent to which scale choice depends on empirical facts, theories about the quantities measured, or measurement conventions. Steven's system, on the other hand, may be more useful to the practicing scientist because it provides a method of assessing the appropriateness of different descriptive practices for use on particular scales (Ellis, 1966). This section discusses Steven's classification system in order to provide a framework for assessing the appropriateness of various methods of representing variability in behavioral data.

The fundamental assumption of Steven's classification scheme is that scales of measurement should be classified on the basis of their "mathematical group structure." This is determined by establishing what types of mathematical operations result in an invariant scale form. For example, if measurements of response rate are made in terms of count per second as a unit of measurement, this scale may be changed to count per minute by multiplying each value by a constant. This transformation results in a different scale, related to the original one by the transformation function $y = mx$, where m is the constant of multiplication. Although the new scale has different values, the form and purposes of the original one are preserved under the transformation. Thus, the scale has a mathematical group structure that may be defined by invariance under transformations of multiplication by a constant.

When an investigator measures a natural phenomenon, he or she assigns numbers to objects or events on the basis of mathematical rules that take into account the nature of the phenomenon. These rules then limit the kinds of statements that the investigator may make. In other words, the nature of the phenomenon determines the measurement scales that are permissible. In addition, the nature of the obtained data further limits acceptable scale options for display and quantitative procedures. The investigator may select among these to suit particular interests.

The basic empirical operations that any particular set of data allow are closely related to the mathematical group structure of the scale. What the investigator needs to know in order to select the correct scale for a set of data in a particular experimental context is (a) the nature of the phenomenon to be measured, (b) the nature of the obtained data, (c) the kinds of statements that might be made about variability, and (d) the types of quantitative transformations that are valid. Within this framework, the five kinds of scales that are commonly distinguished are listed in Table 10.1.

Nominal scales are required when measurement only labels objects or events in any manner that distinguishes between them. Any phenomenon that can be quantified thus permits this scale. For example, an investigator who measures presses on one lever as Response Class A and those on another lever as Response Class B is conducting measurement on a nominal scale. In this case, it is the labeling itself that constitutes measurement, and there would be no interest in counting or otherwise quantifying such responses. The only empir-

TABLE 10.1
Measurement Scales, Measures of Variability, and
Examples of Phenomena Measured on Each Scale

Scale	Measure of Variability	Phenomena
Nominal	Information	Labeling response classes or stimuli Numbering subjects
Ordinal	Percentiles	IQ test raw scores Street numbers Ordering racers
Linear	Standard deviation Average deviation Absolute mean deviation (AMD)	IQ standard scores Temperature (C or F)
Logarithmic	Absolute mean ratio (AMR)	Changes in response frequency
Ratio	Any of the above Percent variation	Length, Weight, Time Intervals, Count, Frequency

ical operation that nominal data allow is the determination of qualitative equivalence, and the types of statements that may be made about variability are only
ones of class inclusion or exclusion. The structure and purpose of nominal
scales are invariant under any permutation transformation because equality
is uninfluenced.

Ordinal scales are permitted when measurement distinguishes between objects or events and indicates order. Measurement on ordinal scales is often conducted when the data of interest involve unspecified changes in magnitude
or level of a dimensional quantity. For example, rank ordering participants
in a bicycle race as they cross the finish line (without measuring their elapsed
time) constitutes ordinal measurement. In other words, if the degree to which
data values differ is unimportant, an ordinal scale may suffice.

Thus, with ordinal data, the experimenter may either speak of the assigned
values that distinguish objects or events (a nominal statement) or of the order
of those objects or events (an ordinal statement). However, ordinal measures
provide no information about the extent of the differences. Ordinal scales may
be transformed without any loss of structure or purpose by any mathematical
function that preserves order (i.e., any monotonic increasing function). Therefore, adding a constant to shift the origin or multiplying by a constant to change
units of measurement will not alter the scale.

For obvious reasons, nominal and ordinal scales are fairly crude levels of
description and do not permit the full potential of scientific measurement. It
is usually possible to assign nonarbitrary values to objects or events, which
permits one or more of the following scales to be used.

Linear interval scales support descriptions of phenomena that allow the
determination of equality, order, and the equality of intervals between data
values. Measures such as temperature, IQ, and calendar time are examples of
data that may be described on linear interval scales. The advantage of these
scales over nominal and ordinal scales is that such descriptions may reference

the equality or inequality of intervals between values, although the data may still be used to support nominal or ordinal statements as well.

Aside from nominal or ordinal statements, the kinds of meaningful statements that one may make with linear interval data are also narrowly defined. For instance, one may say that the difference between the November 30 and November 15 is 15 days, but it is meaningless to say that November 30 represents twice as much calendar time as November 15. Similarly, it is correct to report that John's IQ of 150 is 50 points higher than Mike's score of 100, but it is not acceptable to say that John's intelligence is 1.5 times higher than Mike's. In other words, statements of comparison may be made only in terms of intervals between values, not ratios among values.

The only type of transformation that leaves the structure and purpose of interval scales intact is a linear one (i.e., $x' = a x + b$). An example of one such transformation is the conversion from the Centigrade to the Fahrenheit scale by the equation F = 1.8C + 32. The arbitrary origin of an interval scale may be changed by a linear function where $a = 1$. Also, a change in unit of measurement may be accomplished by a linear function where $b = 0$.

Logarithmic interval scales are permissible when the phenomenon measured allows the determination of equality, order, and equality of ratios among values. Logarithmic interval scales represent equal ratios by equal differences on the scale. For example, an increase in response frequency from 4 cycles per minute to 12 cycles per minute is proportionally equivalent to an increase from 40 cycles per minute to 120 cycles per minute. This is because the difference between two values on a logarithmic scale is equivalent to a ratio of the two values. In the present case, $ln(12) - ln(4) = ln(12/4) = ln(3)$ is equivalent to $ln(120) - ln(40) = ln(120/40) = ln(3)$. Thus, a logarithmic interval scale represents equal ratios as equal differences, as these data show in the top graph in Fig. 10.1.

However, logarithmic interval scales do not provide any means of assessing absolute differences between values in terms of subtraction (a linear interval statement). This is because logarithmic interval scales are based on ratios among values. For example, a decrease in response rate from 30 cycles per minute to 5 cycles per minute is not the same proportional change as is represented by a decrease from 100 cycles per minute to 75 cycles per minute. In the first case, the amount of change is 83%, whereas in the second case, it is only 25%, and the bottom graph in Fig. 10.1 appropriately represents this difference. Thus, on a logarithmic interval scale, it is not meaningful to make statements regarding absolute change because the meaning of absolute change is relative to the level at which it occurs.

The structure and purpose of logarithmic interval scales are invariant under transformations of the form $y = kx$. The origin of a logarithmic interval scale is arbitrary because there is no absolute zero point. Therefore, multiplying or dividing by a constant to shift the origin is permissible.

Ratio scales permit the operations allowable with all of the other scales (see Table 10.2). Stevens (1959) argued that ratio scales are possible only when the phenomenon measured allows the determination of equality, order, equal

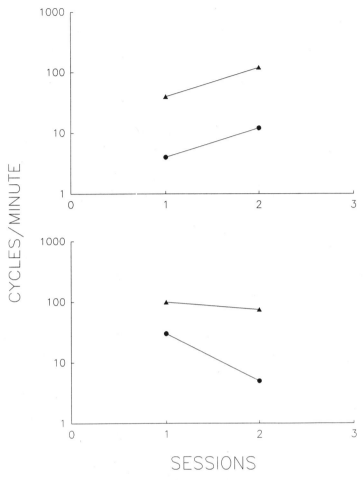

FIG. 10.1. Logarithmic interval scales representing equal proportional change (top graph) and equal absolute change (bottom graph).

TABLE 10.2
Hierarchy of Measurement Scales and Permissible Operations

Scale	Permissible Operation
Nominal	Equality or inequality
Ordinal	Equality or inequality Greater or less than
Linear	Equality or inequality Greater or less than Equality or inequality of differences
Logarithmic	Equality or inequality Greater or less than Equality or inequality of ratios
Ratio	Equality or inequality Greater or less than Equality or inequality of differences or ratios

differences between values, and equal ratios among values. Ratio scales allow the calculation of fractions, multiples, and ratios of data values, as well as differences. For this reason, ratio scales are generally considered to be the most useful in science.

Most physical quantities such as length, weight, and numerosity are examples of dimensional quantities that may be measured with ratio scales. Similarly, behavioral quantities such as latency, duration, IRT, rate, and count may also be measured with ratio scales because it is meaningful both to form ratios of their quantities and to determine differences between values. That is, ratio scales allow the advantage of comparative descriptions in terms of ratios, such as "one-third as much" or "four times as slow." Furthermore, one may report that a subject completed ten more problems than another subject, or that a subject showed a reduction of five responses compared to a previous session.

Thus, a linear interval scale permits one to report only that Subject A responded at a rate of .75 responses per minute and Subject B responded at a rate of 1.5 responses per minute, whereas a logarithmic interval scale allows the description that Subject B responded at twice the rate of Subject A. A ratio scale permits both types of statements. Statements about variability may reference proportional change or absolute change. It is therefore meaningful to speak of logarithmic interval and linear interval properties of ratio data.

The only type of transformation that results in an invariant ratio scale form is multiplication by a constant (i.e. $y = mx$). Because ratio scales imply an absolute zero, the origin is nonarbitrary and may not be shifted by adding or subtracting a constant. However, units of measurement may be changed by multiplying a constant.

Recall that measurement is simply the assignment of numbers on the basis of observation and mathematical rules. Measurement scales are rules that serve to bring the experimenter's behavior under control of certain aspects of the phenomenon, as limited by particular measurement procedures. The question now is how our interest in specific features of behavior and our pursuit of them with specific measurement procedures come together to provide these measurement scale rules. In other words, how will the nature of behavioral data be influenced by measurement scale decisions?

SCALES AND THE NATURE OF BEHAVIORAL DATA

Behavioral data are ratio data. The physical properties characteristic of behavior can vary in all of the ways specified by ratio scales and all subordinate scale forms, as shown in Table 10.2. For example, latency measures may vary in terms of linear or logarithmic intervals or even order of occurrence. Because the general nature of behavior is such that dimensional quantities may vary in ways described by any scale, it is important to design measurement procedures so as to capture any potential form of behavior change.

Ratio scales are generally considered more desirable than others because they provide valuable advantages. An investigator who measures behavior on ratio scales creates the opportunity to examine features of the data that are not available when other, more restrictive, scales are used. Conversely, an investigator who measures behavior with procedures that limit the scale to either a linear or a logarithmic interval form will be unable to detect those aspects of variability that would be evident if measurement was conducted on a ratio scale. For instance, using a manipulandum that allows force of responding to be measured only on a linear interval scale prevents detection of exponential change.

Although all levels of measurement scales are available whenever real dimensional quantities of behavior are observed and recorded, when observation procedures limit the record of responding to a particular scale, only that scale or subordinate scales are permissible. For example, if observers assign ordered values to subjective judgments (as in rating scales), only ordinal or nominal scale operations may be used. However, even when objective counts are made, a narrow interest in order of occurrence may limit measurement to ordinal scales (as in typical stimulus equivalence procedures). In both cases, variability that would be revealed by other measurement scales will not be detected.

It is important to appreciate the different points at which the investigator must understand the role of measurement scales in behavioral experimentation. As Fig. 10.2 outlines, the fundamental nature of behavior circumscribes all subsequent scale considerations. Representations of variability in the obtained data are then limited by the measurement scale selected by the experimenter.

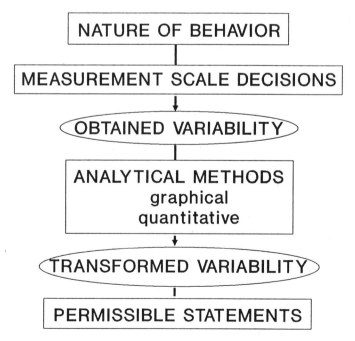

FIG. 10.2.   Graphic representation of the relation between behavior, measurement and analytical scale decisions, and permissible statements.

The nature of obtained variability in the data also provides the choices for the experimenter's selection of scales used for analytical purposes. Because the experimenter must explicitly choose or construct graphic scales, we tend to be at least generally aware of this decision. However, the scale implications of quantitative procedures are usually only implicit, thus camouflaging the importance of scales to this choice. The kinds of statements permitted may follow directly from the raw data or be influenced by the scale restrictions on the analytical procedures.

We began this reading by considering how variability in data may be determined by both the nature of response class observed and by measurement scale decisions. The remainder of the reading extends these issues to a focus on analytical tactics that may be used to augment the control that the data exerts over the experimenter's verbal behavior. Although we mention a number of specific graphic and quantitative techniques, the following discussion is primarily intended to emphasize a general approach to analyzing variability.

GRAPHIC DISPLAY

Linear and Logarithmic Interval Scales

The term *variability* is a fully inclusive reference to all aspects of a set of data. We are usually interested in particular features of variability in a set of behavioral data, but it is wise to be cautious about having strong prejudices about what aspects of variability will be extant or most important in a data set. Behavior analysts tend to show interest in changes in level of responding, overall range, local range or bounce, trend, and variation around some measure of central tendency, although changes in level and range tend to dominate researchers' attention. Although one of these indices of variability may indeed be relevant to the effects of the independent variable, unexamined convictions that a particular feature will be important (e.g., average level of responding) may lead investigators to ignore other aspects (e.g., trend or dispersion) that require different techniques of analysis to discover. An important strategy of graphic display, then, is to determine the types of displays that will reveal *any* features of variability that might be valuable.

A graph is a transformation of sets of dimensional quantities ($x, y, z, \ldots$) describing an observation into another metric ($dx, dy, dz, \ldots$), where d is a linear distance. The issue is whether the set of relations among data points $(x_1 y_1)$, $(x_2 y_2)$, $\ldots$ remain invariant under this transformation. Decisions about graphic display of variability require distinctions between the scales used as a basis for measurement and the scales used for displaying data. In graphic analysis, all of the issues concerning scales of measurement and the nature of variability in the data often reduce to the treatment of the vertical axis. The earlier discussion of the effects of various transformations on measurement scale values provides one way to determine the appropriateness of different graphic displays. For instance, it is appropriate to attach linear (equal) interval display scales to vertical axes for displaying data quantified with linear interval measurement scales because both scales are invariant under transformations that result in an invariant scale form.

In other words, the variability that is captured by linear interval measurement scales will bring the viewer's verbal behavior under better control of relevant features of the data if they are displayed on linear (equal) interval vertical axes. An analogous point may be made for logarithmic interval measurement and display scales. If measurement employs a ratio scale, the investigator has the luxury of fitting the display scale to the nature of the data's variability.

To illustrate this tactic, Fig. 10.3 shows two hypothetical ratio data sets plotted on a linear interval scale vertical axis in the upper panel and a logarithmic

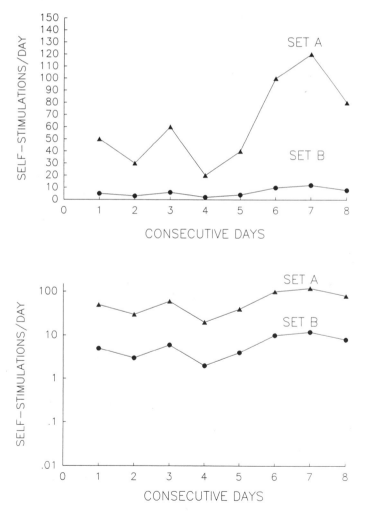

FIG. 10.3.   Effects on linear interval and logarithmic interval displays when Set A is transformed to Set B by division by a constant of 10.

interval scale vertical axis in the lower panel. Set A has been transformed to
Set B by dividing each value by 10. The linear interval representation suggests
that Set B is more variable than Set A, whereas the logarithmic interval representation indicates identical variability. This clearly depicts the graphic effects
of the transformation invariant nature of a logarithmic interval scale axis when
data are multiplied by a constant by comparing them to the effects of such
multiplication on the data displayed on an linear interval scale axis. The figure
also shows the dramatic differences in the graphic appearance of ratio data
plotted on the two scales.

Figure 10.4 shows two more data sets plotted on linear interval and logarithmic interval axes. In this case, Set A has been transformed to Set B by adding
a constant of 50 to each value. As can be seen from the graphs, the addition

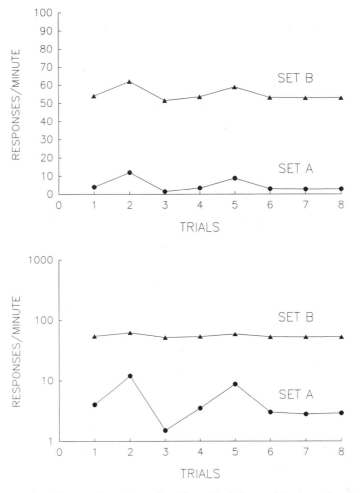

FIG. 10.4. Effects on linear interval and logarithmic interval displays when Set
A is transformed to Set B by addition of a constant of 50.

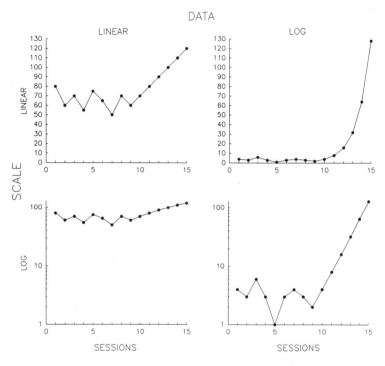

FIG. 10.5. Linear data plotted on linear and logarithmic interval scales in the left column and logarithmic data plotted on linear and logarithmic interval scales in the right column.

of a constant suggests decreased variability on the logarithmic interval axis but not on the linear interval axis. This illustrates the superiority of linear interval display scales for representing linear interval variability in ratio data because such axes are transformation invariant by addition. Analogously, logarithmic interval displays will produce changes in the appearance of variability under any transformation other than multiplication by a constant.

The tactic this discussion suggests is that if the data to be analyzed are measured on ratio scales, they may be displayed on either linear or logarithmic interval vertical axes. However, it is paramount that the scale chosen for the vertical axis corresponds to the type of variability observed in the data. For instance, if the data vary linearly, the investigator should assess them on a linear interval vertical axis, whereas data that change exponentially over time are best described on logarithmic interval scales. In fact, some have argued that changes in rates of responding tend to change exponentially and should generally be displayed on logarithmic interval scales (e.g., Koenig, 1972; Pennypacker, Koenig, & Lindsley, 1972; White & Haring, 1976).

The consequences of displaying ratio data on vertical axes that do not correspond to the observed pattern of variability are illustrated in Fig. 10.5, which shows the graphical effects of displaying data that change in linear and logarithmic fashion on linear and logarithmic vertical axes. Note that plotting linear interval data on a logarithmic interval axis has the effect of dampening the appearance of variability in the second phase compared to its pattern on a linear interval axis. In contrast, displaying logarithmic interval data on a linear interval axis makes the changes in responding in the second phase appear to increase dramatically, although the effect on the logarithmic interval axis shows a more moderate change. In summary, using a scale that is improper for the nature of the data may make it difficult to detect the true nature of the obtained variability.

In passing, note that the previous discussion has assumed that the data subjected to analysis are unmodified from those collected through the measurement process. However, it is possible to perform mathematical procedures that change the raw data before they are analyzed by graphical (or quantitative) means. Under these or any other conditions, alterations of the data can change only the appearance of variability, not the nature of variability in the phenomenon. Recall that the more restrictive the scale, the less restrictive the changes to the data. Thus, linear interval raw data may be changed by any function that preserves equal intervals, and logarithmic interval data may be modified by functions that retain equal differences between equal ratios.

Finally, when measurement detects no instances of the target response class, another set of graphic guidelines is required. When using linear interval scales, zero may be assigned to the horizontal axis and zeros plotted accordingly. When a logarithmic interval scale is used, zeros are not possible, and there is no proper way to display them. However, Pennypacker, Koenig, and Lindsley (1972) suggested a procedure that provides a useful graphic result in the case of frequency. They argued that we cannot say that a rate is zero because that is not mathematically true and would imply that the behavior never occurs. The minimum frequency possible is only known to be less than one response divided by the time of observation. This value is called the record floor (Pennypacker, Koenig, & Lindsley, 1972) and is considered to be a lower limit on observable frequencies. Plotting the record floor assigns a non-zero value to a measurement interval in which no observations occurred, although this introduces systematic error. This procedure is merely one of many possible ways of representing zeros on a logarithmic interval scale, but none can be correct.

Selecting the Appropriate Display Scale

Determining the nature of variability is not always an easy task because this characteristic can itself vary across and even within phases. The typical circumstance under which behavior analytic investigators face these decisions involves data from multiple phases of an experiment across multiple, individual subjects. These data may exhibit variability that show either linear or logarithmic trend or no trend at all. Thus, the challenge of the display scale decision is to represent multiple aspects of variability that will suit a number of sets of data with different characteristics.

This would be an impossible task if one were limited to a single display scale. Although the scale decision may be made separately for each phase or portions of a phase, it will usually be simplest to begin by plotting all of the data from an experiment on both linear and logarithmic interval scales. This practice may help evaluate the appropriateness of the display scale for each data set phase by phase. It may also focus the investigator's deliberations on choosing the best scale for making experimental inferences.

This tactic requires considering which display scale is most appropriate for analytical purposes at the level of each distinguishable pattern of data, whether they constitute an entire phase or only a portion of a phase (such as the transition at the beginning of the phase or the steady state at the end of the phase). Having constructed both linear and logarithmic interval graphs, one then searches each graph for patterns of variability that indicate the type of display scale required for effective inferences. It might be easiest to begin by looking for trends. Although a trend may be suggested on one or the other graph, the nature of the change may not be obviously linear or exponential, and it may be necessary to calculate the mathematical function that describes the data set. Although this step is unfamiliar in most behavioral research, the now extensive role of computers in data storage and analysis can make it simple and fast. If it is determined that the change in data is clearly linear or exponential, then one or the other graphic scales is unequivocally required, as Fig. 10.5 shows.

When the data do not exhibit relatively consistent change or trend on either graph, the decision about a graphic scale for analytical purposes is more difficult because it involves some complex judgments. The general rule in this case is to use (a) the scale that is required by the nature of the data (which is determined by the phenomenon and the measurement scale used to observe the data), (b) the nature of the variation in the data, (c) the inferential needs of the experimental question and the literature, (d) the directions of the investigator's curiosity, and (e) the history of the audience. Having already discussed the options provided by the nature of the data, we consider each of the remaining factors.

Aside from these other considerations, trendless data may be usefully analyzed on either scale. However, the scale choice may determine the aspects of the data that the investigator comes in contact with. For instance, vertical "bounce" appears different depending on the display scale chosen. If data are displayed on a logarithmic interval scale, variability will be represented in terms of proportional change, but if data are displayed on a linear interval scale, variability will be represented in terms of absolute change. In other words, an increase of two responses per minute is proportionally less on a logarithmic interval scale if responding is generally at a level of 100 responses per minute versus a level of one response per minute but equivalent on a linear interval scale. Figures 10.3, 10.4, and 10.5 show the importantly different consequences of these alternatives on the pictures that the viewer sees.

If the experimental question or the literature directs the investigator's attention to absolute changes in data, a linear interval scale may be the most appropriate choice because the logarithmic interval scale can dampen the appearance of such variation. However, if the investigator is interested in making inferences about stability of data in order to implement phase change procedures, a logarithmic interval scale may be the most appropriate choice so that decisions are not influenced by minor variations in data.

Whatever the scale decisions, the impact of the scale attached to the vertical axis is sufficiently powerful in controlling viewer interpretations that assuring the proper scale for graphic analysis is mandatory. But what defines "proper"? Is there a correct or right scale for each set of data? In a sense, there is, and it is the "bottom line" of all science referred to in an earlier section. The best or correct display scale is the one that leads to interpretations of the data in light of the experimental question that, in turn, lead to effective actions on the part of users of the scientific literature. This rule is inviolate because it comes from nature rather than logical systems, traditions, training histories, or individual biases.

It is these other influences over scale decisions that have tended to dominate display practices. For instance, the almost rigid tradition in behavior analysis is to plot data on linear interval scales. This has so biased our interpretation of data that linear interval scales now function as a de facto standard for informally evaluating other scales. Thus, many might view logarithmic interval axes as "distorting" the data or hiding the "true" pattern of variation. However, as we have pointed out, behavior is usually measured on ratio scales, which provides both logarithmic and linear interval possibilities for analysis. We therefore have no general reason to impose linear interval display characteristics. Neither alternative is generically more "right" than the other (unless behavior change is generally proportional or absolute—as with biological versus chemical phenomena, for example).

QUANTIFICATION

Appropriateness of Descriptive Statistics

When the nature of variability in the data and the investigator's interests suggest that an increased level of descriptive precision might be useful, the data may be subjected to a number of quantitative procedures. In doing so, many of the same points discussed in the context of graphic display remain relevant. In general, Stevens' classification of measurement scales on the basis of invariance provides an equally useful method of assessing the appropriateness of statistical measures of variability.

A statistic is appropriate for use on a particular scale if it is invariant when permissible mathematical transformations are made on the scale values. Stevens (1951) argued that this invariance may be of two types. First, if a statistic is dimensionless (i.e., unitless), the numerical value of the statistic will remain fixed when the scale is transformed. Unitless statistics are those that are calculated from ratios of like dimensional quantities, which results in cancellation of the attached units. These statistics are the most useful in science because they allow general comparisons that are independent of the original quantities represented by the data.

Second, if the statistic has a dimension, the numerical value will change under scale transformations, although the measured property will remain invariant. For example, the standard deviation will vary in proportion to the constant of multiplication required to change measurement units (i.e., $s' = ks$). This is not invariance of the statistic, but invariance of the dimensional quantity of the phenomenon. The result of including this second type of invariance is that many statistics are appropriate for use on various scales, and virtually all statistics are appropriate for use on ratio scales (see Table 10.1), which Stevens acknowledged (1959).

However, Ellis (1966) proposed more stringent criteria for determining the appropriateness of statistics that renders Stevens' classification system more restrictive and, therefore, more useful. He argued that only those statistics that are numerically invariant under permissible transformations for a particular scale are appropriate for use on that scale, regardless of whether units of measurement are still attached.

This classification system provides a convenient method for assessing the appropriateness of statistics. However, they are not exhaustive frameworks in the sense that they solve all judgments concerning quantification of observations. Stevens (1951) stated:

> As I see this issue, there can surely be no objection to anyone computing any statistic that suits his fancy, regardless of where the numbers came from in the first place. Our freedom to calculate must remain as firm as our freedom to speak. The only question of substantial interest concerns the use to which the calculated statistic is intended. What purposes are we trying to serve? (p. 29)

How, then, are we to choose between statistical measures of variability such as the range, the variance, the standard deviation, or the coefficient of variation? If our purpose is to make statements regarding the logarithmic interval properties of behavioral data, the appropriate statistics are those that are invariant under permissible logarithmic transformations. On the other hand, if our intent is to make statements about the interval properties of behavioral data, statistics that are invariant to linear transformations are appropriate.

As a descriptor of variability, the range has limited value because it considers only two values in a set. Furthermore, unless expressed as a ratio (the larger value divided by the smaller), it retains the data's units of measurement and cannot be used to compare across different measurement quantities.

The standard deviation (and variance) considers all values in a set, but defines variability as deviations from a measure of central tendency (the mean). In doing so, it also retains the units of measurement, although its definition of variability in terms of the mean is a more serious problem. For instance, if a data set has some extreme values, the mean will be affected by these outliers.

The standard deviation is appropriate for use on linear interval data because it is invariant under transformations allowable on linear interval scales. The standard deviation is not appropriate for use on logarithmic interval data, however, because its numerical value varies under transformations allowable on logarithmic interval scales. The standard deviation is transformation variant by multiplication because deviations about the mean are altered in proportion to the constant of multiplication. Table 10.3 shows the effects of addition (a linear interval transformation) and multiplication (a logarithmic interval transformation) on standard deviation values.

One strength of the standard deviation is that it considers all values in a set. However, it does so in terms of deviations from the mean, which is not consistent with the traditional conception of variability as the degree to which each value differs from every other value in a set, whether comparisons are accomplished by absolute or relative methods. Of course, the standard deviation has the advantage of tradition. Those trained in the social sciences are familiar with its meaning because we have so often related standard deviation values to other representations of the data. However, tradition alone cannot be a secure defense for scientific practices.

Therefore, we might consider other descriptive statistics that meet the following requirements: (a) independence from the mean, (b) involvement of all possible comparisons of each value with every other value, and (c) appropriateness to scale requirements. A great many descriptive techniques have been developed to serve particular needs, and many meet some of these requirements. Volumes such as Hoaglin, Mosteller, and Tukey (1983) and Tukey (1977) contain excellent discussions of ways of using such techniques, but we cannot review this large statistical literature in the context of the issues raised in this reading.

Instead, we introduce two descriptive statistics that do meet all of our requirements and, in the process, provide a brief, informal model for evaluating the appropriateness, performance, and utility of such quantification techniques. Although these statistics have properties that warrant exploration and comparison to traditional techniques, we are not proposing that they are generally superior to other methods. Finally, even though it is possible to evaluate statistics from a purely mathematical perspective, the discussion of these two statistics will approach matters from the perspective of the behavioral scientist, who is sensitive to the function of statistics in controlling verbal behavior.

Absolute Mean Difference

Definition.   The absolute mean difference (AMD) takes an average of the absolute value of all possible differences $\| X_i - X_j \|$, such that $i < j$. The formula for the AMD is given in Fig. 10.6. The AMD therefore represents variability by reflecting the average degree to which we might expect any one value to differ from every value.

For instance, if we calculate the AMD on a data set that contains four values, we would form the following differences:

$$\| X_1 - X_2 \| \quad \| X_1 - X_3 \| \quad \| X_1 - X_4 \|$$
$$\| X_2 - X_3 \| \quad \| X_2 - X_4 \|$$
$$\| X_3 - X_4 \|$$

TABLE 10.3
Standard Deviation, Absolute Mean Difference, and Absolute Mean Ratio Values
Resulting From Data Transformations

Data	Standard Deviation	Absolute Mean Difference	Absolute Mean Ratio
A = {4,2,3,1,3}	1.14	1.4	1.89
A + 10 = {14,12,13,11,13}	1.14	1.4	1.12
A * 10 = {40,20,30,10,30}	11.4	14	1.89

There are $n(n - 1)/2$ such differences. Therefore, the AMD is the sum of the indicated differences divided by 6.

Properties Related to Linear Interval Scales. The appropriateness of the AMD for use on linear interval data may be determined by evaluating its performance under particular transformations of scale values. Consider again the values in Table 10.3. When initial values of X are changed by addition of a constant of 10, the calculated value of the AMD does not change. The reason for this is that differences are not altered by adding a constant to each value. Given this information, we may state the first property of the AMD: that it is transformation invariant by addition or subtraction of a constant.

A second property of the AMD is that it is transformation variant by multiplication or division of a constant. Consider once more the values in Table 10.3. When each value is multiplied by 10, the AMD changes because differences are altered by transformations of multiplication and division. Thus, the AMD is an inappropriate measure of variability on logarithmic interval scales because it varies under transformations that preserve the logarithmic interval features of the scale (see Ellis, 1966). It can also be shown that the AMD, like linear interval graphic displays, will vary under any transformation other than addition of a constant.

Additional Properties of the AMD. There are several other properties of the AMD that are useful, though not directly related to an evaluation of its appropriateness for use as a measure of behavioral variability. Consider the two graphs in Fig. 10.7. Which function appears more variable? Close inspection reveals that they are drawn from a rearrangement of the same data points and are in fact equally variable, but the order of occurrence may have in-

$$\text{AMD} = \frac{2 \sum_{i<j}^{n} |X_i - X_j|}{n(n - 1)}$$

FIG. 10.6. Definitional formula for the Absolute Mean Difference (AMD).

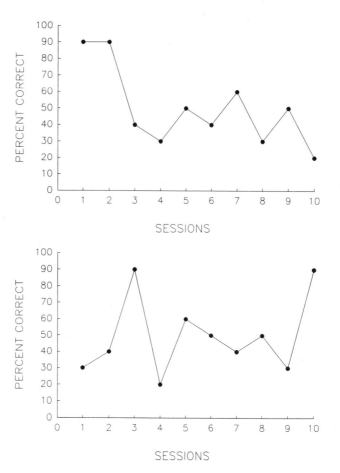

FIG. 10.7. Linear interval graphic representation of two data sets constructed by rearranging the sequence of the same values.

fluenced your judgment. In fact, the AMD values are equivalent for the two sets of data. This illustrates a third property of the AMD—that it is permutation invariant, or not influenced by order of occurrence. This property is important because subjective interpretations based on graphic displays of variability may be influenced by clusters of similar values or extreme differences when they occur in temporal proximity.

A fourth property of the AMD is that it retains the units of measurement of the raw data. The AMD is therefore not a good general descriptor of variability and may not be used to compare variability in behavioral data sets resulting from different dimensional quantities. However, when comparing data sets involving the same quantities, the attached units present no problems.

A fifth property of the AMD is that it has a lower limit of zero and no upper limit. If there is no variability in a set of values (as when all values are equal to each other), computing the AMD will yield a value of zero. If there is a great deal of variability in a set of values, the AMD will reflect this with an appropri-

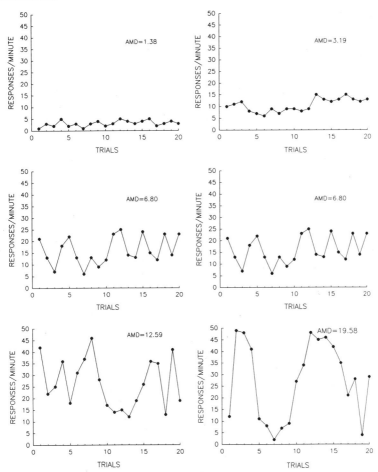

FIG. 10.8.   Six data sets of increasing amounts of variability and obtained AMD values.

ately high value. It has no upper limit. Figure 10.8 shows six hypothetical data sets constructed so as to relate a familiar graphic representation of variability to the AMD values.

Finally, recall that the process of subtraction leaves the units of measurement attached to the AMD values. Whether this is a problem depends on the use to which the statistic is put. If a comparison involves AMD values calculated from measures of the same dimensional quantities and units, there is no problem. If the comparison involves values based on the same quantity (such as duration), but different units (e.g, seconds versus minutes), one of the values must be converted by multiplication or division in order for the comparison to be meaningful. If, however, the dimensional quantities represented by the raw data are not the same (e.g., duration versus force), a comparison in terms of AMD values is not meaningful.

In other words, statistics such as the AMD, which retain the data's units of measurement, limit comparisons to those based on data of like dimensional quantities and cannot serve as a general descriptor of variability. This does not weaken their utility under more parochial circumstances, but it does give ratio-based statistics an important advantage. Aside from the mathematical operations underlying different statistics, the general practice of looking at variability in terms of ratios encourages the development of a more coherent scientific data base than is likely to emerge from a focus on differences. Such an approach allows us to relate our observations to any others in terms of scalers (e.g., "Jones' baseline data from his 1981 paper are 2.4 times as variable as Smith's treatment data in the 1987 article"). The following discussion provides an example of a ratio-based statistic.

Absolute Mean Ratio

Definition. The absolute mean ratio (AMR) is calculated in a similar manner to the AMD except that it takes an average of all possible ratios (X_i/X_j) such that $i < j$. The formula for the AMR is given in Fig. 10.9. (The AMR is the same statistic called Kappa in chapter 17 of Johnston & Pennypacker, 1980.) As can be seen, the formula for the AMR may also be represented as "geometric absolute mean ratio," which may be easily approximated on semilogarithmic graphs. The AMR represents variability by reflecting the average degree to which we might expect any one value to differ from every value (Johnston & Pennypacker, 1980, chapter 17).

For instance, if we calculate the AMR on a data set that contains four values, we would form the following ratios:

$$\| \ln X_1/X_2 \| \quad \| \ln X_1/X_3 \| \quad \| \ln X_1/X_4 \|$$
$$\| \ln X_2/X_3 \| \quad \| \ln X_2/X_4 \|$$
$$\| \ln X_3/X_4 \|$$

There are $n(n - 1)/2$ such ratios. Therefore, the AMR is the sum of the indicated ratios divided by 6.

Properties Related to Logarithmic Scales. Because the AMR is calculated on the basis of ratios, it has a number of properties that are unique to a statistic of this type. For example, the AMR is affected by changes in data that would not affect a statistic that is calculated from differences, such as the AMD. Therefore, the appropriateness of the AMR for use on logarithmic interval data may be determined by evaluating its performance under particular transformations of scale values. Consider again the values in Table 10.3. When initial values of X are multiplied by 10, the calculated value of the AMR does not change. The reason for this is that ratios are not altered by multiplying

$$AMR = antilog \left[\frac{2 \sum_{i<j}^{n} |\ln X_i - \ln X_j|}{n(n - 1)} \right]$$

FIG. 10.9. Definitional formula for the Absolute Mean Ratio (AMR).

each value by a constant. Given this information, we may state the first property of the AMR: It is transformation invariant under multiplication or division by a constant. Note the contrast with the AMD, which varies under multiplication.

A second property of the AMR is that it is transformation variant by addition or subtraction of a constant. Consider once more the values in Table 10.3. When 10 is added to each value of X, the AMR changes because logarithmic interval values are altered by transformations of addition and subtraction. Thus, the AMR is an inappropriate measure of variability on interval scales because it varies under transformations that preserve the linear interval features of the scale. It can also be shown that the AMR, like logarithmic interval graphic displays, will vary under any transformation other than multiplication of a constant.

Additional Properties of the AMR. There are several other properties of the AMR that are useful, though not directly related to an evaluation of its appropriateness for use as a measure of behavioral variability. For instance, as with the AMD, the AMR is permutation invariant. The calculation of the AMR from the data in Fig. 10.7 provides values of 1.77 in both cases.

However, unlike the AMD, the AMR is unitless because like measurement units cancel when placed in ratio to each other. Therefore, the AMR may be used to compare variability in behavioral data sets resulting from different dimensional quantities. Furthermore, because the AMR is invariant to transformations by multiplication and division, it may be used to assess variability across different units of measurement.

A fifth property of the AMR is that it has a lower limit of one and no upper limit. If there is no variability in a set of values (i.e., when all values are equal to each other), the AMR will yield a value of one. If there is a great deal of variability in a set of values, the AMR will reflect this with an appropriately high value. It has no maximum value. In order to suggest the meaning of different values of AMR in a familiar context, the graphs in Fig. 10.10 indicate a wide range of variability and the associated AMR values.

Lastly, the AMR is undefined for zero data values because it is calculated from all possible ratios in a set. If zero occurs in the denominator, division by zero occurs and the result is undefined. This apparent problem raises an interesting but challenging issue that has broad implications for both graphic and quantitative techniques. Should we interpret reports of measurement that detect zero responding in the same manner that we interpret reports that describe some responding? Unfortunately, this topic goes beyond the scope of the present discussion because the solution requires consensus on the meaning of "zero" responding.

Tactics of Descriptive Statistics

The field of behavior analysis partly defines itself by its insistence on maintaining the critical qualities of behavioral data in undiluted form throughout the tortuous processes of inferential statistical machinations (see Reading 8). As a result, we have learned to revere methods of graphic analysis; but, even

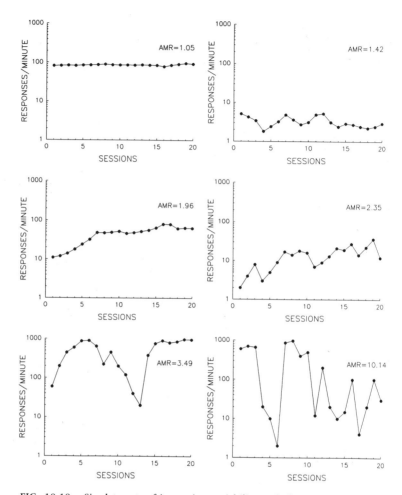

FIG. 10.10.   Six data sets of increasing variability and obtained AMR values.

when used well, they have their limitations and can even be misleading. Describing graphed features of variability in words is often simply too imprecise for our needs. After all, variability is the data of science, and we should work toward the goals of quantification that are so successfully reflected in the natural sciences. It should not be sufficient to say that "responding increased over baseline" when one investigator's "increase" may be quite different from another's.

When properly used, descriptive statistics can increase precision of reference. It is probably more difficult than most realize to detect all of the useful aspects of variation in a set of data merely by examining a graph or two. For instance, consider the five data sets in Fig. 10.11 displayed on linear (left) and logarithmic (right) interval graphs. Attempt to rank each set in terms of variability from least to greatest. Which one is most variable? What are your criteria for this decision? Are you just looking at vertical bounce?

Table 10.4 displays the results of both AMD and AMR calculations from these five data sets. You can see that the question of which set is most variable is

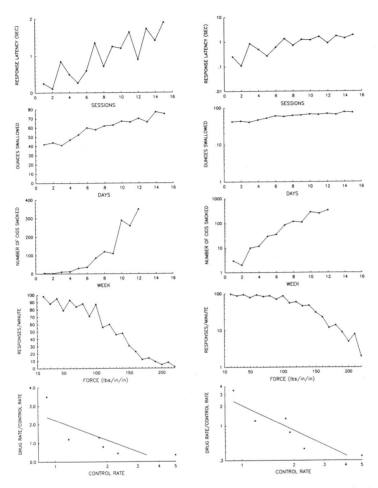

FIG. 10.11.   Five data sets plotted on linear interval scales (left) and logarithmic interval scales (right) representing different degrees of variability.

difficult to answer without quantitative guidance. Furthermore, the answer partly depends on the aspect of variability that is represented by the graphic scale or the statistic that one uses. According to both the AMD and the AMR, Data Set C is the most variable, but the agreement between these two statistics ends there. The AMD finds Data Set E the least variable, whereas the AMR assigns this status to Data Set B. There is no agreement between the two statistics on the other rankings.

The AMD produces its rankings by looking at differences between values, and the larger the differences, the larger the AMD value. Thus, the large differences among Data Set C contrast with the small differences in Data Set E's data, even though the linear scale and its representation on the vertical axis make Data Set E look more variable. If you find it difficult to accept Data Set E as less variable than Data Set C, it is because we have uncritically fallen into the trap of informally evaluating variability primarily in terms of vertical bounce.

In contrast, the AMR makes its evaluations in terms of ratios between values,

TABLE 10.4
Absolute Mean Difference (AMD), and Absolute Mean Ratio (AMR)
Values for Sets A–E in Figure 10.11

Set	AMD	AMR
A	.71	2.64
B	13.72	1.27
C	136.24	8.13
D	28.24	1.61
E	.33	2.52

which often do not correspond to differences. Although it agreed with the AMD on the most variable data set, it found the average ratio in Data Set B less than the average ratio in Data Set E. The AMR also found Data Set A the second most variable set, whereas the AMD described those data as the second least variable set.

Which ranking is correct? This question cannot be answered without specifying the reasons for comparing variability and the aspects of variability that are relevant to the experimental question and the data. For instance, if Data Sets E and B were both generated in support of the same experimental question concerning effects of pharmacological agents on some aspect of behavior, small differences might be quite important. Under this circumstance, the data in Graph E might be described as less variable than those in Set B, as ranked by the AMD. On the other hand, if the question of amount of variability is asked in the abstract, the correct answer depends entirely on how you choose to assess variability.

Although making a general assessment of the degree of variation in these five sets of data is challenging, there are a number of other kinds of information about variability that one might wish to examine. For instance, although one rarely has to rank order data sets in terms of their variability, we often need to know how much variability characterizes sets of data. In the absence of quantifications of variability, this question cannot be answered. Another general aspect of variability is whether it changes under certain conditions and in what specific ways. Applying this curiosity to any of the graphs in Fig. 10.11 should convince one of the need for statistical aids. We briefly consider some of the more common ways of using quantitative procedures.

In describing changes in variability or lack of change, descriptive statistics provide the needed precision and continuity of reference. For example, experimental comparisons that depend on repeated measures of responding under constant conditions within phases require the investigator to make judgments about the stability of growing sets of data in order to decide when a representative picture of responding has been attained.

This task is easily aided by the appropriate statistic. The problem requires a statistic that involves comparisons of all observations with each other (range is often too crude a measure for this task). The simplest approach is to determine the proper scale of analysis based on the characteristics of the data, to calculate either the AMD or the AMR (or some other appropriate statistic) for each phase (or portion of a phase) in question, and then, to compare the outcomes. Although the values generated by this practice would at first be unfamiliar, their pairing with graphic representations of data would soon encourage experimenters to compare the degree of stability attained across phases and even experiments.

A variation of this procedure is to recalculate the AMD or the AMR for the entire data set as each new data point is added. Fig. 10.12 shows graphs of AMR values on the bottom left and right that were calculated from the baseline and experimental phases, respectively, of the upper graph. Notice from the baseline graph of AMR values (lower left) that the function approaches a horizontal asymptote. This indicates that the data are increasingly stable.

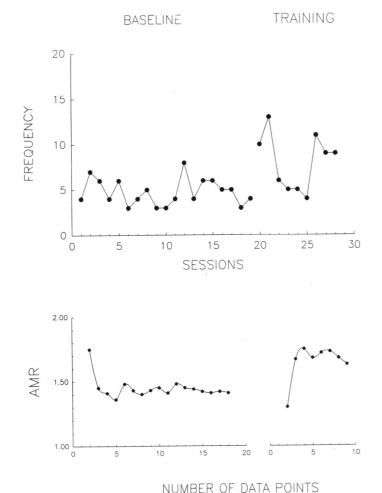

FIG. 10.12.   Graphs of baseline and experimental phases of an experiment (top graph) and graphs of AMR values calculated as data points accumulate for the baseline phase (lower left graph), and for the experimental phase (lower right graph).

However, also notice that the graph of AMR outcomes obtained from the experimental phase (lower right) is not approaching an asymptote, indicating that a steady state has not been achieved. Care should be taken in using this technique because the influence of additional data values decreases as the total number of values in the calculation increases. This problem can be avoided by calculating the statistic based on a fixed number of the most recent consecutive sessions.

In the event that the data show change correlated with the passage of time, we may still assess stability by performing a time-series analysis and calculating one of these statistics based on comparisons among the actual data values and the predicted ones from the time-dependent function. Figure 10.13 is taken from Johnston and Pennypacker (1980, chapter 17) to illustrate this tactic in the case of the AMR. The time series generated the smooth line, and ratios were calculated between observed values and their predicted counterparts. This process yields a value that will vary inversely with the stability of the data.

Another common analytical need is to evaluate changes in variability in order to relate them to systematic variations in treatment conditions. The AMD and the AMR can similarly be used to evaluate changes in variability across and within experimental phases. Consider the data plotted in Fig. 10.14 on logarithmic interval (bottom) linear interval (top) scales. We may calculate the same statistic for each phase and compare the outcomes in the form of a ratio to get a measure of relative change in variability across phases (note that the units of measurement attached to AMD values cancel as a result). When this is done, we see that the experimental phase is only 63% as variable as the baseline phase in terms of the AMR and 67% as variable in terms of the AMD. This is difficult if not impossible to determine from the graphic display alone.

We have described some analytical tactics that may enhance the likelihood that the experimenter's interpretations will be under effective control of the study's procedures and the real variability represented in the data. We have argued that no single analytical technique should be considered sufficient or correct. A search for those procedures that may be usefully revealing should take into account the implications that the phenomenon of behavior have for

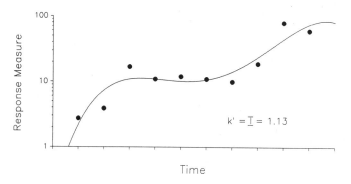

FIG. 10.13. Graph illustrating the difference between an obtained time-series function and actual data points used to quantify time-dependent variability.

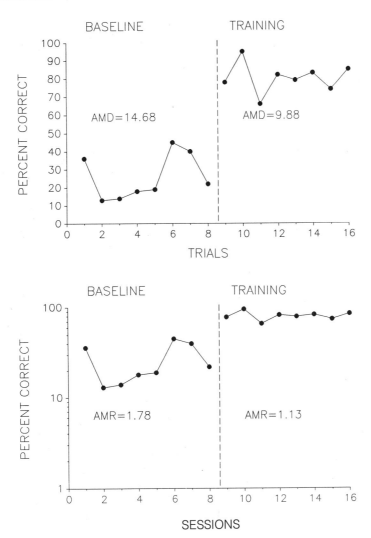

FIG. 10.14. AMD and AMR values for baseline and experimental phases that may be placed in ratio to each other to get a measure of relative change in variability across phases.

how we describe and talk about variability. Measurement scales are the mathematical rules under which we conduct and describe measurement of behavior, and analytical techniques must be evaluated under these constraints.

The field of behavior analysis is unique among the natural sciences in being able to approach the behavior of its researchers with the same understanding that it brings to the investigation of its subjects' behavior. We should therefore be able to appreciate that our understanding of the nature of behavioral variability and our approach to its experimental treatment and interpretation provides unavoidable and powerful limits to the effectiveness of our scientific and technological research enterprise. Although we have not tried to describe contemporary practices in the field, even casual inspection will show that the treatment of variability in behavioral data can be improved. In doing so, we should remember that the most general strategy is to bring our verbal behavior under effective control of the behavior of our experimental subjects.

Logic, Reasoning, and Verbal Behavior

INTRODUCTION

Skinner outlined a conceptual framework for the experimental analysis of verbal behavior in 1957 with the publication of his book, *Verbal Behavior*. However, experimental research based explicitly on this framework has emerged only in recent years. This still sparse body of work included research on the verbal operant classes of mands and tacts (Hall & Chase, 1986; Lamarre & Holland, 1985), echoics (Boe & Winokur, 1978a, 1978b), and intraverbals (Braam & Poling, 1983; Chase, Johnson, & Sulzer-Azaroff, 1985). In addition, research on the independence of speaking and listening (Lee, 1981) and on self-editing (Hyten & Chase, 1986) has been inspired by Skinner's work. This conceptual framework has also been utilized in analyses of verbal discourse in group psychotherapy (McLeish & Martin, 1975), maladaptive verbal behavior of the psychotherapy client (Glenn, 1983), auditory hallucinations (Burns, Heiby, & Tharp, 1983), and instructional design (Johnson & Chase, 1981).

Skinner (1957b) also devoted a chapter of his book to an analysis of logical and scientific verbal behavior (chapter 18), and this analysis has been elucidated by Schnaitter (1980). Human logicality and reasoning have been topics of investigation in psychology for decades (for reviews, see Evans, 1982; Falmagne, 1975; Revlin & Mayer, 1978; Watson & Johnson-Laird, 1968). However, logic and reasoning involve verbal behavior and both interpretative and experimental analysis based on Skinner's framework are therefore appropriate. In this reading, the concepts of logic and reasoning are briefly analyzed in this conceptual context. First, we describe and interpret the concept of proposition in behavioral terms. Then, we analyze premises and conclusions, rules of logic, deductive reasoning, and inductive reasoning as verbal behavior.

THE PROPOSITION

The proposition is a basic component of logic and reasoning. Traditionally, the proposition has been conceptualized in the following manner. There are acts in which one may engage that require some sort of object for their execution. These acts are depicted by the transitive verbs. For example, in order to *hit*, there must be *something* to hit. This something, the object of the action, is depicted by the accusative of the transitive verb. Some transitive verbs depict what have been called acts of thinking (e.g., to know, believe, or assume). To "know, believe, or assume" requires knowing, believing or assuming something. These somethings, the accusatives of the acts of thinking, have come to be called propositions. A proposition is what it is that one can know, believe, think, judge, assume, opine, and so forth (Ryle, 1971). When an individual states or expresses what it is that he or she knows, that individual has emitted behavior that can be analyzed in Skinner's framework (1957b).

To begin such an analysis, consider the behavior–environment relation that Skinner (1957b) called the tact (chapter 5) because it will later be shown that tacts and propositions are closely related. A particular form of verbal response is consistently reinforced in the presence of a particular object or event (e.g., a ball) or a property of an object or event (e.g., its roundness). If the object or event controls the response, it is typically called a pure tact. If only some property of the object or event controls the response, it is called an abstract tact. Therefore, any given object may evoke several verbal responses, some that are pure tacts and others that are abstract tacts controlled by the object properties.

Rather than simply emitting the different forms of tacts separately (e.g., "ball," "round"), an additional response is often emitted that connects the tacts (e.g., "The ball *is* round"). Skinner (1957b) called this additional response, "is," the assertive autoclitic and stated that its function is to enjoin the listener to "accept a given state of affairs" (p. 326). One might say that the roundness of the ball is the state of affairs asserted by the speaker. However, it may be more useful to consider that the proposition, "The ball is round," tacts a relation between the pure and abstract tacts "ball" and "round." It is not the roundness of the ball that evokes the entire response, "The ball is round." It is the relations among the object and each of its properties, as well as the respective tacts controlled by them, that evoke the utterances of the proposition. This is essentially a case of predication (see Skinner, 1957b, pp. 334–335).

The concept of the tact relates verbal behavior to nonverbal characteristics of the environment (e.g., objects and properties of objects). However, a substantial portion of the human environment includes verbal stimuli (e.g., the verbal behavior of other individuals). Verbal behavior related to these aspects of the environment is called intraverbal (see Skinner, 1957b, pp. 71–78). Sometimes, subjects and predicates of propositions may be related intraverbally, rather than tactually, to the environment. The emission of such a response tacts the relation between the intraverbals and their stimulating circumstances (e.g., " 'John' is a proper noun").

Finally, it is not unusual for the proposition to include a quantifying autoclitic (see Skinner, 1957b, p. 329–330). Under certain circumstances, the tact "swan" becomes "the swan" or "a swan." Other circumstances may evoke discriminative behavior in the form of the response "some swans," "all swans," or "no swans." Skinner asserted that, as autoclitic components, these responses do not modify the subject of the proposition. Instead, their effect is to modify the reaction of the listener to the responses they accompany. "All" is "more appropriately taken as equivalent to *always* or *always it is possible to say*" (Skinner, 1957b, p. 329). Schoenfield (1969) described a relationship between the universal proposition (e.g., "All swans are white") and the behavioral tendency toward generalization. Such a response cannot possibly be under the control of all the swans in the universe. Yet, enough exposure to reinforcing consequences in the presence of variations of stimulus conditions will result in highly generalized stimulus control. The universal proposition tacts the relation between the stimuli, the responses, and the generalization of stimulus control.

In summary, the proposition is a complex verbal response that comprises tacts or intraverbals modified by particular autoclitics, such as "is," "all," or "some." As a unit of behavior, the proposition functions as a tact in that it is controlled by the objects of simple tacts or intraverbals and the relations between verbal behavior and its environmental control. In other words, when we say, "The ball is round," we tact not only the ball and its roundness, but our tendency to predicate roundness to the ball (Skinner, 1957b, pp. 334–335).

Having described the speaker's verbal behavior involved in uttering a proposition, we may now examine the effects of such behavior on a listener. If behavior produces reinforcing consequences, we may say that it is effective. Responses producing consequences that reduce the likelihood of future occurrences of a response class may be considered ineffective. This argument is analogous to the adaptiveness of characteristics that are exhibited during the evolution of a species (Skinner, 1984a). The verbal utterance of a proposition may be effective or ineffective in producing reinforcing consequences. The emission of a proposition may be reinforced when a listener accepts or believes it. According to Skinner (1957b), "Our belief in what someone tells us is . . . a function of, or identical with, our tendency to act upon the verbal stimuli which he provides" (p. 160). Therefore, the utterance of a proposition may be effective (i.e., accepted or believed by a listener) regardless of its correspondence to any state of affairs or whether it is considered to be true. Likewise, all utterance may be ineffective (i.e., rejected or ignored by a listener) regardless of its truth.

Additionally, the listener's behavior in response to the proposition may also be classified as effective or ineffective. Again, behavior that produces reinforcement is considered effective. Whether the behavior of accepting or rejecting a proposition produces reinforcing consequences may have something to do with the "truth" of the statement. Skinner (1974) stated that "a proposition is true to the extent that with its help the listener responds effectively to the situation it describes" (p. 235). This statement applies to tacts in general. Again, according to Skinner (1957b), "behavior in the form of the tact works for the benefit of the listener by extending his contact with the environment, and such behavior is set up in the verbal community for this reason" (p. 85).

In summary, the utterance of a proposition has been defined as effective in two ways. First, if the listener accepts or acts upon the proposition as a verbal stimulus, it has been effective. Second, if the behavior of accepting it produces reinforcing consequences, the proposition is again effective. A precise definition of truth as an epistemological issue is not required by a behavioristic analysis of the utterance of propositions. According to Zuriff (1980):

> Because of a specific phylogenetic and cultural history, humans have evolved so that they are affected in certain ways by verbal behavior, that is they believe certain verbal behavior to be true. For the most part they do so without applying any explicit criteria of truth but rather because of human nature. (p. 348)

Exactly how and why any given proposition comes to be accepted as true by a listener is a problem for empirical psychology (Popper, 1959).

REASONING

Premises and Conclusions

If the listener's behavior of accepting a proposition is reinforcing to a speakers's behavior, the speaker may engage in responses that will increase the probability of that reinforcing consequence. This supplementary behavior may be considered verbal to the extent that it is also reinforced by the listener's response. For example, a speaker may increase the probability of a listener accepting a proposition (i.e., reinforcing the speaker's behavior) by emitting other propositions that are more readily accepted by the listener. In the traditional language of logicians, these more readily accepted propositions are called premises, and the proposition whose acceptability is subsequently enhanced is called the conclusion. The acceptance of the premises is assumed to be at a greater strength in the listener's behavioral repertoire than the acceptance of the unpremised conclusions. In some cases, the speaker may preface the premises with the mand "Suppose that . . ." This utterance may then facilitate the acceptance of the conclusion.

In colloquial language, the speaker is attempting to "prove a point," "support a conclusion," or "convince" the listener of a proposition's truth, viability, or possibility. For example, a prosecutor may assert or propose that a defendant is guilty of some crime. The acceptance of this proposition by the members of a jury will be reinforcing to the prosecutor. By itself, the single proposition may have a minimal effect on the jury members' behavior. Therefore, the prosecutor produces other assertions that members of the jury readily accept as true. These assertions essentially describe the evidence for the conclusion (e.g., defendant was present at scene of crime; weapon was found in defendant's possession; defendant's alibi is weak, etc.). If these premises have the intended effect on the jury's behavior, it is more likely that a guilty verdict will be returned. Thus, the members of the jury will have accepted the prosecutor's original proposition and probably reinforced that verbal behavior.

The emission of propositions in such a manner constitutes a pattern of verbal behavior that is traditionally called *reasoning*. Speakers reason with listeners when they emit verbal behavior that alters the probability of the listener accepting certain propositions. In the previous example, the prosecutor provides reasons for the jury to accept the proposition that the defendant is guilty. Speakers are also said to reason when they emit propositions with higher levels of acceptability (premises) and thereby produce verbal stimuli that facilitate the emission of a concluding proposition. Premises may be emitted in spoken or written form and may occur in different orders or sequences. The products of this behavior, the verbal stimuli, may then set the occasion for new propositions to be emitted. We say that conclusions have been drawn or inferred from the premises. Acceptance of conclusions, or, rather, effective behavior in response to conclusions may reinforce the pattern of behavior that produced them.

Examples of this kind of behavior are ubiquitous in science. The behavior of the scientific theoretician includes a "set of manipulative responses directed, not at the natural subject matter of the science, but at the verbal record of that subject matter, the data" (Schnaitter, 1980, p. 159). Verbal responses tacting the results of experimental manipulations set the occasion for the emission of other verbal responses (i.e., conclusions are drawn and theories are proposed). Similarly, some scientists may respond to a number of different theories by emitting a proposition that must be true if the theories (or premises) are true (i.e., a hypothesis). The research scientist then goes on to test this proposition experimentally.

Nonscientific verbal behavior may also involve inferring or drawing conclusions. For example, a salesperson may provide reasons for buying a particular product at a particular time. The reasons may be acceptable to a potential buyer and ultimately occasion the emission of the conclusion, "Now is the time to buy this item."

In summary, a speaker may emit statements in ways that influence a listener's acceptance or emission of other statements. Specifically, the emission of the premises affects the acceptance or emission of conclusions. Two senses of such verbal reasoning have been described in terms of the behavior of the speaker and listener. In one sense, a listener's behavior of accepting a conclusion is modified when a speaker emits more readily accepted premises. In another sense, a listener's behavior of emitting a conclusion is modified when premises are emitted in a particular manner. In either case, the speaker and listener may be two (or more) different people or may be the same person. One may prove a point to oneself as well as to someone else. Likewise, one may draw one's own inferences as well as inspire someone else to draw them.

The manner in which premises have such effects on conclusions is the topic of the remaining sections of this paper. After a discussion of "rules" as descriptions of regularity in patterns of behavior, we present analyses of the concepts of deductive and inductive reasoning.

Logicality and Rules

Physical events occur in time, and the temporal sequence in which they occur may be described as a pattern of events. As a subset of physical events, behavior also occurs in temporal sequences or patterns. Some patterns occur at a higher frequency than others, and these patterns come to be recognized as regularities or consistencies in nature. Verbal behavior may tact patterns of events in the same way that it tacts single events. Verbal behavior that tacts consistent patterns in nature generally results in statements that are typically called rules. For example, certain forms of verbal behavior described as grammatical are patterns of behavioral regularities with which we are familiar as rules. As verbal responses, rules tact not specific events but the relationships among the events (i.e., the consistent or regular patterns in which the events occur).

These verbal responses (rules) may originate as descriptions of regularity; however, they may very often become prescriptive by aiding in the verbal control of human behavior. For example, the rules of grammar describe some consistencies in the reinforcement practices of members of a verbal community (Skinner, 1957b). These descriptions of reinforcement contingencies do not necessarily affect the events they describe. They are verbal descriptions, not the contingencies themselves. However, the rules may be "helpful in instruction and in maintaining verbal behavior in conformity with the usages of the community" (Skinner, 1984b, p. 585).

It is important to distinguish between rule-governed or rule-following behavior and rule-characterized behavior. Although any given set of responses may be described as corresponding to some rule, the rule, as a description of the contingency, does not necessarily control the behavior. The contingency itself may control the behavior. For example, an individual may be described as speaking grammatically, although the verbal behavior is entirely under the control of the prevailing social contingencies. This behavior may be called rule-corresponding or rule-characterized, but it is not rule-following or rule-governed. However, the cautious writer or a speaker of a foreign language may consult a rule book, such as a style manual or dictionary, before emitting a statement. Such verbal behavior may be considered rule-following to the extent that the verbal stimuli, the rules, control the behavior; however, additional control exerted by prevailing social contingencies is not to be understated.

Furthermore, the degree of control exerted by a verbal statement of contingencies may shift in the ontogenetic development of behavior (Buskist & Miller, 1986; although cf. Hayes, Brownstein, Haas, & Greenway, 1986). An individual learning a second language may first learn the rules of grammar for that language, and for some time those rules may be meticulously consulted before each utterance. However, once fluent, the speaker usually no longer consults rules before speaking. Rather the verbal behavior comes under the control of the foreign verbal community's reinforcement contingencies.

With regard to reasoning, there are consistencies in the way premises might be emitted in altering the probability that a conclusion will be emitted or accepted. Certain patterns or arrangements of premises are more effective than others in facilitating the emission or enhancing the acceptability of conclusions. A description of these consistencies may be stated in terms of the reinforcement practices of a particular verbal community, such as the logical/ scientific or the lay verbal communities. Furthermore, descriptions of consistencies in reinforcement practices with regard to the emission and acceptance of propositions might be called the rules of logicality.

The rules of logic, sometimes called the rules of deductive inference (which are discussed more extensively in the next section), may be considered as a more formalized subset of the rules of logicality. At this point, the rules of logicality may be described as the broad set of verbal responses that are tactually related to regularities in propositional verbal behavior (i.e., patterns of proposition utterances). When the emission of propositions corresponds to such rules, the probability of reinforcement (i.e., the acceptance of the conclusion or the emission of an effective conclusion) is maximal. Because arranging and emitting propositions is a verbal process, the rules of logicality may, along with the rules of grammar, be considered a subset of the rules of language (i.e., the descriptions of consistencies and regularities in the general reinforcement practices of a verbal community).

Again, any given set of responses, such as those constituting a logical discourse, may be considered rule-characterized or rule-following depending on the nature of the controlling variables. A student of logic may consult the rules of deductive inference to draw a conclusion from a set of premises; yet an experienced logician may derive conclusions from premises much in the same way that the experienced poet thinks in a particular poetic meter (Skinner, 1957b, p. 422). In fact, it is highly probable that logical verbal behavior emerges or develops in the normal course of human development under processes similar to those in the development of verbal behavior in general (e.g., Inhelder & Piaget, 1958, 1969).

Deductive Reasoning

In the traditional language of logicians, it is possible to arrange propositions in such a manner that the conclusion is necessarily true, given premises that are true. That is, given an arrangement of propositions that may be said to correspond to an actual state of affairs, a concluding proposition can be formulated that also corresponds to the particular state of affairs. The form of such arrangements these propositions must take are characterized by the formal rules of logic, sometimes called the rules of deductive inference. Behaviorally restated, patterns of verbal response forms may consistently produce effective behavior on the part of the listener (i.e., acceptance of emission of effective conclusions). The rules of deductive inference describe the patterns of behavior that have a high probability of reinforcement. As a subset of the rules of logicality, these rules are verbal responses that tact the relations among behavioral events of emitting premises and emitting and accepting conclusions (i.e., verbal reasoning).

To illustrate, consider three ways that logicians describe the relations among propositions: conjunction, disjunction, and implication. A conjunction is a combination of two propositions. The verbal response "and" functions to connect two responses that may just as easily have been emitted separately (e.g., "It is Friday, and I am writing"). The emission of two propositions connected in such a manner constitutes a more complex propositional response, if only for the effect it has on the listener. If a listener accepts any two simple propositions, it is most probable that a conjunctive proposition (i.e., the two simple propositions connected by the response "and") will be accepted. This is the deductive inference rule called conjunction. Alternatively, if a listener accepts a conjunctive proposition, the behavior of emitting any one of the conjuncts will most likely be accepted. This is the rule of simplification.

Two propositions are said to be disjuncted when they are connected by the response "or" (e.g., "Either class has been canceled, or I'm in the wrong room"). If a disjunctive proposition is accepted as a premise, and if a second premise negating one of the disjuncts is also accepted, it is most probable that a conclusion in the form of the other disjunct will be accepted. This is the rule of disjunctive syllogism. Acceptance of the premises "Class has been canceled, or I'm in the wrong room" and "I'm not in the wrong room" facilitates the acceptance or emission of the conclusion, "Class has been canceled."

Another pattern of behavior is described in the deductive rule called addition. Any single true proposition may be disjunctively connected to any other proposition. This pattern of behavior may not occur very often in ordinary discourse. According to Braine (1978), "If p is already established, there is no reason to want to infer the weaker statement, p or q, which suggests doubt about p" (p. 14). It may be true that anyone who accepts the simple proposition will also accept the disjunctive proposition (although it is an empirical issue), but it is unclear what function such a pattern of verbal behavior might have.

An implication is another case of two simple propositions connected by an additional verbal response. The responses that make this connection take various forms, such as "If . . . , then . . ." or "implies." This kind of proposition may function as a tact of intraverbal relations, such as class inclusion (e.g., "If you have a cat, then you have a pet") or definition (e.g., "If one of the angles is 90 degrees, then it is a right triangle"). It may also tact a contingency (e.g., "If you are late, then I'll leave without you") or a causal relation (e.g., "Combustion implies the presence of oxygen"). If a listener accepts such a proposition, and if the listener further accepts a simple proposition that constitutes the antecedent of the implication, it is most probable that the listener will accept the simple proposition that constitutes the consequent of the implication. This is the rule of *modus ponens*. Acceptance of the proposition that combustion implies oxygen and that combustion is present facilitates the acceptance of the proposition that oxygen is present. Alternatively, if a listener accepts an implication and further accepts a proposition negating the consequent, it is most probable that the listener will accept a conclusion negating the antecedent. This is the rule of *modus tollens*. Acceptance of the premises that combustion implies oxygen and that oxygen is not present will facilitate the acceptance of the conclusion that combustion is not present.

Other rules of deductive inference (e,g., hypothetical syllogism, De Morgan's theorem, exportation) may be described in a similar manner. A person reasons deductively when the emission of propositions corresponds to these formal rules of logic. Again, deductive reasoning is not necessarily an instance of rule-governed behavior. An individual's behavior may be partially under the control of verbal stimuli constituting these rules. "Rules of evidence in a court of law restrict the verbal behavior of witnesses, the rules of chess restrict the movements of the pieces, logical rules have a comparable effect on the logician" (Skinner, 1957b, p. 423). However, evidence of rule following is not required. The reasoning is deductive simply if the behavior can be characterized or described by these rules.

Inductive Reasoning

We have suggested that rules of deductive inference are descriptions of reinforcement contingencies for effective sequences of proposition utterances. Premises can be constructed and arranged in ways that may enhance the acceptability of a conclusion but do not correspond to the rules of deductive inference. This kind of verbal behavior may be called inductive reasoning. We do not argue for a functional distinction between inductive and deductive patterns of verbal behavior. The distinction originated in the writings of logicians, but from a behavioral perspective, the distinction seems topographical in nature. Behavior is called deductive reasoning simply if it can be related to the rules of deductive inference, whether legitimate or fallacious. Although logicians find the definition of inductive reasoning difficult, behavior is generally labeled as inductive if it leads to conclusions that are only probably true. In other words, inductive reasoning is not defined in terms of a set of formal rules. There are consistencies in the patterns of behavior called inductive reasoning, and these consistencies may be described as rules from a behavioristic perspective.

Consider, for example, J. S. Mill's (1843/1973) methods of inductive inference. Mill maintained that there are some consistencies in the way one discovers and demonstrates causal relations in scientific investigation. If one observes a common variable in several otherwise disparate circumstances, that variable may be inferred to be the cause, or effect, of the phenomenon under investigation. This is Mill's Method of Agreement. If a number of people all exhibit some similar disease symptomatology and these people have no common history except a deficit of fresh fruit and vegetables in their diet, it might be inferred that the lack of fresh fruit and vegetables is a cause of their illness.

Mill's Method of Differences may be considered in a similar manner. If an event occurs in the presence of some other event, and never in its absence, it may be inferred that the two events are causally related. This kind of causality may be more widely accepted as necessary conditionality. Combustion may occur in the presence of oxygen (as well as additional necessary conditions), but never in the absence of it.

Another inductive practice is reasoning by analogy. A number of events, objects, or circumstances are described as having a number of common properties or characteristics. If several of these events, objects, or circumstances have an additional common characteristic, it is inferred by analogy that the remaining circumstances also have the additional characteristic. For example, if John, Bob, and Paula are all graduates of the same school and have all attained satisfying careers, and Jane is also a graduate of that school, we may conclude that Jane is likely to attain a satisfying career. This kind of reasoning may be the result of the behavioral phenomenon of stimulus generalization. If verbal responses are reinforced in the presence of a particular discriminative stimulus, other stimuli that have physical characteristics in common with the discriminative stimulus may also control similar verbal responding.

Other patterns of verbal behavior in which premises affect the acceptability of conclusions are described as logical fallacies. It is common for the affirmed consequent of an implication to increase the acceptability of an affirmed antecedent as a conclusion. Logicians call this pattern of discourse *illicit modus ponens*. For instance, "If it rained last night, then the ground will be wet this morning. It did not rain last night, therefore the ground is not wet."

Although these patterns do not correspond to the rules of deductive inference, they may occasionally, if not frequently, produce reinforcement (i.e., effective behavior of accepting the conclusion). These patterns of behavior are considered to be cases of fallacious reasoning, although sometimes what superficially appears to be a case of illicit modus ponens (or tollens) is actually deductively legitimate. For example, denying the antecedent or affirming the consequent of an implication that functions as a definitional tact is deductively valid (e.g., "If 90 degrees, then right angle").

Mill's methods, analogical reasoning, and some of the deductive fallacies are examples of verbal behavior patterns that may have a high probability of reinforcement. The legitimacy of inductively derived conclusions, in terms of correspondence with actual states of affairs, has been an epistemological controversy since the time of Hume (1748/1955). The probability that such conclusions are accepted by a listener and the effects of various propositional manipulations on that probability are empirical issues suitable for experimental psychology.

If a pattern of behavior produces more reinforcement than other patterns, we may expect that pattern to be of greater strength than other patterns in the repertoire of an individual. The behavior is explained or justified by reference to the reinforcement process that maintains the behavior. To say that deductive reasoning is justified by the rules of deductive inference may mean nothing more than that the behavior is adequately reinforced in the verbal community, and the rules of inference describe the reinforcement contingencies. If patterns of inductive reasoning are similarly maintained by the verbal community, they are similarly justified. We may call this justification psychological rather than logical.

In other words, the psychological justification of behavior lies in an understanding of reinforcement contingencies. The reinforcement contingencies for inductive behavior have been studied in the context of generalization. In fact, "inductive inference" and "induction" are expressions that have been used traditionally to describe the same phenomena that we now call generalization from experience or stimulus generalization. Consider Mill's observation, "The child, who having burnt his fingers, avoids to thrust them again into the fire, has reasoned or inferred, though he has never thought of the general maxim, Fire burns" (1843/1973, p. 188). Skinner (1953) described it in behavioristic language: "The spread of effect to other stimuli is called generalization or induction" (p. 132). Finally, Sidman (1960) explicitly stated, "Induction is a behavioral process. . . . Whether or not we make an inductive inference, and the degree of tenacity to which we cling to that inference, will depend upon our behavioral history (experience)" (p. 59).

The patterns of nonverbal behavior that may be called inductive reasoning or inference are the same patterns that are explained in the body of knowledge constituting the science of behavior. Skinner (1957b) proposed that verbal behavior be analyzed in the same manner as nonverbal behavior, and there is no reason to account for verbal inductive reasoning in any other way. The present analysis extends this approach to the deductive patterns that have been the subject of traditional logical investigation.

SUMMARY

An analysis of verbal reasoning and logical verbal behavior begins with an analysis of the proposition. Stating propositions involves emitting verbal responses that are related as tacts to their environmental circumstances and to typical relations between similar circumstances and verbal behavior in general. This kind of verbal behavior may be considered effective if it produces reinforcing consequences, such as acceptance by a listener.

Some propositions may be rendered more acceptable to a listener when they accompany other, more readily acceptable propositions called premises. Verbal reasoning involves altering the probability that conclusions will be accepted or emitted by emitting and manipulating premises. Any consistencies in patterns of reasoning that have high probabilities of reinforcement may be described by a set of contingencies that may be called the rules of logicality. Behavior that corresponds to such rules, but is not necessarily under the control of verbal descriptions of the contingencies, has a high probability of producing reinforcement.

One subset of the rules of logicality is the set of rules of deductive inference. It is said that correspondence to these rules guarantees the truth of conclusions given the truth of premises. The rules may describe patterns of reasoning that have a high probability of being accepted by a listener. There are no formal rules of inductive inference, but consistencies in patterns of inductive reasoning can be described and related to basic principles of behavior. Consistencies in the reinforcement practices for verbal inductive reasoning remain a topic for behavior analysis.

An experimental analysis of the verbal behavior involve in logic and reasoning may uncover functional relations that will enhance a person's effectiveness with regard to the reinforcing environment. Some of the relevant behavioral issues have already been raised. How does logicality develop in the human repertoire? How do propositions develop or emerge from simple tacts and intraverbals? What factors control the acceptance of the premises of a logical discourse? How well do the rules of deductive inference describe the behavioral effects of deductive reasoning? What are the variables that affect the acceptance (or emission) of inductive conclusions? These are only a few of the questions that the science of behavior must address in the study of reasoning and logical verbal behavior.

On the Relation Between Generalization and Generality

The astute student of behavioral psychology may have noticed the terms generalization and generality share the same stem word. At first glance, this relation may appear simple enough—both have something to do with the "generalness" of environmental control over behavior, generalization referring to a particular behavioral process and generality referring to one kind of characteristic of behavioral data. However, the relation between these two ubiquitous terms is more complex and subtle than this, and how well we understand this relation has important and pervasive consequences for our science and our technology. The purpose of this reading is to examine these terms and their relation to one another so as to improve progress toward a more mature science and more effective technology.

Stimulus generalization and response generalization are related but different behavioral processes (Sidman, 1960). Stimulus generalization refers only to the fact that when responses are reinforced in the presence of one stimulus, they may also occur (although possibly with lesser frequency) to other similar but different stimuli. Response generalization adds that with such a training history, similar but different responses may be evoked by the stimulus previously paired with reinforcement. These brief descriptions are more fully developed in many sources, and their explanation is relatively well understood (Mackintosh, 1977; Rilling, 1977; Terrace, 1966).

These two effects of differential reinforcement are understandably important in applied sciences. Therapeutic efforts are of little value if their effects are exhibited only under a single set of stimulus conditions or in the presence of a single stimulus, such as the therapist or experimenter. In the interest of both effectiveness as well as efficiency, it is imperative that behavioral changes produced under special training conditions often also occur under nontraining circumstances.

This is the goal with which behavior modifiers have long been preoccupied.

However, an uncritical use of terminology and a general misunderstanding of behavior processes has led to a serious misinterpretation of the problem. The term generalization is often used as a shorthand for the phrase stimulus generalization or as an incomplete reference to both stimulus and response generalization. These are only minor matters, however, compared to the more serious error of using generalization as a catch-all description and explanation of any appropriate change occurring in a nontraining setting. This kind of usage is misleading in that it suggests that a single phenomenon is at work when actually a number of different phenomena need to be described, explained, and controlled. The consequences of this problem pervade our understanding of behavioral change in nontraining settings and thus our efforts to engineer such changes successfully.

The assumption that obtaining generalization is the essence of the challenge is a serious underestimation of the task of behavioral control that must be faced. To the extent that training procedures have established some degree of stimulus control, it is indeed important to so design modification efforts in other settings that the utility of this control over responding is maximized in a therapeutic direction. But even this is an inadequate perspective. It is necessary to design the training procedure from the beginning in such a way that stimulus control is created in training settings that will have maximum behavioral influence in nontraining settings (Baer, Wolf, & Risley, 1968). For example, in an elementary school setting, we might take pains to establish other children as discriminative stimuli for appropriate behavior instead of the homeroom teacher. When the child was in other classes, we would not lose control of the homeroom teacher but would possibly benefit from the influence of the continued presence of other children setting the occasion for appropriate behavior (Johnston & Johnston, 1972).

However, carefully designing procedures to optimize the contributions of stimulus and response generalization would hardly exhaust our repertoire of tactics for getting the subject to behave in a desirable way in nontraining settings. Our successes will be more frequent when we realize that maximizing behavioral influence in such settings requires careful consideration of all behavioral principles and processes. We are expecting too much from the phenomena of stimulus and response generalization under the conditions of a nontraining setting (regardless of how well our training procedures are designed to facilitate generalization) if we think that it is robust enough to maintain or produce desired responding in the face of a different set of environmental stimuli. Although this might on occasion be the case, more often, appropriate behavior change in nontraining settings will require implementing a somewhat different set of therapeutic conditions, preferably more closely approximating the natural characteristics of the untampered-with environment with less interference from the therapist (e.g., Risley, 1968; Risley & Wolf, 1967).

This burden cannot be placed on the back of generalization alone. Behavioral practitioners must consider extending the initial behavior change to other settings as a necessary and integral part of the overall project, which must receive the same care and attention in environmental design and arrangement as is given to the setting and behavior of primary interest—though perhaps with the different goal of less artificial sources of control (Baer et al., 1968).

At this point, however, we are no longer talking only about generalization. Stimulus and response generalization are only two of the many weapons in our arsenal that can be used to extend initial training to other responses and circumstances. All of the other principles of behavior that were used to modify responding in the first place must be a part of the modification efforts under any other conditions of interest. Describing or explaining such changes solely as generalization is incorrect. Indeed, the applied literature rarely provides empirical evidence that generalization is the behavioral process at work when changes in target responding are observed in nontraining settings. Nor does it seem that the more general term transfer is necessary or adequate. Ever since Thorndike (1903) talked about the identical elements theory of transfer, it has merely been a less popular synonym for generalization.

In fact, there does not appear to be a distinct phenomena, effect, or process to describe, and there is a danger in any summary term that disguises the actual principles at work. It is simply that the behavior modifier's job is not finished until the subject is behaving appropriately in all of the desired settings. It is only an apparent misunderstanding of that task that seems to necessitate a distinct characterization. Instead of referring to how generalization or transfer was or was not obtained, we should describe the exact procedures (and their rationale in behavioral principles) by which environmental control was arranged in the necessary settings of interest (primary and secondary) and the results that were forthcoming. Even the traditional distinction between training and nontraining settings is somewhat misleading in that it encourages the view that variables are manipulated only up to a certain point, and then the behavior modifier stops and hopes that further changes occur. If behavioral change in some setting is of any interest (even secondary), perhaps it should not be considered a nontraining setting.

This perspective may have stemmed from the dangerous belief that, by producing behavioral change, the individual has somehow been changed and that it is this changed person who goes into other settings. It must be remembered that we do not change or control the individual's behavior—the environment does. We only control the environment, and its influence on the behavior of the individual must be continuing. At no point does behavior become permanently self-supporting or independent of environmental control (Skinner, 1953).

Of course this is not to deny that, eventually, no further artificial manipulations may be needed in a project to produce appropriate responding in all desired settings. But to describe that fact as the result of the process of generalization is to ignore the many other processes of environmental control that may contribute to such a result, such as (a) the nature of the response class originally selected for modification, or (b) the contingencies of reinforcement that were arranged, or (c) the contingencies for that response class that exist in other settings, or (d) uncontrolled behavioral changes that indirectly result from treatment.

It can also be argued that this whole perspective surrounding generalization is dangerously close to a mentalistic concept masquerading in behavioral raiment. This view of generalization subtly forces our use of it as a hypothetical cognitive process, much like retention, for example. The same philosophical/methodological arguments we would quickly raise regarding retention apply exactly to the use of generalization criticized here.

Some of these problems of perspective and strategy are epitomized by a recent article by Stokes and Baer (1977). Their paper is mainly addressed to elucidating a number of general tactics from the applied literature for producing desired responding in nontraining settings. Although these may indeed include useful procedures, the general approach taken in the article exemplifies the problems posed here. For example, they are explicit about their definitional position.

> The notion of generalization developed here is an essentially pragmatic one; it does not closely follow the traditional conceptualizations (Keller & Schoenfeld, 1950; Skinner, 1953). In many ways, this discussion will sidestep much of the controversy concerning terminology. Generalization will be considered to be the occurrence of relevant behavior under different, nontraining conditions (i.e., across subjects, settings, people, behaviors, and/or time) without the scheduling of the same events in those conditions as had been scheduled in the training conditions. Thus, generalization may be claimed when some extra manipulations are necessary, but their cost or extent is clearly less than that of the direct intervention. (p. 350)

Thus, generalization is intentionally defined in conflict with its formal and standard use in the field to include behavior changes that are certainly the result of other behavioral processes. This kind of terminological slippage between our science and our technology may have pervasive and enduring consequences that make maintaining symbiotic relations difficult. This usage discourages any understanding of the behavioral processes that are at work in training and nontraining settings and encourages a technological literature more in a bag-of-tricks style than in a behavior–analytic style. Although there is no question that we need to develop procedures for obtaining desired responding in settings of secondary interest with a minimum expenditure of resources, it is important to understand that progress toward this goal will be facilitated by the proper description and an empirical understanding of the variables and processes that are at work in such efforts.

This overdependence on generalization as a means of getting behavioral changes in nontraining settings or in explaining such changes if they occur seems, at least in part, to result from an inadequate understanding of the questions that are actually being raised when we ask how to extend initial changes or how successful changes in nontraining settings were produced. The issue is, not so much how to get "generalization," but how to arrange control over different environmental conditions that result in desired influences on behavior. This in turn becomes the larger question of what are the environmental sources of control, and for both the behavior analyst and the behavior modifier, this is a question of generality. When we ask how we are going to get Johnny to behave in the second-period class as we have so carefully trained him to do in his homeroom class, we are asking about generality. When we want to know why he did indeed show homeroom treatment effects in the third-period class, where we did nothing, but why he continues to be a disaster in the second-period class, we are asking about generality. When we use the same procedures with Jane but see no changes in her behavior in the third-period class, we will again be asking about generality.

Generality refers to universality or replicability. It may be formally defined as the characteristic of numerical data or verbal interpretations of data that describes some meaning or relevance (effect) beyond the circumstances of its origin. It must be distinguished from the concern for reliability of effect, which simply raises the question, "If I repeat certain procedures, will I get the same result?" A broad statement of the question raised by generality is, "If I take part or all of the procedures that produced a result and apply them under circumstances that are in some degree different, will I get the same kind of effect?" (see *Strategies and Tactics*, chapter 13). This formal definition is still insufficient, however. There are a number of distinguishable emphases in meaning that can be described. These differences concern the kinds of information about generality that are the object of experimental efforts. These meanings are not always easy to delineate clearly, and the usual process of experimentation provides information on a number of dimensions of generality simultaneously, although particular manipulations can be directed at specific dimensions of interest.

In order to understand these various dimensions of generality, it is helpful to realize that they include dimensions, across which we investigate the generality of functional relations between variations in a subject's responding and the experimental environment; these in addition to dimensions concerning aspects of the generality of functional relations that we want to clarify. In other words, the difference is between "generality across" versus "generality of," and in any experimental instance, emphasis may be on one type of dimension or the other, if not both.

Figure 12.1 depicts this distinction and the various meanings of generality. Generality across species is obviously important when the entire spectrum of behavioral research is considered. Subject generality has to do with the representativeness of a finding across subjects and is less important than it might seem. As Sidman (1960) exhaustively pointed out, this usually has nothing to do with the size of a group of subjects; the distribution of some quan-

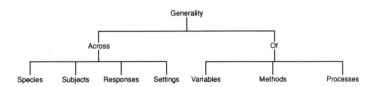

FIG. 12.1.   Dimensions of generality.

titative aspect of the data in the population is actually of little importance. However, if the same kind or type of orderliness occurs widely among individuals in the population as a result of some procedure, we would say that the finding has great subject generality. We can also examine the generality of a functional relation across response classes in the same (or different) subject(s), just as we may be interested in the generality of a finding across different settings.

In examining generality across these dimensions, we are also unavoidably probing the generality of certain other dimensions. We can subdivide these meanings as having primarily to do with the independent variable (generality of variables and methods) or the dependent variable (generality of processes). It must be pointed out, however, that it is possible to fractionate both categories further if desired. For example, we could examine the generality of any number of data characteristics or we could investigate particular parameters of some variable in a search for generality. Whatever the particular interest, however, we are always assessing the generality of both sides of a functional relation. We can look at variables and methods only through their associated effect, and a behavioral process cannot be studied independently of its environmental determinants.

Process generality refers to either the generality of the interaction of different variables that we might call a behavioral process (such as extinction or the generality of a wide range of quantitative values of a single variable (such as FI values). *Methodological generality* refers to the replicability of the effects of procedures or techniques, usually of environmental control over behavior, such as the time-out procedure. *Generality of variables* is at the base of all other types. Here we are talking about the universality of effect of a variable or class of variables, such as intermittency of reinforcement.

Both the researcher and practitioner are really asking about generality when they ask how to extend behavioral changes from one setting to another. In particular, most of the time we are interested in the generality of methods and, ultimately, of variables. For example, in asking how to get the same effects in Situation B that we produced in Situation A, we are actually asking particular questions about the generality of that method of environmental control and about the generality of the arrangement of the different variables which constitute that control. For example, in the case of time out, these might be the typical questions.

- Will time out produce the same effects in other situations?
- What variations of the procedure will continue to reproduce those effects?
- What variables that are crucial in time-out can be used in a different way to yield the same effect?
- What elements of the time-out procedure can be omitted while still retaining its effectiveness?
- What variables of all those used are minimally necessary to produce the same effect in Situation B?

It is our understanding of how the effect in Situation A was produced that will provide the answers for Situation B; this has to do with the thoroughness of our analysis and understanding of the procedures and their elements we use—that is, their generality. If our knowledge is such that we are confident about the generality of methods of environmental control and their component variables, the question of how to extend or maintain a behavioral change becomes a much easier one. Instead of making educated guesses about proper techniques and their likely effects, or reaching into a bag of tricks for a procedure that may not be applicable, we will increasingly be able to select confidently with relative precision the procedures that will yield maximum effect with minimum artificial environmental arrangement in any setting of interest.

This perspective seems to be more than slightly at variance with prevailing attitudes and practices in our field. How can we ameliorate this situation? What must be our research strategies? A catalog of inadequately replicated techniques (the components of which have not been analyzed), each of which worked at least once for the investigator who published it, may hold the appearance of an interwoven and established literature, but it will prove to be a disappointing facade that does not live up to its seeming utility. Investigators must concurrently work to conduct both applied and laboratory research specifically designed to establish and extend the generality of the various aspects of such variables and techniques (including procedures for maximizing the effects of the processes of stimulus and response generalization). This generality is not necessarily a natural outgrowth of any accumulation of studies. It must be a strong theme of the research in an area, and it must be the central focus of at least some carefully and skilled investigators who can specifically design programs that will weave together the results of many independent studies.

This style of research may be described as thematic, in contrast to the more demonstration-style, one-shot projects that are independent of the needs of an area of behavioral literature (see *Strategies and Tactics*, Box 3.2). A thematic study may be conducted in any setting with any kind of subject; what makes the study thematic is the nature of the question addressed and the methodological style that characterizes the effort. The thematic study fits into a carefully predetermined position in a larger research program. The program may be directed by one person or a collaborative team; it may exist as a program only through the complementary, but independent, efforts of investigators whose contact is primarily through the formal channels of communication (e.g., journals, etc.). The questions addressed by thematic research are less likely to result from a local opportunity to work in a certain setting or with a particular population than from the specific needs of a coherent and relatively integrated, yet still incomplete, literature.

In thematic behavioral research, when there is a conflict between experimental and service goals, the scales are tipped in favor of science so that the resulting interpretations may be unambiguous. Thus, it may be expected that the quality of methodological decisions may be somewhat higher in thematic efforts than in the more independent demonstration studies. After all, in thematic research, the goal is not just to change behavior but to determine its controlling variables in a relatively detailed manner. This in no way vitiates service delivery. The work of Lovaas and his colleagues with autistic children is an excellent example of thematic applied behavior analysis that is successful from both analytical and service perspectives. Furthermore, the studies reviewed by Lovaas and Newsom (1976) comprising the language training literature with normal, autistic and retarded populations describe an area of investigation largely resulting from thematic research efforts that have not compromised therapeutic or educational responsibilities.

It may indeed be that, when we work for behavioral changes in one setting, we happily observe changes appearing in other settings without any special efforts on our part. However, most often we will have to direct specific efforts at such changes, and the seemingly simple questions we then ask must be seen as a part of a larger and more important range of questions about generality.

Within Subject Versus Between Groups Designs: Comparing Experimental Outcomes

INTRODUCTION

The experimental literature concerning procedures for addressing severe behavior disorders in developmentally disabled individuals embodies two fundamentally different approaches to designing and conducting experiments. These are known as *within subject* and *between groups designs*, although this dichotomy oversimplifies the methodological variations represented. The differences between these two approaches to asking and answering experimental questions present serious difficulties when we try to review this literature in order to summarize its findings.

In order to fully appreciate this problem, we must first review some of the key features of each methodological approach; how each approach asks experimental questions, arranges comparisons, addresses the need for experimental control, analyzes data, and draws inferences offers some clear contrasts. This will facilitate consideration of what these differences mean for how we evaluate literatures that embody both approaches.

Before beginning this comparison, however, it is important to be clear about the nature of the subject matter under study. Perhaps the most fundamental fact about behavior for present purposes is that it is a biological phenomenon. Behavior results from an interactive condition between individual organisms and their environments. It is therefore a phenomenon that occurs only at the level of the individual. This means that it is only at this level that we can see the orderly relations that are the focus of our interest. Another important feature of behavior is that the organism–environment interactions that result in behavior occur through time. The methodological consequence of this fact is that we have to measure behavior over time in order to see the effects of these interactions clearly.

In considering these attributes, it is important to remember that as with all

181

sciences, we need to adapt our experimental methods to the characteristics of the phenomenon, rather than forcing the subject matter to fit our research methods. This means that the ways that we study behavior must accommodate these and other characteristics if we are going to learn how these organism–environment interactions work and what factors can influence them. We might also remember that the behavioral technology now widely used in many settings has emerged from a basic and applied experimental literature that exemplifies this methodological priority.

EXPERIMENTAL QUESTIONS

The divergent methods of within subject and between groups designs begin with the strategic issue of experimental questions. At least formally, the curiosities of these approaches are quite different. The generic experimental question in between-groups designs is, technically, not a question at all. The logical device required to lend the practice of hypothesis testing the illusion of deductive validity precludes an official question. Instead, we make the prediction that there will be no difference between experimental and control groups. When the data reveal that we are wrong (with an acceptable risk of being wrong by chance), we gratefully turn to the alternative hypothesis, which suggests the independent variable as the most likely (or, at least, the most preferred) culprit—our real interest all along.

Putting aside the logical legerdemain, the generic form of the experimental question hidden in this practice asks "Is there a difference (between experimental and control groups)?" Of course, there is almost always a difference, the only issue is whether there is enough of a difference to satisfy the requirements of the underlying mathematical model used to answer the question. What is more revealing, however, is what is *not* being asked. This approach does not address the size of the difference or the nature of its other characteristics, although statisticians are always trying to find new ways of manipulating the data to permit us to say whatever we want to say. Remember, however, that all that we can officially conclude is that there is, or is not, a difference between experimental and control groups, yielding the possibility of causal assignment to the independent variable.

In contrast, within subject designs are guided by a rather different type of question. Its most generic form asks "What are the relations between the independent variable and the dependent variable?" This is an especially open and searching curiosity. It encourages an approach to measurement and design that accommodates an interest in learning anything and everything about the effects of the independent variables on the dependent variable, and it does not impose any particular content or form on the answers that data might support. Satisfactory answers might describe any and all aspects of the relationship.

EXPERIMENTAL COMPARISONS

The essence of experimental design lies in how we bring the behavior of subjects into contact with various conditions so as to permit comparisons whose data will suggest inferences that answer the experimental question. Within-subject designs expose subjects individually to a sequence of conditions. Each subject's contact with a condition occurs across a series of successive sessions. What determines the number of sessions under each condition is evidence that the subject's behavior is, to the extent deemed necessary, under control of the variables defining that condition, so that a clear and complete picture of its effects is available. When behavior is under control of a constant set of conditions, and reasonable attention is paid to controlling extraneous variables, it usually exhibits relatively good stability across repeated sessions. These decisions are made individually for each subject because different subjects react to the same condition in varied ways.

An important feature of this approach is that it permits the target behavior to have sufficient contact with each condition being compared to provide a complete and clear picture of the effects of each on behavior; however, the value of this evidence is lost if it is not done individually for each subject. Although there is no limit on the number of subjects employed, it is typical to use only a small number in comparison to between groups designs. As we see, the success of this approach partly depends on how well the researcher uses the opportunity it offers to establish good experimental control, but the result can be a database that clearly and fully describes *how* the behavior of each subject was affected by each condition.

The between groups approach could not be more different. First, each subject typically experiences only one of the conditions being compared. This means that comparisons of the effects of independent variable and control conditions must involve different subjects, which confounds the effects of treatment conditions with between subject variability. The seriousness of this problem depends, not on the number of subjects involved, but the nature of the data being compared. Within subject designs sometimes make comparisons between subjects as well, but they do so using individual data collected in a repeated measures style. As its name promises, between groups designs make this comparison using grouped data representing as few as one observation per subject.

Second, although the between-groups approach typically exposes each subject to a single condition as little as once, or no more than a few times, it does this for a relatively large number of subjects. Although this tactic provides many observations, it does not provide the same picture of behavior as does repeated within subject observations. Recall that behavior is a continuous phenomenon, which means that we can be sure of seeing a clear picture of how a particular response class is influenced by some condition only if we expose the behavior to the condition for a sufficient amount of time. A between groups design does not usually provide enough time to obtain such a picture. This means that each subject's values may represent different points on his or her individual function, or even the influence of extraneous variables. In other words, different subjects usually take different amounts of time to respond to a new condition. A single observation may catch one subject early in this transition but another after the transition is complete. The result is two different pictures of the effects of the condition, and averaging these pictures does not make it any clearer.

EXPERIMENTAL CONTROL

One of the more subtle but important differences between these two research styles lies in their approach to experimental control. The emphasis on obtaining a clear and complete picture of responding under each condition separately for each subject, which typifies within subject designs, encourages efforts to improve control by each condition, while minimizing control by extraneous variables. The fact that each subject's behavior is repeatedly measured under each supposedly constant condition permits behavioral variability to serve as a metric of the degree of control attained. This allows the researcher to improve control over the variables defining the condition or to identify and hold constant or eliminate extraneous influences, all while assessing the effects of these manipulations on each subject's behavior.

This approach to experimental control enhances the generality of the study's conclusions. In other words, improvements in the consistency and purity with which data reflect the effects of the conditions being compared improve the chances that the independent-dependent variable relations identified by the conclusions will be true and will hold up when examined or used under different circumstances.

Although the need for experimental control may not be viewed any less seriously in between groups designs, its approach to experimental comparisons does not facilitate efforts to assess or improve it. The relatively few measurements of each subject's behavior under its assigned condition does not permit the researcher to assess the clarity with which each condition's effects are represented by the data. Neither does it provide very much of an opportunity to improve the purity of each condition's control over each subject's responding. Other considerations aside, this means that the data from each subject in a between groups design may be likely to represent more extraneous influences than for each subject in a within subjects design.

Instead of controlling its sources before the fact, the between groups approach instead emphasizes controlling variability statistically after the fact. These two tactics do not have the same effects on the database, however. Whereas efforts to control actual variability lead to improved control over responding and, thus, a clearer picture of the effects of each condition, statistical manipulation of variable data cannot remove the influences already represented in the data. What is manipulated is how we talk about the data, a tactic that is less likely to enhance generality.

DATA ANALYSIS

Although the number of observations available for analysis can be similar for the two approaches, the databases represent different information, notwithstanding the fact that in both cases each raw value might represent an observation of the behavior of a single subject. By collecting a large number of observations on each of a relatively small number of subjects, within subject designs allow the researcher to examine individually each subject's response to each of the conditions being compared. The most basic form of analysis usually involves displaying measures of each subject's responding graphically as a function of time. Given the degree of control that can usually be attained, the clarity of this picture is often convincing without further analysis (although this analytical technique is not as obvious as many assume and requires some training). If a more wide-ranging examination is warranted, it may involve additional graphic representations of particular features of the data or descriptive statistical manipulations (e.g., see Tukey, 1977).

The strength of this approach to data analysis lies less with its reliance on graphic displays than with the nature of the data being displayed. Data that represent the repeated performance of individual subjects under each of the conditions being compared, their clarity having been enhanced by tactics that augment experimental control, will tend to be revealing as long as their handling respects the fundamental qualities of the subject matter. As in other natural sciences, graphic displays serve nicely most of the time, in spite of the fact that this analytical style does not embody rigid inferential rules.

As is well known to every student in the social sciences, the analysis of between-groups data is conducted in accordance with elaborate mathematical and interpretive models, collectively called inferential statistics. For present purposes, the most important feature of this approach is that it typically involves analyzing grouped data representing the combined performance of all subjects exposed to each condition being compared. This feature alone guarantees that orderly and revealing relations between the independent variable conditions and behavior (an intraorganismic phenomenon) will be difficult if not impossible to detect. Such an achievement is quite different from showing statistical significance, and it is probably a more difficult goal to attain. Furthermore, although the size of the groups being compared may affect the likelihood of getting a significant result, it has nothing to do with discovering orderly relations between environmental variables and behavior.

EXPERIMENTAL INFERENCES

With between groups designs, the process of reaching experimental conclusions is fully scripted by the mathematical model used to analyze the data. The rules of the statistical test being used generally require that, if the difference is significant, the researcher must conclude that the independent variable was responsible. This inferential practice is relatively automatic, although arguments about the possible role of extraneous influences can always vitiate any inferences.

One of the problems with this way of determining experimental inferences is that its focus is too narrow in at least three ways. First, as the tail end of the hypothesis testing game, it strongly encourages researchers to make conclusions out of the original predictions, hardly a practice that stimulates open and critical thinking. In other words, by virtually requiring simple causal inferences about the role of the independent variable, attention is not adequately given to other aspects of its effects on the behavior of subjects.

Second, in spite of this complaint, conclusions about the size of the effect, its other characteristics, or the effects of other variables may not always be logically permitted by the inferential model underlying such statistics. On the other hand, this may be just as well because various features of between groups designs may preclude the kind of database that would support more varied or analytical inferences.

Third, by licensing causal statements upon receipt of a significant statistic, this inferential approach does not encourage attention to the many details of experimental method or to extraneous factors that might bear on the conclusions. As a result of this relatively restricted focus, the formal outcomes of between groups designs tend to be overly simplistic statements to the effect that "Effect Y was caused by Procedure X," unqualified by detailed description of the characteristics of the relation or by methodological limitations on its generality.

Again in stark contrast, conclusions drawn from within subject designs are guided by no inferential model or set of rigid rules. Researchers are free to describe whatever findings they think the data support, focusing on whatever features of the data seem revealing, without regard for their original expectations or curiosities. The only counsel for this exercise lies in a few overarching strategies: (a) Inferences should be about the relations between physical (environmental) variables and the behavior of individual subjects, (b) Inferences are appropriate only when the data result from methodological practices that accommodate the fundamental characteristics of behavior, and (c) Inferences should be supported by data approximating functional relations. The effect of these strategies and their supporting tactics is to focus attention on what the experiment really says about how variables influence behavior, even if the findings are unanticipated or contrary to those originally suspected.

Although this dependence on informal and flexible strategies instead of rigid inferential rules bothers those in the social sciences who do not understand this approach very well, it is just as effective in the study of behavior as it is in the natural sciences when studying other natural phenomena. Unfortunately, the history that social scientists have with inferential statistics seems to have led to the belief that a quantitative decision rule is required to certify the truthfulness of a study's results. Inferential statistical traditions have, in effect, replaced the goal of accurate conclusions with the concept of statistical significance. As a result, some attempt to append various forms of inferential statistical analysis to within subject designs in a misguided attempt to avoid the subjectivity that is an inherent and valuable aspect of experimental method in the natural sciences.

One of the most important criteria for the effectiveness of any design concerns the extent to which it leads to conclusions that have good generality. Generality is a much misunderstood topic that is at the root of inferential differences between within-subject and between groups designs. Generality is a characteristic of data that describes some meaning or relevance beyond the circumstances of its origin. The generality of a proposed relation between independent and dependent variables should be distinguished from its reliability, which simply raises the question, "If I repeat certain procedures, will I get the same result?" Generality asks "If I take a certain result and apply the procedures that produced it under circumstances that are somewhat different, will I get the same effect?" (*Strategies and Tactics*, chapter 13; Reading 12).

Questions about generality may have varying emphases, which, because we are always asking about a relation, necessarily have two parts. For example, we may ask about the generality *of* variables, methods, or processes *across* subjects, behaviors, settings, or species. Perhaps the most important point about what generality is asking, however, is that the answers must describe variables that influence the relation under study. In other words, our knowledge about the extent to which we may expect our findings to hold under other circumstances depends entirely on the how well we understand the variables required to produce the effect and variables that can modulate it. This kind of information can only be obtained from experimentally identifying such variables and determining their impact on the relation of interest.

The two experimental styles under consideration manifest fundamentally different perspectives on generality. Within subject designs clearly approach generality as an experimental obligation. From the form of the experimental question to the style of data analysis and inference, there is a pervasive focus on obtaining a behaviorally meaningful and accurate picture of independent–dependent variable relations, so that there will be a sound foundation for the subsequent search for their generality. It is understood that the generality of a study's findings may be contemplated in its discussion section, but that it can be clarified only with additional research. Because the ability to predict the conditions under which the relation of interest will and will not hold depends on how well contributing variables are understood, within subject studies tend to focus less on making predictions and more on identifying controlling variables.

Between-groups designs approach generality as an actuarial or sampling issue. By misperceiving the question to be how well the sample represents the population (Fisher, 1935), the primary interest tends to lie in the generality of a finding across subjects, which ignores the many other facets of generality that are important. (In within subject designs, generality across subjects is often a relatively minor interest because it is more important to first understand controlling variables and because subject generality is usually so easily obtained once the relation is well understood.) Unfortunately, the methods required to pursue this actuarial perspective tend to preclude obtaining a clear picture of the relations of interest in the first place. For example, the use of large numbers of subjects and grouped data prevents or discourages various practices that are necessary to study behavior effectively.

Approaching generality as a question of how well the sample represents the population has other problems as well. For instance, it misstates our real scientific interest, which is in the individual, not the population. Because behavior is a phenomenon that only occurs with individuals, it is at this level that we must identify sources of control and pursue generality. Of course, as Fisher (1935) recognized, it is improper to generalize from the sample to the individual, but we fail to realize that our apparent interest in the universality of a finding in the population confuses the scientific obligation to establish generality (which requires understanding sources of control) with our practical desire that the finding be broadly applicable. In fact, because behavior is an intraorganismic phenomenon, we should only be interested in generality to the individual. When we understand what controls an effect at this level, we are in a much better position to assess whether the effect will be obtained for any particular individual or class of individuals.

A related problem is that this actuarial perspective discourages a crucial distinction between assessing versus obtaining generality. The drive to assess the generality of each experiment's conclusions on the spot by making it a sampling question misdirects attention away from the far more important matter of determining the kind of evidence that will be required to establish the generalness of the findings. Whether a study's results will hold under other conditions is entirely a function of the extent to which the variables responsible for the effect are present under those conditions. Knowing this requires discovering those variables (see Reading 9).

EVALUATING EXPERIMENTAL LITERATURES

This brief comparison of the general features of within subject and between groups designs that directly concern experimental inferences should make it clear that there are few similarities and that the differences are fundamental. In fact, the differences are such that it may be said that they result in qualitatively different subject matters. When well done, the procedures of within-subject designs preserve the pure characteristics of behavior, uncontaminated by intersubject variability. In contrast, the best between groups design practices obfuscate the representation of behavior in various ways, particularly by mixing intersubject variability with treatment-induced variability.

We argued that this difference in the subject matter represented by the experimental database constitutes a distinction between pure versus quasi-behavioral research (see Reading 9). Pure behavioral research results from experiments embodying methodological practices that preserve the fundamental qualities of behavior in undisturbed and uncontaminated form. What is pure is the representation of the complete array of fundamental qualities of behavior in the experimental data. Quasi-behavioral research results from experiments whose data originated with observations of behavior but whose methods prevent the data from representing behavior's fundamental qualities fully and without distortion or contamination. The prefix denotes the potential problem; such research seems to be about behavior although it is not, according to the standards of the phenomenon itself.

Where does all of this leave us when we are trying to make sense of a literature that includes both kinds of approaches? Frankly, we are left in a very difficult position. It is clear that if we are looking at, for instance, two studies that address the same intervention procedure for reducing self-injurious behavior, one using a within subject design and the other a between groups design, it would be improper simply to view their conclusions as equivalently believable. Furthermore, the inherent superiority of within-subject designs for the study of behavior certainly does not mean that any instance of this approach automatically leads to true or even more accurate conclusions than its competitor. As with between groups designs, there are plenty of inferior examples, and it is hardly the case that conclusions from a methodologically weak within subject study are better than conclusions from any between groups study; and it is never the case that they are better than nothing. There are no guarantees here. Sound examples of this approach can always lead to erroneous findings.

In reviewing a methodologically diverse literature, it is important to understand that the "study" is not the proper unit of inferential analysis. The only meaningful unit is the functional relation. One study may contribute no such instances, whereas another may suggest more than one. Thus, reviewing a literature is not a democratic process of tallying the number of studies that do and do not support a particular finding, regardless of each's methods. Even the more sophisticated version of this practice represented by meta-analysis cannot help here (although it can be a useful technique for evaluating certain kinds of literature). The reason is that there is no straightforward way to equate or compare the findings from these two types of designs. Because of differences in how these designs collect and treat raw behavioral observations, their findings cannot be simply integrated. They do not usually ask the same question, and they clearly do not represent and compare behavioral data in equivalently interpretable forms.

This certainly does not mean that we should ignore the findings from between-groups designs when trying to understand what a literature tells us about behavior or methods for controlling behavior. Just because this approach is generally ill-suited to the study of behavior certainly does not mean that the conclusions of each instance are necessarily wrong. It is not unusual for an especially strong effect to override the weaknesses of experimental methods, whether between groups or within subject. But how do we know when this is or is not the case? How do we decide, when reviewing a literature, which study's findings are true and which are false, or at least indeterminate?

This is not a challenge only encountered when comparing the results of differing methodological approaches. The customary practice of evaluating any study's conclusions by critically assessing the details of its methods remains a necessary technique. Following the arguments briefly outlined here, this will place between groups designs in a weak position relative to within subject designs. However, we then look at the pattern of findings across those studies whose methods are at least minimally appropriate to the subject matter and the question. At this point, the results of the studies remaining will still not be weighed equally. Because of detailed differences in their methods and the data, some will be given more credence and others, less. Only then can we attempt some kind of summary of the literature's findings, assuming that enough studies remain to justify general conclusions.

This process of evaluating scientific literatures is necessarily idiosyncratic to each reviewer, a fact that some might see as a disadvantage. It may be argued, however, that this is often a valuable characteristic of scientific reviews. Only some kinds of literatures warrant the formalities of meta-analysis, and they are not usually found in the social sciences. The fact that each reviewer brings a certain point of view to the task of reviewing a literature should be considered a strength of the traditional (nonquantitative) approach. Although this perspective or bias may encourage differences among the conclusions of different reviewers of the same literature, who is to say which are correct? Why should different reviewers come to the same conclusions anyway? Assessing any study's findings is always a subjective process, even if a statistical decision rule is used. Although science strives for accuracy in all things, it gets there by a series of judgments, an observation that Bertrand Russell noted when he said, "Although this may seem a paradox, all exact science is dominated by the idea of approximation."

In summary, although we might like a simple procedure for reviewing methodologically diverse literatures that guarantees accuracy, there is none. What we should want, instead, is better literatures. What we should be doing is improving our experimental methods, which will require us to improve the way that we think about and pursue behavior as a scientific subject matter. What we must do is to become more concerned with learning about behavior than following methodological traditions. Anyone with graduate training in the social sciences has had no less than a year's worth of formal instruction in inferential statistical approaches to conceptualizing and conducting research, and often much more. What proportion have had an equivalent amount of training in within subject methods or exploratory data analysis?

Some concluding caveats are required. First, these arguments concern only research in which the goal is to learn about the relations between behavior and other variables. When behavioral data are used to answer other kinds of questions, such as the administrative aspects of one procedure versus another, between groups designs may be quite appropriate. (This point must be considered in light of some important issues concerning research whose goal is to compare two procedures, however. See Reading 9 for further discussion.)

Second, these critical comments about between groups designs and inferential statistics should be interpreted in a narrow context. These methods do what they do perfectly well, and it is important that all students of behavior learn at least their basics. Although they are often misapplied in psychological research, a useful role remains, although it should be a much smaller role that present traditions suggest. They are inherently inappropriate for the task of learning about behavior in any fundamental or analytical sense, however, and their dominance in psychology lies at the root of psychology's continuing failure to build an importantly useful science and technology.

References

Adams, C. K., Hall, D., Rice, P., Wood, K., & Willis, R. (1975, November). *Stimulus control problems in developing an animal model for prothetic vision.* Paper presented at the meeting of the Psychonomic Society, Denver, CO.

Baer, D. W., Wolf, M. M., & Risley, T. R. (1968). Some current dimensions of applied behavior analysis. *Journal of Applied Behavior Analysis, 1,* 91–97.

Barber, T. X. (1976). *Pitfalls in human research.* Elmsford, NY: Pergamon Press.

Barenblatt, G. L. (1987). *Dimensional analysis.* New York: Gordon & Breach.

Bernard, C. (1957). *An introduction to the study of experimental medicine.* New York: Dover. (Original work published 1865)

Barrera, R. D., & Sulzer-Azaroff, B. (1983). An alternating treatment comparison of oral and total communication training programs with echolalic autistic children. *Journal of Applied Behavior Analysis, 16,* 379–394.

Barry, A. E. (1986). Behavior, psychology, and praxics: Where does science fit in? *The Behavior Analyst, 9,* 225–226

Blough, D. S. (1966). The study of animal sensory processes by operant methods. In W. K. Honig (Ed.), *Operant behavior: Areas of research and application.* New York: Appleton-Century-Crofts.

Boe, R., & Winoker, S. (1978a). A procedure for studying echoic control in verbal behavior. *Journal of the Experimental Analysis of Behavior, 33,* 495–520.

Boe, R., & Winoker, S. (1978b). Echoic control in conversational speech. *Journal of General Psychology, 99,* 299–304.

Boole, G. (1854). *The laws of thought.* New York: Dover.

Boring, E. G. (1920). The logic of the normal law of error in mental measurement. *American Journal of Psychology, 31,* 1–33.

Boring, E. G. (1942). *Sensation and perception in the history of experimental psychology.* New York: Appleton-Century-Crofts.

Boring, E. G. (1950). *A history of experimental psychology* (2nd ed.). New York: Appleton-Century-Crofts.

Boring, E. G. (1961). Measurement in psychology. In H. Woolf (Ed.), *Quantification* (pp. 108–127). New York: Bobbs-Merrill.

Braam, S. J., & Polling, A. (1983). Development of intraverbal behavior in mentally retarded individuals through transfer of stimulus control procedures: Classification of verbal responses. *Applied Research In Mental Retardation, 4,* 279–302.

Braine, M. D. S. (1978). On the relation between the natural logic of reasoning and standard logic. *Psychological Review, 85*, 1–21,

Bridgeman, P. W. (1922). *Dimensional analysis.* New Haven, CT: Yale University Press.

Burns, C. E. S., Heiby, E. M., & Tharp, G. G. (1983). A verbal behavior analysis of auditory hallucinations. *The Behavior Analyst, 6*, 133–143.

Buskist, W. F., & Miller, H. L. (1986). Interactions between rules and contingencies in the control of human fixed-interval performance. *The Psychological Record, 36*, 109–116.

Campbell, N. R. (1920). *Physics, the elements.* Cambridge, England: Cambridge University Press.

Campbell, D. T., & Stanley, J. C. (1966). *Experimental and quasi-experimental designs for research.* Chicago: Rand-McNally.

Carlin, G. (1973). *Occupation: Fool.* New York: Little David Records.

Carnap, R. (1966). *Philosophical foundations of physics.* New York: Basic Books.

Chase, P. N., Johnson, K. R., & Sulzer-Azaroff, B. (1985). Verbal relations within instruction: Are there subclasses of the intraverbal? *Journal of the Experimental Analysis of Behavior, 43*, 301–313.

Chertov, A. G. (1964). *Units of measurement of physical quantities.* New York: Hayden Book Company.

Cochran, W., & Cox, G. (1950). *Experimental designs.* New York: Wiley.

Cook, T. D., & Campbell, D. T. (Eds.) (1979). *Quasi-experimental design and analysis issues for field settings.* Chicago: Rand-McNally.

Cook, N. H., & Rabinowicz, E. (1963). *Physical measurement and analysis.* Reading, MA: Addison-Wesley.

Crombie, A. C. (1961). Quantification in medieval physics. In H. Woolf (Ed.), *Quantification* (pp. 13–30). New York: Bobbs-Merrill.

Cronbach, L. J., & Meehl, P. E. (1955). Construct validity in psychological tests. *Psychological Bulletin, 52*, 281–302.

Dampier, W. C. (1942). *A history of science and its relations with philosophy and religion.* New York: Macmillan.

Dews, P. B. (1987). An outsider on the inside. *Journal of the Experimental Analysis of Behavior, 48*(3), 459–462.

Durbin, P. R. (1968). *Logic and scientific inquiry.* Milwaukee, WI: Bruce Publishing Co.

Ellis, B. (1966). *Basic concepts of measurement.* London: Cambridge University Press.

Epstein, R. (1984). The case for praxics. *The Behavior Analyst, 7*, 101–119.

Estes, W. K. (1979). Experimental psychology: An overview. In E. Hearst (Ed.), *The first century of experimental psychology* (pp. 623–667). Hillsdale, NJ: Lawrence Erlbaum Associates.

Evans, J. (1982). *The psychology of deductive reasoning.* London: Routledge & Kegan Paul.

Falmagne, R. J. (1975). *Reasoning: Representation and process in children and adults.* Hillsdale, NJ: Lawrence Erlbaum Associates.

Fisher, R. A. (1925). *Statistical methods for research workers.* London: Oliver & Boyd.

Fisher, R. A. (1935). *The design of experiments.* London: Oliver & Boyd.

Fisher, R. A. (1956). *Statistical methods and scientific inference.* London: Oliver & Boyd.

Ford, R. G., & Cullmann, R. E. (1959). *Dimensions, units, and numbers.* New York: Teachers College, Columbia University.

Fraley, L., & Vargas, E. A. (1986). Separate disciplines: The study of behaviorism and the study of the psyche. *The Behavior Analyst, 9*, 47–59.

Galton, F. (1889). *Natural inheritance.* London: McMillan.

Geller, E. S., Winett, R. A., & Everett, B. (1982). *Preserving the environment: New strategies for behavior change.* Elmsford, NY: Pergamon Press.

Glenn, S. S. (1983). Maladaptive functional relations in client verbal behavior. *The Behavior Analyst, 6*, 47–56.

Goldstein, M. K., Stein, G. H., Smolen, D. M., & Perlini, W. S. (1976). Bio-behavioral monitoring: A method for remote health measurement. *Archives of Physical Medicine and Rehabilitation, 57*, 253–258.

Gossett, W. S. (1908). The probable error of a mean. *Biometrika, 6*, 1–25.

Hall, S. A., & Chase, F. N. (1986, May). *Functional transfer between mands and tacts.* Poster presented at the meeting of the Association for Behavior Analysis, Milwaukee, WI.

Hayes, S. C., Brownstein, A. J., Haas, J. R., & Greenway, D. E. (1986). Instructions, multiple schedules, and extinction: Extinguishing rule-governed from schedule-controlled behavior. *Journal of the Experimental Analysis of Behavior, 46*, 137–147.

Herrnstein, R. J. (1987). Reminiscences already? *Journal of the Experimental Analysis of Behavior, 48*(3), 448–453.

Herson, M., & Barlow, D. (1976). *Single case experimental designs.* New York: Pergamon Press.

Hoaglin, D. C., Mosteller, F., & Tukey, J. W. (1983). *Understanding robust and exploratory data analysis.* New York: John Wiley & Sons.

Hopkins, B. L. (1987). Comments for the future of applied behavior analysis. *Journal of Applied Behavior Analysis, 20*, 339–346.

Hume, O. (1955). *An inquiry concerning human understanding.* New York: Liberal Arts Press. (Original work published 1748)

Hursch, D. E. (1976). Personalized systems of instruction: What do the data indicate? *Journal of Personalized Instruction, 1*,(2), 91–105.

Hyten, C., & Chase, P. N. (1986, May). *Experimental analysis of self-editing.* Poster presented at the meeting of the Association for Behavior Analysis, Milwaukee, WI.

Inhelder, B., & Piaget, J. (1958). *The growth of logical thinking from childhood to adolescence.* New York: Basic Books, Inc.

Inhelder, B., & Piaget, J. (1969). *The early growth of logic in the child.* New York: W. W. Norton & Co.

Ipsen, D. C. (1960). *Units, dimensions, and dimensionless numbers.* New York: McGraw-Hill.

Johnson, K. R., & Chase, F. N. (1981). Behavior analysis in instructional design; A functional typology of verbal tasks. *The Behavior Analyst, 4*, 103–121.

Johnson, K. R., & Ruskin, R. S. (1977). *Behavioral instruction: An evaluative review.* Washington, DC: American Psychological Association.

Johnson, L. M., & Morris, E. K. (1987). When speaking of probability in behavior analysis. *Behaviorism, 15*(2), 107–129.

Johnston, J. M. (1975). Alphabet soup, generality, and the good old days. In J. M. Johnston (Ed.), *Research and technology in college and university teaching* (pp. 9–13). Champaign, IL: Research Press (distributor).

Johnston, J. M. (1979). On the relation between generalization and generality. *The Behavior Analyst, 2*, 1–6.

Johnston, J. M. (1985). Controlling professional behavior: A review of *The effects of punishment of human behavior* by Axelrod and Apsche. *The Behavior Analyst, 8*, 111–119.

Johnston, J. M. (1988). Strategic and tactical limits of comparison studies. *The Behavior Analyst, 11*, 1–9.

Johnston, J. M. (1991). We need a new model of technology. *Journal of Applied Behavior Analysis, 24*(3), 425–427.

Johnston, J. M. (in press). A model for developing and evaluating behavioral technology. In R. Van Houton and S. Axelrod (Eds.), *Effective behavioral treatment: Issues and implementation.* New York: Plenum.

Johnston, J. M., & Johnston, G. T. (1972). Modification of consonant speech sound articulation in young children. *Journal of Applied Behavior Analysis, 5*, 233–246.

Johnston, J. M., O'Neill, G. W., Walters, W. M., & Rasheed, J. A. (1975). The measurement and analysis of college student study behavior: Tactics for research. In J. M. Johnston (Ed.), *Behavior research and technology in higher education.* Springfield, IL: Charles C. Thomas.

Johnston, J. M., & Pennypacker, H. S. (1971). A behavioral approach to college teaching. *American Psychologist, 43*, 219–244.

Johnston, J. M., & Pennypacker, H. S. (1980). *Strategies and tactics of human behavioral research.* Hillsdale, NJ: Lawrence Erlbaum Associates.

Johnston, J. M., & Pennypacker, H. S. (1986). Pure versus quasi-behavioral research. In A. Poling and W. Fuqua (Eds.), *Research methods in applied behavior analysis* (pp. 29–54). New York: Plenum Publishing Co.

Judd, C. M., & Kenny, D. A. (1981). *Estimating the effects of social intervention.* New York: Cambridge University Press.

Kazdin, A. E. (1976). Statistical analyses for single-case experimental designs. In M. Hersen & O. H. Barlow (Eds.), *Single-case experimental designs: Strategies for studying behavior change* (pp. 265–316). Elmsford, NY: Pergamon Press.

Kazdin, A. E. (1982). *Single-case research designs.* New York: Oxford University Press.

Keller, F. S. (1968). "Goodbye teacher . . ." *Journal of Applied Behavior Analysis, 1,* 79–89.

Keller, F. S., & Schoenfield, W. N. (1950). *Principles of psychology.* New York: Appleton-Century-Crofts.

Kerlinger, F. N. (1986). *Foundations of behavioral research.* New York: Holt, Rinehart, & Winston.

Koenig, C. (1972). *Charting the future course of behavior.* Kansas City: Precision Media.

Kolata, G. (1986). What does it mean to be random? *Science, 231,* 1068–1070.

Krantz, D. L. (1972). The separate worlds of operant and nonoperant psychology. *Journal of Applied Behavior Analysis, 4*(1), 61–70.

Kuhn, T. (1970). *The structure of scientific revolutions* (2nd ed.). Chicago: University of Chicago Press.

Kyburg, H. E. (1984). *Theory and measurement.* London: Cambridge University Press.

Lamarre, J., & Holland, J. G. (1985). The functional independence of mands and tacts. *Journal of the Experimental Analysis of Behavior, 43,* 5–19.

Lazarfeld, P. F. (1961). Quantification in sociology. In H. Woolf (Ed.), *Quantification* (pp. 147–203). New York: Bobbs-Merrill.

Lee, V. L. (1981). Prepositional phrases spoken and heard. *Journal of the Experimental Analysis of Behavior, 35,* 227–242.

Leighland, S. (1985). Praxics and the case for radical behaviorism. *The Behavior Analyst, 8,* 127–128.

Levin, J. R., Marascuilo, L. A., & Hubert, L. J. (1978). N = Nonparametric randomization tests. In T. R. Kratochwill (Ed.), *Single subject research: Strategies for evaluating change* (pp. 167–196). New York: Academic Press.

Lindquist, E. F. (1953). *Design and analysis of experiments in psychology and education.* Boston: Houghton Mifflin.

Lloyd, K. E. (1978). Behavior analysis and technology in higher education. In T. A. Brigham & A. C. Catania (Eds.), *Applied analysis of social and educational behavior* (pp. 482–521). New York: Irvington Publishers.

Lovaas, O. I., & Newsom, C. D. (1976). Behavior modification with psychotic children. In H. Leitenberg (Ed.), *Handbook of behavior modification & behavior therapy* (pp. 303–360). New York: Appleton-Century-Crofts.

Mackintosh, N. J. (1977). Stimulus control: Attentional factors. In W.K. Honig (Ed.), *Operant Behavior: Areas of Research and Application.* Appleton-Century-Crofts, New York.

Malagodi, E. F., & Branch, M. N. (1985). Praxics and behaviorism. *The Behavior Analyst, 8,* 123–125.

Mann, H. (1949). *Analysis and design of experiments.* New York: Dover.

Mason, S. F. (1953). *Main currents of scientific thought.* New York: Henry Schuman.

McDowell, J. J. (1988). Behavior analysis: The third branch of Aristotle's physics. *Journal of the Experimental Analysis of Behavior, 50,* 297–304.

McLeish, J., & Martin, J. (1975). Verbal behavior: A review and experimental analysis. *Journal of General Psychology, 93,* 3–66.

McNemar, Q. (1949). *Psychological statistics.* New York: Wiley.

Michael, J. (1974). Statistical inference for individual organism research: Some reactions to a suggestion by Gentile, Roden, and Klein. *Journal of Applied Behavior Analysis, 7*(4), 627–628.

Michael, J. (1988). *Response probability as a dispositional concept.* Unpublished manuscript.

Mill, J. S. (1973). *A system of logic.* In F. F. McRae (Ed.), *Collected works of John Stuart Mill* (Vols. 7 & 8). Toronto: University of Toronto Press. (Original work published 1843)

Miller, F. (1972). *College physics.* New York: Harcourt, Brace.

Mood, O. (1950). *Introduction to the theory of statistics.* New York: McGraw-Hill.

Moore, J. (1981). On mentalism, methodological behaviorism and radical behaviorism. *Behaviorism, 9*(1), 55–77.

Mosk, M. D., & Bucher, B. (1984). Prompting and stimulus shaping procedures for teaching visual-motor skills to retarded children. *Journal of Applied Behavior Analysis, 17,* 23–34.

Nagel, E. (1961). *The structure of science.* New York: Harcourt, Brace, & World.

Neale, J. M., & Liebert, R. M. (1980). *Science and behavior.* Englewood Cliffs, NJ: Prentice-Hall.

Nevin, J. A. (1974). Response strength in multiple schedules. *Journal of the Experimental Analysis of Behavior. 21,* 389–408.

Nevin, J. A. (1979). Reinforcement schedules and response strength. In M. D. Zeiler & P. Harzem (Eds.), *Advances in analysis of behaviour: Vol. 1. Reinforcement and the organization of behavior* (pp. 117–157). New York: Wiley.

Nevin, J. A., Mandell, C., & Atak, J. R. (1983). The analysis of behavioral momentum. *Journal of the Experimental Analysis of Behavior, 39,* 49–59.

O'Neill, G. W., Walters, W. M., Rasheed, J. A., & Johnston, J. M. (1975). Validity of the study report form (Vol 2). In J. M. Johnston (Ed.), *Behavior research and technology in higher education* (pp. 411–420). Springfield, IL: Charles C. Thomas.

Pavlov, I. P. (1927). *Conditioned reflexes* (G. Anrep, Trans.). London: Oxford University Press.

Pennypacker, H. S., Koenig, H., & Lindsley, 0. R. (1972). *Handbook of the standard behavior chart.* Kansas City: Precision Media.

Popper, K. R. (1959). *The logic of scientific discovery.* New York: Basic Books.

Rast, J., & Johnston, J. M. (1988). Effects of pre-meal chewing on ruminative behavior. *American Journal of Mental Retardation, 93*(1), 67–74.

Rast, J., Johnston. J. M., Allen, J., & Drum, C. (1985). Effects of nutritional and mechanical properties of food on ruminative behavior. *Journal of the Experimental Analysis of Behavior, 44,* 195–206.

Rast, J., Johnston, J. M., & Drum, C. (1984). A parametric analvsis of the relationship between food quantity and rumination. *Journal of the Experimental Analysis of Behavior, 41,* 125–134.

Rast, J., Johnston, J. M., Drum, C., & Conrin. J. (1981). The relation of food quantity to rumination behavior. *Journal of Applied Behavior Analysis, 14,* 121–130.

Repp, A. C., Barton. L. E., & Brulle, A. R. (1983). A comparison of two procedures for programming the differential reinforcement of other behaviors. *Journal of Applied Behavior Analysis, 16,* 435–445.

Revlin, R., & Mayer, R. E. (1978). *Human reasoning.* Washington, DC: V. H. Winston.

Rilling, M. (1977). Stimulus control and inhibitory processes. In W.K. Honig (Ed.) *Operant behavior: Areas of research and application.* Appleton-Century-Crofts, New York, 1966.

Risley, T. R. (1968). The effects and side effects of punishing the autistic behaviors of a deviant child. *Journal of Applied Behavior Analysis, 1,* 21–34.

Risley, T.R., & Wolf, M.M. (1967). Experimental manipulation of autistic behaviors and generalization into the home. In S.W. Bijou & D.M. Baer (Eds.), *Child development readings in experimental analysis.* New York: Appleton-Century-Crofts.

Ryle, G. (1971). *Collected papers* (Vol. 2). London: Hutchinson.

Salmon, W. C. (1966). *The Foundations of Scientific Inference.* Pittsburgh: University of Pittsburgh Press.

Schnaitter, R. (1980). Science and verbal behavior. *Behaviorism, 8,* 153–160.

Schoenfield, W. N. (1969). J. R. Kantor's *Objective psychology of grammer* and *psychology and logic:* A retrospective appreciation. *Journal of the Experimental Analysis of Behavior, 12,* 329–247.

Sidman, M. (1960). *Tactics of scientific research.* New York: Basic Books.

Skinner, B. F. (1938). *The behavior of organisms.* New York: Appleton-Century-Crofts.

Skinner, B. F. (1953). *Science and Human Behavior.* New York: Macmillan.

Skinner, B. F. (1956). A case history of scientific method. *Americal Psychologist, 11,* 221–233.

Skinner, B. F. (1957a). *Schedules of Reinforcement.* New York: Appleton-Century-Crofts.

Skinner, B. F. (1957b). *Verbal Behavior.* New York: Appleton-Century-Crofts.

Skinner, B. F. (Ed.) (1959). *Cumulative Record.* New York: Appleton-Century-Crofts.

Skinner, B. F. (1966). Operant behavior. In W. K. Honig (Ed.), *Operant behavior: Areas of research and application* (pp. 12–32). New York: Appleton-Century-Crofts.

Skinner, B. F. (1969). *Contingencies of Reinforcement: A theoretical analysis.* New York: Appleton-Century-Crofts.

Skinner, B. F. (1971). *Beyond freedom and dignity.* New York: Knopf.

Skinner, B. F. (1974). *About Behaviorism*. New York: Knopf.

Skinner, B. F. (1978). *Reflections on behaviorism and society*. Englewood Cliffs, NJ: Prentice-Hall.

Skinner, B. F. (1979). *The Shaping of a Behaviorist*. New York: Knopf.

Skinner, B. F. (1980). *Notebooks*. Englewood Cliffs, NJ: Prentice-Hall.

Skinner, B. F. (1984a). The phylogeny and ontogeny of behavior. *Behavioral and Brain Sciences*, 7, 669–711.

Skinner, B. F. (1984b). An operant analysis of problem solving. *Behavioral and Brain Sciences*, 7, 583–613.

Snedecor, G. W. (1937). *Calculation and interpretation of analysis of variance and covariance*. Ames, IA: Collegiate Press.

Stein, G. H., Goldstein, M. K., & Smolen, D. M. (1976). Remote medical-behavioral monitoring: An alternative for ambulatory health assessment. In J. W. Cullen, B. H. Fox, & R. N. Isom (Eds.), *Cancer: The behavioral dimensions*. New York: Raven Press.

Stevens, S. S. (1946). On the theory of scales of measurement. *Science, 103*, 677–680.

Stevens, S. S. (1951). Mathematics, measurement, and psychophysics. In S. S. Stevens (Ed.), *Handbook of experimental psychology*. New York: Wiley.

Stevens, S. S. (1957). On the psychological law. *Psychological Review, 64*, 153–187.

Stevens, S. S. (1959). Measurement, psychophysics, and utility. In C. W. Churchman, & Ratoosh, P (Eds.), *Measurement: Definitions and theories* (pp. 34–56). New York: Wiley.

Stokes, T.F., & Baer, D.M. (1977). An implicit technology of generalization. *Journal of Applied Behavior Analysis, 10*, 349–367.

Terrace, H.S. (1966). Stimulus control. In W.K. Honig (Ed.) *Operant Behavior: Areas of Research and Application* (pp. 271–344). New York: Appleton-Century-Crofts.

Thorndike, E. L. (1898). *Animal intelligence*. New York: Macmillan.

Thorndike, E.C. (1903). *Educational Psychology*. New York: Leucke & Buechner.

Tukey, J. W. (1977). *Exploratory data analysis*. Reading, MA: Addison-Wesley.

Van Houten. R. (1987). Comparing treatment techniques: A cautionary note. *Journal of Applied Behavior Analysis, 20*, 109–110.

Walker, H. (1929). *Studies in the history of statistical method*. Baltimore, MD: Williams & Wilkins.

Walters, W. M., O'Neill, G. W., Rasheed, J. A., & Johnston, J. M. (1975). Validity of the study report form (Vol. 1). In J. M. Johnston (Ed.), *Behavior research and technology in higher education* (p. 147). Springfield, IL: Charles C. Thomas.

Watson, P. C., & Johnson-Laird, P. N. (1968). *Thinking and reasoning*. Middlesex, England: Penguin Books.

White, O. R., & Haring, N. G. (1976). Exceptional teaching. Columbus, OH, Merrill.

Woolf, H. (Ed.). (1961). *Quantification*. New York: Bobbs-Merrill.

Zebrowski, E. (1979). *Fundamentals of physical measurement*. Belmont, CA: Wadsworth.

Zuriff, G. E. (1980). Radical behaviorist epistemology. *Psychological Bulletin, 87*, 337–350.

Author Index

Subject Index